READER'S DIGEST

Getting the Most from Your PC

READER'S DIGEST

Getting the Most from Your PC

A Practical Guide to Upgrading, Customizing, and Working Faster with Your Computer

THE READER'S DIGEST ASSOCIATION, INC.

PLEASANTVILLE, NEW YORK • MONTREAL

A READER'S DIGEST BOOK

Copyright © Eaglemoss Publications Ltd 2001

Reader's Digest Project Staff
Project Editor: Don Earnest
Senior Design Director: Elizabeth L. Tunnicliffe
Senior Designer: George McKeon
Editorial Manager: Christine R. Guido

Reader's Digest Illustrated Reference Books
Editor-in-Chief: Christopher Cavanaugh
Art Director: Joan Mazzeo
Director, Trade Publishing: Christopher T. Reggio
Editorial Director, Trade: Susan Randol

Library of Congress Cataloging in Publication Data

Reader's Digest getting the most from your PC : a practical guide to upgrading,
customizing, and working faster with your computer.
     p. cm.
  ISBN 0-7621-0352-3
     1. Computer literacy. I. Title: Getting the most from your PC. II. Reader's Digest
Association.

QA76 .R35 2001
004—dc21

                                                                                    2001048282

This book was designed, edited and produced by Eaglemoss Publications Ltd
in association with VNU Business Publications Ltd,
based on the partwork *PC KnowHow*

Reader's Digest and the Pegasus logo are registered trademarks of
The Reader's Digest Association, Inc.

To order additional copies of this book, call 1-800-846-2100.

Visit our website at rd.com.

Printed in Singapore

1 3 5 7 9 10 8 6 4 2

Contents

1

Time-saving tips

Keep it tidy

The Desktop in Windows is just like a real desk, and keeping it organized can make using your PC easier.

When you start up Windows, what you see after it has finished loading is called the Desktop. Like a real desktop, you can organize it to keep the things you use frequently close at hand, and you can cover it with files you are working on. You can work better with your PC if your Desktop is well organized and you put some thought into making it suit you.

The Windows Desktop is just a folder on your hard disk, albeit a special one in the way its contents are displayed. Anything you can put in an ordinary folder you can store on the Desktop. However, it's best to use the Desktop sparingly and not clutter it up. Spend some time organizing your Desktop and you'll work more efficiently.

How to keep your Desktop tidy

1 Windows automatically installs some standard icons onto every Desktop. The My Computer icon lets you access information about your computer. The Recycle Bin lets you recover files that you have deleted. You cannot delete these icons, but you can drag them to a convenient position where they won't always be obscured by other windows. It is possible to get rid of other icons you don't need. For example, My Briefcase is useful only if you have two computers and want to transfer files between them. So if you are just using one computer, it's not necessary and you can get rid of it.

Likewise, the Internet, and icons for online services such as the Microsoft Network (MSN), are useful only if you have a modem. If you don't need these icons, delete them by dragging them to the Recycle Bin. If you change your mind after deleting them, all is not lost. Just right-click on the Desktop and choose Undo Delete.

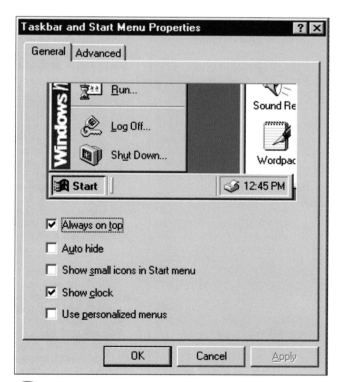

2 The taskbar lets you run applications and switch between the windows you have open. If you find other windows are obscuring it, you can change the settings to make the taskbar always appear in front. Right-click on a blank part of the taskbar and select Properties. When the Taskbar Properties dialogue box appears, check Always on Top. The taskbar will now always appear in front of other windows. If you would prefer not to see the taskbar except when you need it, check the Auto Hide option. This makes the taskbar slide out of the way when you are not using it. When you need it, move the mouse to the edge of the screen where the taskbar is hiding and it will slide back into view.

3 The taskbar doesn't have to be at the bottom of the screen. You might prefer to have it on one side, or at the top. Just click on a blank part of the taskbar, hold down the button and drag the mouse to the edge of the screen. To change the width of the taskbar move the mouse to its edge. The pointer becomes a double-ended arrow, and you can drag the edge to the width you want.

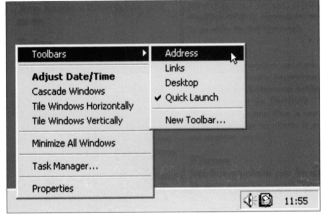

4 The Windows Me taskbar has several optional toolbars. To add them to the taskbar, right-click an empty part of the bar, select Toolbars from the pop-up menu and pick a toolbar you want from the cascading menu. If there is a check against the toolbar, it is already present. To remove a toolbar, uncheck it from the pop-up menu.

Jargon buster

Shortcut A link to a program, file or folder.
Shortcut icons have an arrow in one corner, and are often named "Shortcut to..." although this can be changed by using programs such as Tweak UI. Shortcuts let you run a program or open a file or folder from an icon on the Desktop, even if the object isn't located there. To create a shortcut, hold down the right mouse button and drag the object you want to the Desktop, then choose Create Shortcuts Here from the pop-up menu. If you delete a shortcut, you are deleting the link, not the file itself.

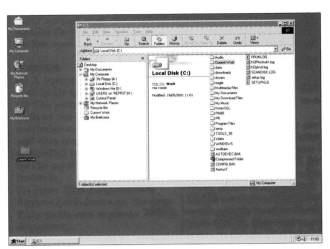

5 It can be time-consuming hunting for files you frequently use. To make them easily accessible from your Desktop, you can create shortcuts to the folders you store them in. If you use Microsoft Office, for example, and store files in a folder called current work, use Explorer to locate this folder on your C: drive. Right-click on the folder icon and drag it over to the Desktop. When you release the button, choose Create Shortcut Here from the pop-up menu that appears. You can now open the folder directly from your Desktop.

Repeat this for your other work folders. If you have files cluttering your Desktop, you can create a folder to store them in. Just right-click on the Desktop and select New, followed by Folder. Type a name for the folder. Simply drag files onto the folder icon in order to store them there. (For details on shortcuts, see pages 19–20.)

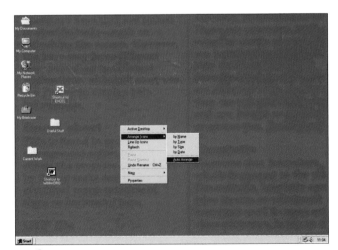

6 After you have created a number of shortcuts and folders on your Desktop, you will probably want to arrange them in some sort of order. If you right-click on the Desktop and choose Arrange Icons from the pop-up menu that appears, you will see that Windows can arrange your icons by name, type, file size or creation date. If you click on Auto Arrange, Windows will automatically rearrange the icons when you create new ones.

That's all very well for an ordinary folder, but for the Desktop you'll probably want to choose your icon locations yourself. You can drag them into position, but you may find that it's difficult to line them up neatly. Windows can do that for you. Just choose Line up Icons from the pop-up menu and your icons will be arranged neatly into rows and columns.

Desktop accessories

Make your Windows Desktop work harder for you with the addition of a few useful Desktop accessories.

Before Windows there was DOS. This was a text-based operating system that worked without a mouse and required users to enter commands in words, but at the time nobody thought it strange. This text-based approach had one tremendous advantage, which was that it was so small you could fit it onto a single floppy disk and still have room for a word processor and several days' work.

Pop up any time

DOS had many flaws, the main one being that it could run just one application at a time. This led to the invention of pop-up tools, or tiny programs loaded into memory before a main application. Typically they were calculators, calendars and notepads which would appear on top of the main program when hot-key combinations were pressed.

Windows killed off pop-up accessories because it let users run several programs at once and arrange the programs in windows on a work surface called the Program Manager. In later versions, Program Manager became the Desktop but its usefulness as a repository for accessory programs was unchanged.

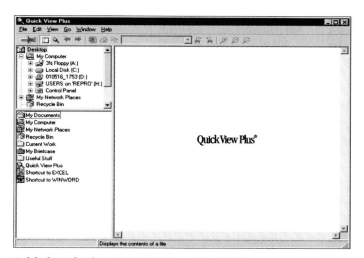

QuickView Plus has its own Explorer-like interface so you can browse files on your hard drive and view them without opening the original program that created them.

Watch out!

Desktop accessories are invaluable, but they do tend to overwhelm an ordinary sized monitor with screen clutter. What's worse is that the presence of a Desktop accessory may indicate that valuable memory and processing resources are being eaten up. In the screenshot below, three major Desktop accessories are running on the Desktop and there's also an anti-virus program running in the background.

A PC with a fast processor and plenty of memory will not be significantly slowed down by running four accessories, but an older PC might. And there's always the danger that running several programs at the same time will cause conflicts rather than prevent them.

Where possible, avoid loading too many Desktop accessories at the same time unless they are part of a portmanteau of programs from a single supplier. Such compilation packages contain modules which are designed to work together and are therefore less likely to waste system resources. Good examples are McAfee Utilities and Norton Utilities from Symantec.

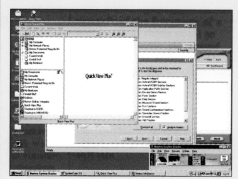

When your Desktop accessories take over the screen, it's time to work out which of them you really need.

Top five brands

- **QuicKeys** www.quickeys.com
- **Microsoft** www.microsoft.com
- **McAfee** www.mcafee.com
- **Powerquest** www.powerquest.com
- **Symantec** www.symantec.com

Buying tips

● Desktop accessories must perform flawlessly with every program on a hard disk, so never buy or install more than one at a time. If you do and you find there's a problem, you won't know which program is to blame.

● Choose accessories that can easily be disabled or unloaded from memory. This is useful when setting up new software, which sometimes won't install properly if other programs are running. Being able to disable an accessory also helps when troubleshooting.

● If an accessory program incorporates an address book you should consider which main applications you'll be using with it. Many spreadsheets and databases can exchange address information with some, but not all, accessory programs. You'll save yourself a lot of typing if you find one that's compatible.

At its simplest, QuicKeys lets you start programs using hot keys, but the QuicKeys wizards can automate almost any Windows activity.

Fact file

● **Accessory Toolbar** Used as a convenient store for several accessories. Toolbars can be freely moved around the screen or docked against one edge.

● **Active Desktop** In Windows 98 and later, this enables your PC to display material from the Internet on the Windows Desktop without having to use a separate browser program.

● **Quick Launch Toolbar** In Windows Me and 98, this is an area of the Taskbar to which users can drag an icon for any program they wish to be accessible at all times.

● **Taskbar** The bar at the bottom of the Windows Desktop. It shows which programs (tasks) are running.

Windows freebies

Of the accessories supplied with Windows, everyone tries Paint and WordPad, and many people become regular users of Calculator, Notepad and Clipboard. If you're prepared to dig deeper, you can find a system resource meter (see page 25), a network monitor and a fax image editor. But generally, the most interesting accessories come from third parties —they tend to identify and satisfy the needs neglected by Windows.

Personal organizer accessories provide a range of features, including a calendar, diary and address book. Other accessories are more focused. They often perform just one task, but they do it well. QuickView Plus makes it easy to view any file, even if you don't have the program that created it; PowerDesk replaces the clumsy Windows Explorer; and WinZip compresses data, making it easier and cheaper to transmit or store.

New interfaces

Since Windows 98, suppliers of Desktop accessories have had to rethink how their products are used. Windows now includes an Active Desktop capable of displaying multimedia information. Rather than obscuring the Active Desktop, accessories are attached to context-sensitive menus, accessed by right-clicking. They may also be placed on toolbars, such as the Quick Launch Toolbar, and on the Windows Taskbar.

With the arrival of utilities such as QuicKeys, the wheel turned full circle and Windows accessories are being assigned to keyboard shortcuts. It's as hard as ever to remember which shortcuts are linked to what, but anyone struggling with a 14in monitor will appreciate reduced screen clutter.

With QuickView Plus it is possible to view files created by more than 200 programs – text, graphics, spreadsheets, e-mail, databases– even if you don't have those programs on your computer.

Managing files

Make life easier by using a proper system to store all your work files on your computer.

Unless you use your PC exclusively for games, the work that you do using your applications will result in files being created. These files must be stored somewhere on your hard disk.

Where you store your files is up to you. Many people just save their files in whatever location a program uses by default. But this means work done in different programs is stored in different folders, which makes files hard to find using Explorer.

Windows Me and 98 make things a bit easier. When you save a file the default location is a folder called My

Documents. If you accept this location all your work will be in one place. If you have more than a few files it's probably better to create sub-folders named after topics or tasks, and store your files in these rather than a single My Documents folder.

Windows makes it easy to create new folders and move files around so that each one is kept in a logical place. It's worth learning how to use Windows' file-management tools so you can organize your work and use your PC efficiently.

How to tidy up your filing system

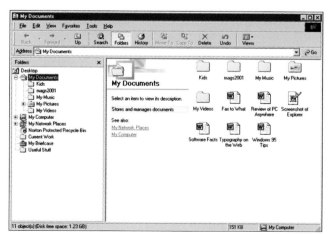

1 Files on your hard disk are organized into a structure of nested folders. There is a root folder called C:. This contains a number of sub-folders, such as the Windows folder, where all the Windows software is stored, and the Program Files folder which contains many of your applications.

Explorer's left-hand pane displays your folder structure as a collapsible outline view. Any folder that contains other folders has a little box with a plus sign next to it. Clicking on the plus sign expands the folder and displays the sub-folders. When all the folders are expanded, the plus becomes a minus sign: clicking on this collapses the sub-folders back into their parent folder.

2 Explorer's right-hand pane shows the files and folders in whichever folder is selected on the left. You can choose how those files and folders are displayed from the View menu, or by clicking the Views toolbar button. If you choose Large Icons, each folder or file is shown by a large icon, with its name underneath. This is convenient for folders containing small numbers of files. If you choose Small Icons, each file and folder is represented by a small icon with its name alongside. List is similar to Small Icons, but you only see one column of names.

If you choose Details, the contents of a folder will be shown as a directory list, with icon, name, size, file type and the date and time the file was last modified all shown. You can sort the list according to any of these categories by clicking on the heading at the top of the list. Click again to sort them in reverse order.

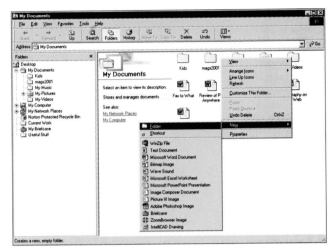

3 To create a new folder, first select the folder in the left-hand pane of Explorer that you want the new folder to be created in. Move the pointer to the right-hand pane, right-click and select New then Folder. A new folder will appear in the Explorer window, with the name New Folder. Replace the default name with the name you want the folder to have.

To change the name of any file or folder, click to select it, wait briefly—so Windows won't think you are double-clicking it—and then click it again. Alternatively you can select it and press the F2 key. The name will appear in a small Edit box. You can type a new name, then hit Enter to accept it or Esc to cancel your change.

4 Start to organize your work logically. A quick and easy way to move files around is using drag and drop. Click on a file you want to move, and hold down the mouse button. Now drag the file to the folder you want. When the folder changes color to show it is selected, release the mouse button. Windows displays an outline of the file icon as you drag it, with a No Entry symbol on it when the pointer is over something you can't move the file to.

Filing tip

Finding files Sometimes icons in a folder can become superimposed on one another. If you can't see a file in a folder and you think it should be there, select View, Arrange Icons to make Windows rearrange the icons. If the icon was hidden under another icon, it will now be visible.

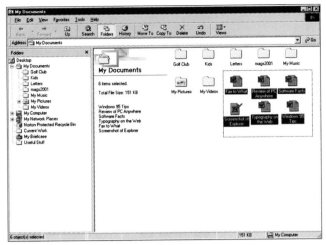

5 If you want to move several files from one place to another, you can select all the files then move them in a single operation. To select a group of individual files, hold down the Ctrl key while you click on them. To select a block of files, hold down the Shift key and click the first and last file in the block. To select all the files in a folder, click Edit, then Select All, or hold down the Ctrl key and press A for All.

Another way to select a group of files shown in Icon View is to drag a selection box around them. Click and hold down the mouse button while the pointer is to the top left of an icon, then drag the pointer down and to the right. As the selection box expands to include the files, the icons change color to show they are selected.

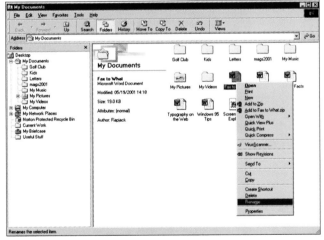

6 There are many things you can do with files in Explorer. Select a file, then click the right-hand mouse button. A menu pops up. This is called a Context menu. From this menu you can click Rename, which like the F2 key, enables you to rename files. You can also delete a file from here. Other ways to delete a file are to drag the icon to the Recycle Bin or to select the file and press the Del key.

To copy a file select Copy. Nothing seems to happen. This is because the file has been copied to the Windows Clipboard. Now select the folder to which you want to copy the file, right-click the folder background and select Paste. A copy of the file will appear. You can also use Cut and Paste as another way of moving files.

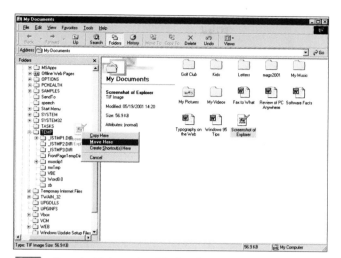

7 If you hold down the right-hand mouse button (instead of the left-hand one) while you are dragging a file, Windows displays a small menu of options when you release the button. You can choose whether to move a file, create a separate copy of it or create a shortcut.

This is a good way to drag and drop files because it lets you choose what action Windows takes. When you drag and drop using the left-hand mouse button, Windows chooses a default action which isn't consistent. If the location you're dragging to is on the same drive, Windows moves the file, but if it's on a different drive it copies it. But if the file is a program, Windows always creates a shortcut, regardless of the new location.

It can be useful to create shortcuts to files you often use on your desktop (see page 10).

8 Another way of moving files around your hard disk is to use the Send To option on the Context menu. A quick way to make backup copies of your work is to send files to the floppy or other removable drive. Depending on the other hardware and software installed, other options will appear. If you have fax or e-mail you can send files by this method by choosing the appropriate option. You can also send files to the Briefcase if you use this feature for synchronizing copies with those stored on another PC.

Advanced users can add locations to the Send To menu by placing shortcuts to the new location in the Send To folder, which is a sub-folder of the Windows folder.

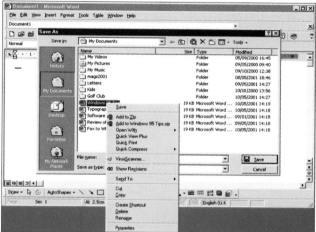

9 To help you find files at a later date, try to choose file names that describe each file clearly. File names can be more than 250 characters long and contain almost any characters except certain punctuation marks.

You should also save files into an appropriate folder. If you don't have a suitable folder when saving a new file, create one. You don't need to open Explorer to do this. The Open and Save dialogue boxes in new Windows applications are mini Explorers. You can use them to do all the things you can do in the right-hand pane of the full-sized Explorer, including changing the way items are displayed, creating new folders and renaming, copying, deleting and moving files using the Context menu.

Filing tip

Create a My Documents folder If you're using Windows 95 and don't have Microsoft Office, you won't have a My Documents folder on your hard disk. If you would like to store your files in a My Documents folder, you can easily create one. Just select your hard disk C: in the left-hand pane of Explorer, right-click in the right-hand pane and select New, then Folder. Change the name of the new folder to My Documents. You will have to use the Open or Save dialogue box to navigate to this folder each time before opening or saving a file.

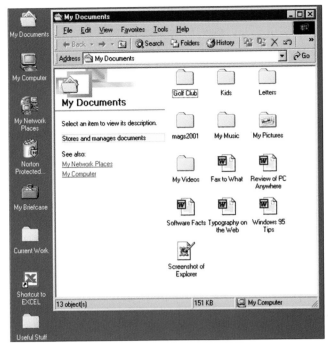

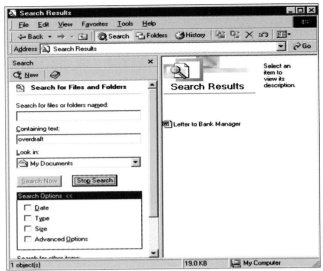

10 If you work in one folder a lot of the time, or want to move files between one folder and another, it's easiest to open windows showing just the folders you want. To do this, double-click on a folder icon in Explorer. A window will open showing the contents of that folder in Large Icon view.

The folder window is the same as the right-hand pane in Explorer. You can change the view to Small or Large Icons, List or Details view (see page 13, step 2). You can drag and drop files to and from Explorer, other folder windows or icons on your Desktop. You can use the Explorer context menu by right-clicking on any icon. Make a shortcut to your My Documents folder, or any other folder you use regularly, on your Desktop (see pages 19–20). You can then open the folder any time you want by double-clicking the shortcut icon.

11 If there are a lot of files on your hard disk, it can be difficult to find the one you want. Windows' Search will help you locate any file. You can run it from Explorer's Tools menu or the Start menu.

If you know the file's name, or just part of the name, type it into the Search for Files or Folders Named: field. Otherwise, click the Search Options, then tick the Type box. Choose the type of file you want to search for, such as a Microsoft Word Document. In the Containing Text box enter a word or two that you know will appear in the file you want. If you have an idea where the file should be, you can tell the Search tool where to look. Otherwise have it search your whole PC by selecting My Computer from the list in the Look in: box. If any files are found that match your criteria, Search will list them. You can double-click the icons to open the files, drag them to another folder or use the context menu to copy, delete, or send them to the printer.

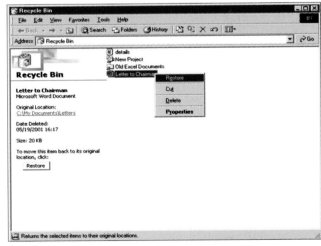

12 Another place to look if you can't find a file is the Recycle Bin. Files deleted using Explorer are sent to the Recycle Bin, where they will remain until either you empty the bin or Windows purges some of the contents because you are running out of hard disk space.

To see what is in the Recycle Bin, double-click on it. This will open an Explorer window showing the contents. In Details view it shows the names of all the files, where they came from, what they are and when they were deleted. To restore a deleted file to its original location, right-click the file name and select Restore from the pop-up menu. Alternatively, click on the Restore button in the left-hand pane.

Easy access folders

Create a quick and easy shortcut to files and Web pages you use most frequently.

On your own hard disk and the Internet there is a lot of information you can access with your computer. It can be difficult to remember where to find the data that you want.

Windows provides a way to get to frequently used files and Web sites quickly. Called Favorites folders, you can access them from a pulldown menu in Windows or Internet Explorer. You can group folders and Web sites into categories so you can find the one you want easily without searching through a long list. If you take the trouble to organize the things you use most often into Favorites folders, you will save time and use your computer more efficiently.

Using Windows' Favorites Folders

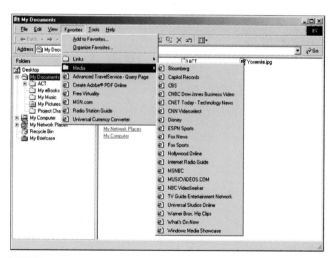

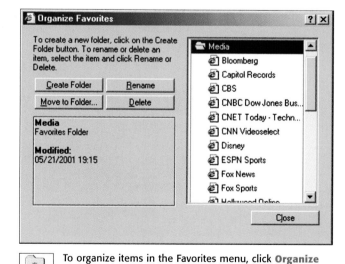

Microsoft felt that Windows **Favorites folders** were such a useful feature that it gave them their own menu in Windows Explorer and Internet Explorer. All you need to do to open a frequently used folder or a favorite Web site is to click on Favorites and then click on the item that you want (or click on a folder and then on the item). Using just two or three mouse clicks like this is obviously a quicker way to get to where you want to go than navigating to the location in any other way.

When you start using your computer you will probably find that the Favorites menu contains some items by default. Microsoft has added links to some World Wide Web sites that it thinks you will want to visit. If you aren't interested in these sites you can delete them. Then you can start to make the Favorites menu really useful by adding items of your own.

To organize items in the Favorites menu, click **Organize Favorites** from the dropdown menu. The Organize Favorites dialogue box opens with the folders on the right and four buttons on the left. You can move, rename and delete items by selecting them and clicking one of the Organize buttons. You can also delete them by highlighting the file or folder and then pressing the Delete key on the keyboard.

Jargon Buster

Context menus The menus that pop up when you right-click on items are often called context menus.

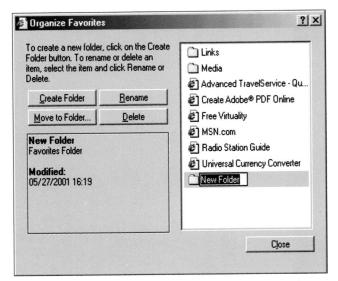

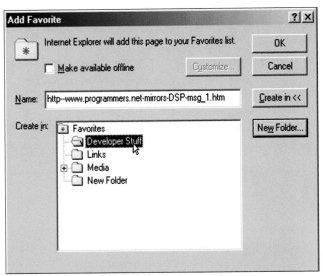

 To create a new folder, click the **Create Folder** button. You can then type a name for the new folder, and move items into it by dragging and dropping.

Favorites aren't only for Web sites. You can drag items from other Explorer windows, and even the Desktop, and drop them on a folder in the Organize Favorites dialogue box. If you drag using the left-hand mouse button, however, you'll usually move the item there. To leave the item where it is and still get the benefit of being able to access it rapidly from the Favorites menu, drag it with the right-hand mouse button. Then when you release the button and the context menu appears select Create Shortcut Here.

When you select Add to Favorites, the **Add Favorite** dialogue box appears. It's easy just to click OK, but that will simply add the folder or site to the main list. If you click the Create In<< button, the dialogue box will expand to show a list of your Favorites folders. Select a suitable one, or click New Folder to create one, to add the item to the most appropriate folder. This will make it easier to find the next time you want it.

Before clicking OK, check the text in the Name field to see that it describes the item. Depending on how the Web page was constructed, this field may contain just a URL, which may not be very meaningful when you see it in the Favorites list. If you want, change the name to something more descriptive.

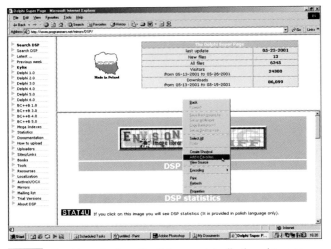

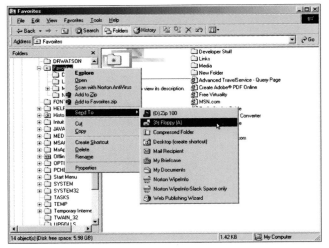

The idea of a Favorites list was originally thought up to make it easy to store links to Web sites that you wanted to go back to. If you are surfing the Internet using Microsoft Internet Explorer it is easy and quick to add sites that interest you to your Favorites list. Either click Favorites, **Add to Favorites** from the main menu, or right-click the Web page itself and select Add To Favorites from the context menu.

You can also add pages to the list when reviewing them offline. Set Internet Explorer to offline mode (click File, Work Offline) then load the page by clicking the Back button or selecting it from the History list. Once it has loaded you can add it to your Favorites list.

If you use the Internet a lot, your Favorites list will become one of the most valuable things on your computer. You should remember to **back it up** regularly. Favorites is simply a folder inside the Windows folder, and the items that appear on the list are shortcuts and folders that are in the Favorites folder. You can back it up just like any other folder.

If you don't have a tape backup device you can save your Favorites on a floppy disk. Locate the folder in Explorer, then right-click it and select Send To, Floppy (A:)—or another location such as a Zip drive. This will make a copy of all your Favorites. As well as a good safety precaution this is a handy way to transfer your Favorites from one computer to another or to make copies of interesting Web links to give to friends.

Shortcuts

Speed up the way Windows works for you by making full use of its shortcut capabilities.

Windows is very flexible in the way it lets you access the programs and data you want. Very often there are several ways to perform a task or access a file. One great feature, first introduced in Windows 95, is the shortcut.

A shortcut is basically a pointer to the program or file that you want to access. The shortcut icon is usually identical in appearance to the icon of the file you want to open, except that it is distinguished from the original by a small black and white arrow in the lower left-hand corner. When you double-click on a shortcut icon, it is as if you clicked on the icon of the program to which the shortcut is pointing.

Shortcuts can point to program files, like Word or Quicken. They can point to data files, such as a frequently used spreadsheet, and to folders—say those you access several times a day. And they can point to objects such as disk drives and Control Panel applets.

Shortcuts can be created in any location on your hard disk, but probably the most convenient and sensible place is on the Desktop itself. This way you have rapid access to the items you most frequently use. Even in its most basic configuration, Windows makes extensive use of shortcuts and most entries on the Program menu are shortcuts.

Speeding up Windows

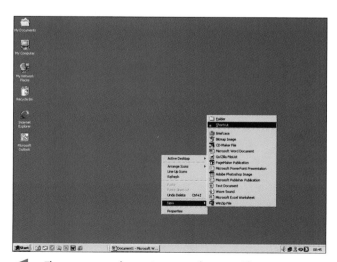

1 There are several ways to create shortcuts. The most thorough way is to right-click the Desktop and from the menu that appears, select New. From the sub-menu, select Shortcut. This launches the Shortcut Wizard. You can then either type in the location and the name of the item, for example, by writing C:\Windows\notepad.exe in the command line box or click on Browse and navigate to the file you want to create a shortcut to.

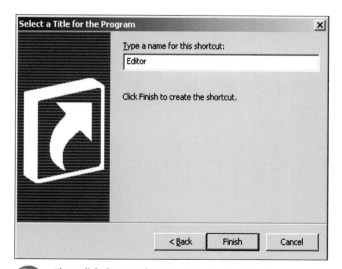

2 Then click the Next button. You can give the shortcut a different name if you want to. By default the file name without the file extension is used, but you can use a different label. Here the Notepad shortcut has been given the label Editor. Click on the Finish button to complete the task. A new icon appears on your Desktop, called Editor, with a shortcut arrow on it to identify it as such.

3 A simpler way to create a shortcut is to right-click an object such as an item on the Program menu and drag the icon to where you'd like the shortcut and release the button. From the pop-up menu select Create Shortcut(s) Here.

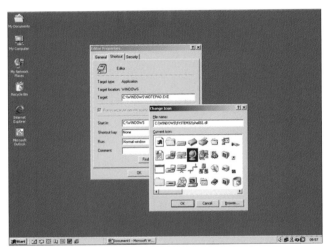

4 You can then right-click the shortcut to fine-tune it by editing its Properties. You could for example give it a different icon. A good source for icons is system file Shell32.dll. Click on Change Icon, then Browse and select it from C:\Windows\System.

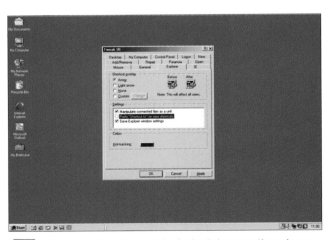

5 You can also customize the look of shortcuts if you have TweakUI. This was one of the Microsoft Power Toys and can be downloaded from www.zdnet.com. TweakUI lets you customize Windows' appearance. Open Control Panel and double-click on TweakUI. Click on the Explorer tab. TweakUI lets you mark a shortcut icon with a less obtrusive arrow or dispense with an arrow altogether. Generally, a shortcut label will be prefixed by the words Shortcut To. An option on this TweakUI tab lets you dispense with this as well. (For more details, see pages 49–52.)

6 One of Windows' best features is its ability to assign a hotkey to a shortcut. You can create a keyboard shortcut to any program you frequently use. Right-click on the Start menu and choose Open. Navigate through the windows until you find the desired program, say Word. Right-click on the program icon and choose Properties. Click on the Shortcut tab and in the Shortcut key box, type over the word None with a letter (such as W for Microsoft Word). Then click on OK. The next time you want to open Microsoft Word, simply press Ctrl+Alt+W and the program will load. Generally hotkeys start with Ctrl+Alt but you can use the Numeric pad as well as function keys.

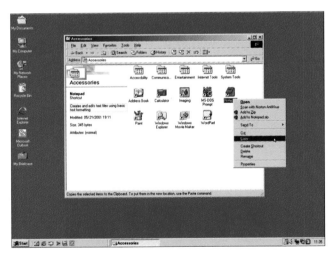

7 If you choose your hotkey letters carefully, you can use hotkeys for all your favorite programs, no matter what you're doing, directly from the keyboard. For example, you could use E for Encarta, I for Internet Explorer, Q for Quicken, W for Word, X for Excel, and so on.

There is one minor restriction. The shortcut key option is effective for shortcuts located on the Desktop or in the Start menu only. The only way to determine the hotkey for a given shortcut is to open its Properties dialogue box. Putting all of your hotkey-equipped shortcuts in a single folder called Keystrokes helps you to keep track of them. You don't have to remove the shortcuts for important programs from the Start menu. You can use a copy of each shortcut instead. Right-click Start and choose Explore. Open the Programs folder and navigate to the folder that contains the shortcut. Right-click on it and select Copy. Now right-click the Keystrokes folder and select Paste. Right-click the new shortcut, select Properties, and click on the Shortcut tab. Click in the Shortcut key box, type the desired key combination, and click OK. Finally, right-click the new shortcut, select Rename and give it a name that reflects the hotkey.

Windows tips

Learn the tricks of the Windows trade to make your computing quicker, safer and more efficient.

Windows is pretty easy to use. But old hands usually discover a whole host of ways to make it even more efficient. The obvious way to do something isn't always the quickest. There are often shortcuts that are faster and make your time spent at the computer more productive.

Here are 40 of the best tips for making common Windows tasks easier and faster. Learn them, and become a real Windows expert.

Windows hints & tricks

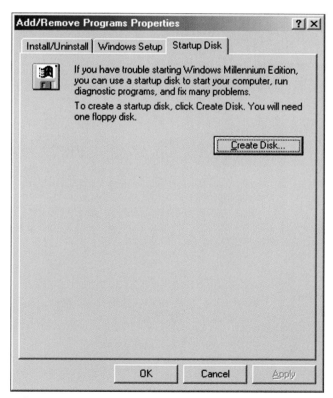

1 Make sure that you always have an up-to-date startup disk in a safe place in case your computer won't start up from the hard disk. Open Control Panel, click Add/Remove Programs and click on Startup Disk. Put a blank disk into the floppy disk drive and click on Create Disk.

2 Use the New option in Explorer menus to create new files of many different types. Open the folder you want to create the file in. Now right-click in the folder and select New. Then choose the file type from the sub-menu that pops up. Rename the new file to give it the name you want.

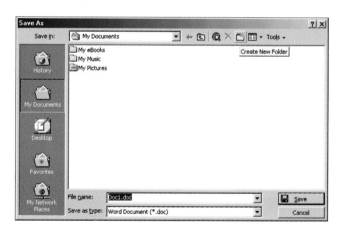

3 Save your work in descriptively named folders to make it easy to find. You can create a new folder in which to save a file, directly from the Save As dialogue box of most applications. Just click the new folder button near the top right of the dialogue box, then rename the folder that is created to give it the name you want.

4 To drag and drop text or data from one maximized application window to another, drag the text to the Taskbar and then drop it on the button for the other application. The text or data will be inserted at wherever the cursor is in the other application.

5 To access Desktop icons that are hidden behind windows quickly, use the Show Desktop button on the Taskbar to bring the entire Desktop to the top. If you have Windows 95 and your Taskbar doesn't have the Show Desktop button, right-click the Taskbar and select Minimize All Windows.

6 Instead of using the mouse, use keyboard shortcuts for faster access to menu commands. Underlined letters in menus are shortcuts. So ⊞+R will open the Run box on the Start menu. If you have an old-style keyboard with no Windows key (⊞), press Ctrl+Esc instead. The Alt key activates the menu of the currently active window, so Alt+F will pull down the File menu of the application you are working in. Applications often have their own shortcuts listed on menus that will directly invoke certain functions. Learn them.

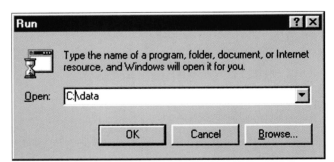

7 A quick way to open a folder or a file is to open the Run box and type the full name (including location) of the folder or file—for example C:\My Documents\Letter.doc. The Run box contains a list of all the most recently opened items, so if you have used it to open a file earlier you may not need to type the name at all.

8 As an alternative to drag and drop when moving files, use Cut, Copy and Paste. Select a file, then select Cut to move it or Copy to copy it from the right-click menu or Explorer's Edit menu. Next, select the target folder, right-click in it—or use Explorer's Edit menu again—and choose Paste.

9 If you aren't sure whether Windows will move, copy or create a shortcut to a file when using drag and drop, drag it using the right mouse button. Then you can choose which action to take from a pop-up menu. The menu also gives you a Cancel option in case you change your mind.

10 If you have second thoughts about moving, copying or deleting a file, Explorer lets you undo the last 10 actions. Select Edit, Undo from the Explorer menu.

11 To delete a file permanently, hold down the Shift key while you delete it. The file will not be moved to the Recycle Bin, so you will not be able to recover it.

12 The quickest way to launch a copy of Explorer is to use the keyboard shortcut ⊞+E, provided you have a Windows keyboard with the Windows key.

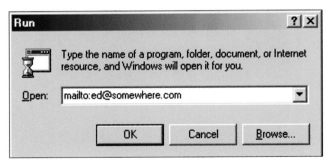

13 A quick way to open your e-mail program is to go to the Run command and type in mailto: followed by the e-mail address of the person to whom you want to send an e-mail. The program will open with a new message that has that address in the To: field.

14 If you want to right-click without clicking at all, just hit Shift-F10. This is the same as pressing the right-hand button on your mouse.

15 To display the parent folder of an open folder in Explorer, simply press Backspace.

16 To close a folder window and the windows of all the parent folders between it and the root folder, hold down the Shift key when you click the Close button.

17 If the text of a Taskbar button is truncated, position the pointer over the button and wait. The full text will appear in a tooltip so you can read it (see left).

18 The traditional way to rename a file is to single-click it to highlight it, single-click it again and write in the name. However, it's easy to double-click on the name and open the program by mistake. To avoid this, single-click on the name and then press F2 before typing the new name.

19 To access the Date & Time Properties quickly to set your computer's date, time and time zone, double-click the clock in the Taskbar.

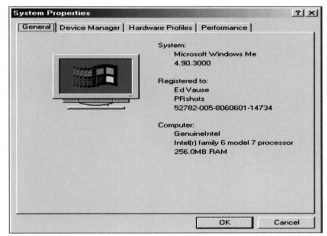

20 To access the System Properties for your PC quickly, use the keyboard shortcut ⊞+Break. Note you can't do this without a Windows keyboard.

21 Want a quick restart? Rather than wait for Windows to reset the hardware before rebooting, select Restart in the Shut Down Windows dialogue box and press down the Shift key as you click OK.

22 To open a file with a different application from the usual files of that type, hold down the Shift key and then right-click the file's icon. You can then use the Open With... menu option to select the program to use.

23 You can create a shortcut to Notepad in your Windows SendTo folder. To do this, find Notepad in the Windows folder, then drag it to the folder SendTo. Once you have done this you will be able to view any file that contains text in Notepad by right-clicking it and choosing SendTo, Notepad. You can also try this with QuickView located in \Windows\System\Viewers.

24 Use drag and drop to open files. Create a shortcut to an application on the Desktop. You can then open files using that application by dragging the files from Explorer and dropping them on the shortcut icon.

25 Save scraps of information from documents so they can easily be located without loading the whole document. Select the text you want and drag it to the Desktop or a folder. A document scrap icon will be created. Double-click the icon to view the selected text in the application.

Create Scrap Here
Move Scrap Here
Create Document Shortcut Here

Cancel

26 Create shortcuts that point to important text or data in a document. Select the text and then use the right-hand mouse button to drag it to the Desktop or a folder. Then choose Create Document Shortcut Here from the pop-up menu.

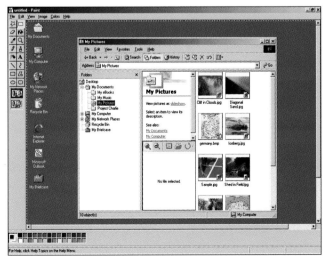

27 To print what's on your screen (including areas that you need to scroll down to), press Print Screen—Print Scrn on the keyboard. Open Microsoft Paint from Programs/Accessories and then press Ctrl+V to paste in the image of your screen, which you can then print off.

28 To assign keyboard shortcuts to the Start menu, right-click the Start button, click Explore, and locate the menu item you want. Right-click it and select Properties. Assign a key combination to the Shortcut Key field. To launch the application, just type the shortcut key combination.

29 When folders are opened, they either appear in the existing window or they open in a new one. To switch between the two options (without changing it for all folders), press the Ctrl key when you double-click on the folder to open it.

30 Use the Task Switcher to switch between open applications. Hold down Alt and press Tab. This calls up the Task Switcher. Pressing Tab while Alt is held down cycles through the list of open windows or applications. When you release Alt control is passed to the selected application.

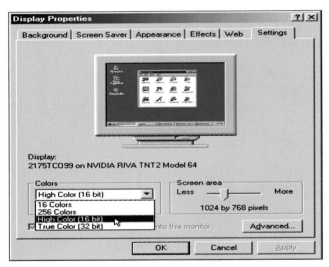

31 If your screen seems to be laboring under too much work and refreshes slowly, try using a different color depth. To change the setting, right-click the Desktop, choose Properties and select the Settings tab and select less colors.

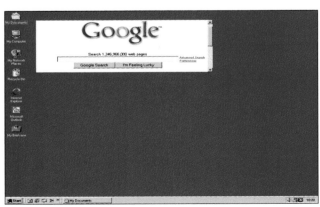

32 If you have the Active Desktop enabled, you can access a Web site from your Desktop. When you reach a Web page you want, right-click the icon next to the URL in the address bar and drag it to the Desktop. Select the option to save it as active content.

33 If your screensaver causes ScanDisk or Disk Defragmenter to keep restarting, click the Start button and leave the Start menu up. While the Start menu is showing the screensaver will not run.

34 If you are using Internet Explorer and want to create a shortcut on your Desktop to a Web site you want to return to, right-click the Web page and select Create Shortcut from the pop-up menu.

35 If you don't want the names of Web sites you've just visited to appear in Internet Explorer's History list, select View, Internet Options. Click Clear History in the History panel, and Delete Files in Temporary Internet Files.

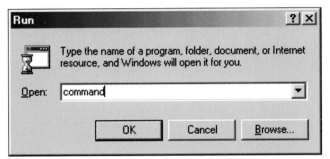

36 In Windows Me, there is no shortcut to an MS-Dos prompt. The quickest way to run DOS under Me is to go to the Run dialogue box on the Start menu and type command.

37 To make life easier when using an MS-DOS prompt, start by typing the command Doskey. Doskey remembers previous commands (press the up and down arrow keys to select them) and lets you edit the commands easily to correct mistakes.

38 To get a printed list of the contents of your My Documents folder, open an MS-DOS prompt and type: DIR "C:\My Documents" /O >prn. You can get a printed list of the contents of any folder by substituting its full path for C:\My Documents inside the quotes. The "/O" is a switch that makes the list appear in alphabetical order.

39 Use the Start command to open a file from a command prompt. For example, Start myfile.txt will open myfile.txt using the program associated with text files. Start followed by a folder name will open that folder.

40 Use the MS-DOS shortcuts for directory names. "." means the current directory, so Start "." will open the directory you are currently in as a Windows folder. ".." means the parent directory of the current directory. Use three or four dots to move two or three levels (grandparent, great-grandparent) up the directory tree.

Peak performance

Windows can help you track down and monitor any bottlenecks in your computer system.

Your computer is a complex system. It contains several different components, all of which have a role to play in how quickly it can carry out commands. If you are interested in getting the best performance from your PC you must monitor the work it does to find out whether there are any bottlenecks.

Windows comes with some built-in tools for monitoring performance. You can use them to find out how well the different components of your computer are performing, and which parts could benefit from upgrading.

How to monitor your system

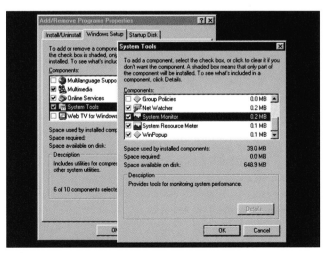

1 Before you can use Windows' system monitoring tools you will have to install them because they are not installed by default. From the Control Panel, click on Add/Remove Programs and then Windows Setup. Scroll down the list of items and select System Tools, then click the Details button. Another window showing the tools available will appear. Check the boxes next to System Monitor and System Resource Meter. Click OK to close the windows, and insert your Windows CD-ROM if prompted.

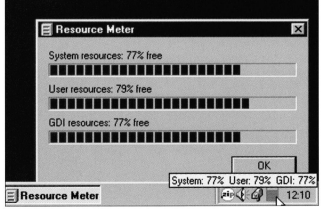

2 Click Start, Programs, Accessories and then select Resource Meter from the System Tools Menu. Resource Meter monitors the usage of three very specific things which are vital to your applications, but which are limited when running Windows. The free resources are shown as a percentage. A small chart showing the overall position will appear in your task bar System Tray. To view the figures for the three types of resource, point to the System Tray icon with the mouse pointer and the results will appear. If you right-click the icon and select Details you can view the results as three progress bars.

If you use programs that tend to run out of resources, consider adding the Resource Meter to your Start menu StartUp folder so it is running, and displaying the meter in the system tray, all the time.

Jargon buster

Resources Small blocks of memory used to store various items of data. GDI resources store data used to create the display on your screen. System resources hold information used internally by Windows. User resources hold information specific to programs. Windows keeps track of these resources using three tables that can store 16,384 items each. If a table becomes full, an application may malfunction.

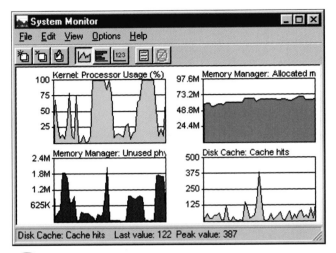

3 System Monitor is also run from the System Tools menu. It displays data about the system as a graph, a bar chart or as raw data. You can toggle between the types of display by clicking the buttons on the toolbar. If you click on a chart, the current value and the peak value for that item are displayed. However, System Monitor consumes resources. If your PC is underpowered, running it could make matters worse. Alleviate the problem by reducing the frequency with which performance snapshots are taken. Select Options, then Chart from the menu, and specify how often the charts should be updated. You can turn System Monitor on and off using the Start Logging and Stop Logging buttons on the toolbar.

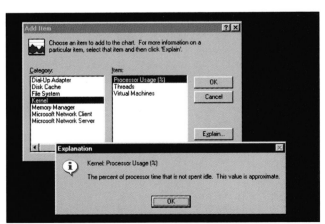

4 To add a new item to the list of things monitored, click the Add button. The Add Item dialogue box displays a list of items you can obtain performance statistics about. Select a category, and a list of items in that category will appear. Each item represents a single measurement or chart. To remove an item from the chart, click the Remove button or select Edit, Remove Item. A dialogue box will appear showing a list of the items. Select the one you want to remove and click OK.

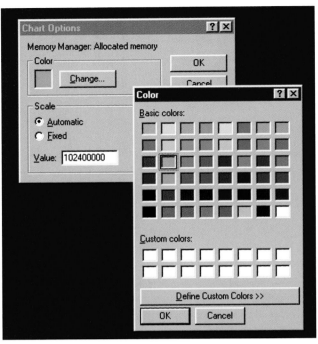

5 The look of the performance monitor charts depends to an extent on space. As you resize the System Monitor window, Windows will rearrange the charts to fill the window.

You can also customize the charts. If you click the Edit button, or select Edit Item from the Edit menu, the Chart Options dialogue box appears. To change the color used for the chart click the Change… button and pick a color from the Color dialogue box that appears.

You can also change the scale used for the graph. In most cases, though, it's best to leave the Scale setting at Automatic. Windows will then set the scale to the most appropriate value for the item.

System Monitor

● **Dial-Up Adapter** This logs data about your Net connection. Choose the Bytes Received/Second item to monitor the speed of downloading items from the Web. Most of the other items are either not useful to know, or else they are error monitors. It may be useful to monitor error items if you are having trouble with your Internet connection.

● **Disk Cache** A high number of cache hits shows that the disk cache is working well. A high number of misses shows that the cache is contributing little to performance. Increasing system memory would allow the cache size to increase.

● **File System** This provides information about the quantity of data written and read, and the number of read/write operations.

● **Kernel** This contains one useful item, Processor Usage. If this is consistently close to 100%, your processor is underpowered. Beware: some programs appear to soak up processor time even when they aren't doing anything useful, so you will always see a high processor usage figure.

● **Memory Manager** This contains items related to your PC's use of memory, but you need an understanding of memory management to make use of most of them. Unused Physical Memory shows you how much RAM is not being used. If there is rarely any unused memory, your PC might benefit from more RAM. You can get an idea of the ideal amount of memory your PC would like by monitoring the Allocated Memory item.

Fine-tuning

Windows is the engine that drives your PC, and just like an engine it benefits from tuning.

Windows is complex. Like a car engine, it has many components working together. And like a car engine, it can benefit from regular tuning, both to negate the effects of wear and tear and to optimize the way that the components perform.

How often you should tune your system is up to you. If the system is well set up, the amount of performance lost through wear and tear is small. In this case it is not worth tuning the PC too often, or spending too much time on it.

If you have never given your PC a tune-up, however, there could be big improvements in performance to be gained. Check out the points shown here to ensure that your computer is working as fast as it should be.

How to fine-tune Windows

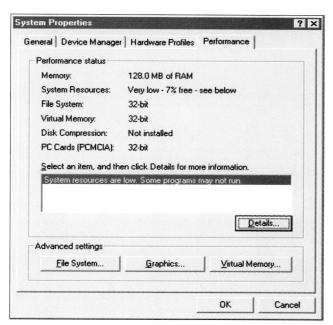

1 Start by checking that the file system and virtual memory are properly set up. Right-click on My Computer and select Properties. Click the Performance tab. Check that both File System and Virtual Memory are shown as 32-bit. If for any reason your system is not running at its best, there will be a message in the box. Here it says that the System Resources are low, which might stop other programs from running properly. If you select the item and click Details, a help box opens with suggestions on how to fix it—in this case, close some of the open programs or restart your computer.

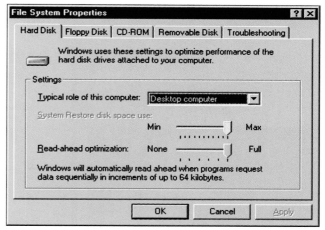

2 Click the File System button under Advanced Settings and check that the Read-Ahead Optimization slider is set to Full. If your PC has plenty of memory you may find an improvement in performance by setting Typical Role of This Computer to Network Server. Under the CD-ROM tab, check that Optimize Access Pattern is set to Quad-speed or higher, and that the Supplemental cache size slider is set to Large.

Click the Graphics button to see the Advanced Graphics Settings dialogue box. Check that the Hardware Acceleration slider is set to Full. This should be reduced only if you experience problems with items not being displayed correctly. Click the Virtual Memory button and make sure that there is adequate free disk space and that no maximum value for virtual memory has been set.

Jargon buster

DMA Direct memory access (DMA) is a way for data to move between a device such as a hard disk or CD-ROM drive and the PC's memory without the CPU getting involved.

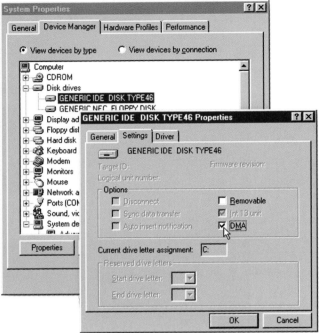

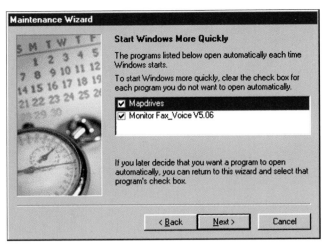

3 Performance can be greatly improved by making sure that your disk drives use DMA. Click on the Device Manager tab in the System Properties dialogue box, expand the Disk drives section, select the IDE Disk entry and click Properties. The DMA check box should be checked. If there is no DMA check box, your system does not support DMA. If the box was not checked, and you check it, Windows displays a warning that enabling DMA might cause problems. The risk is small, but the only way to find out is to ask your PC's manufacturer, or to try it. If you decide to try it, back up your existing configuration and important files first. You will have to restart Windows for the change to take effect.

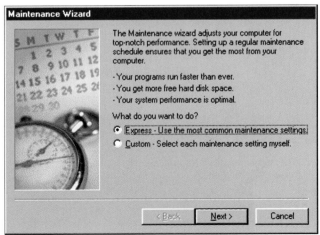

4 If your computer is running Windows Me or 98, you can use the Maintenance Wizard to schedule a regular tune-up. To run the wizard, click Start, Programs, Accessories, System Tools, Maintenance Wizard. The wizard has two options. If you choose the Express option, it will enable your commonly used programs to run faster, it will delete unwanted and temporary files to reclaim disk space and it will check your hard disk for errors.

Some maintenance tasks take a long time to run, and cannot proceed while you are using the PC, so the Maintenance Wizard uses Task Scheduler to run them at a time you choose. You can choose to start them at midday, 8pm or at midnight. Remember to leave your PC switched on so that the wizard can run.

5 Choose the Custom option of the Maintenance Wizard and you will see more options for optimizing performance. One of the options is to enable Windows to start quicker by disabling items from the StartUp folder. To disable an item, clear the check box alongside it. You can re-enable it by running the wizard again and replacing the tick in the check box.

If you have Microsoft Office on your computer you might try disabling the FastFind tool. Uninstallers and system utilities often add programs to the StartUp folder. These programs often provide useful safeguards, but they mean Windows takes longer to start and they can affect performance during normal use, too.

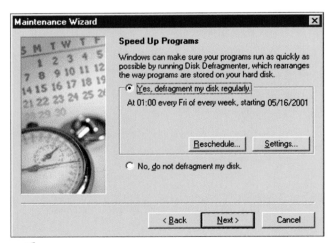

6 If you chose the Custom option you can choose to run the Disk Defragmenter, which speeds up programs by optimizing the way they are stored on your hard disk, or ScanDisk, which scans that hard drive for errors. For further information on these, see pages 29–30.

Finally, you can specify what types of files are deleted to reclaim disk space. The wizard can delete temporary Internet files, which are kept so that you can browse Web sites you have visited offline, and it can empty your Recycle Bin. These options can reclaim a lot of disk space, but it is useful to keep the files unless space is short. The other types of file that the wizard will remove are rarely needed, so it is worthwhile to clear them out on a regular basis.

PC check-up

If you take care to maintain your hard disk properly, your PC will stay as fast and reliable as when you bought it.

One important step you can take to keep your PC healthy is to check the data on the hard disk. If you don't, you might find out that something is wrong only when you try to open a file.

The files and folders in Explorer are a graphical representation of how the data is stored on disk. The files in a folder need not in fact be stored together. Even the blocks holding

parts of a file can be scattered. Windows knows where everything is, in the same way as a book index lets you find specific subjects. But the links—the page references—can be wrong, and then Windows can't find your files. Two disk tools, Defrag and ScanDisk, make sure the links are correct, and that all parts of each file are stored together for faster access.

Maintaining your hard disk

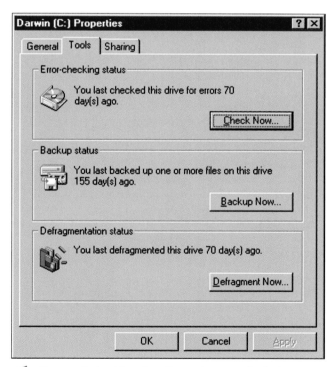

1 You can find out how long it was since you checked on your PC by right clicking on your hard drive (C:), selecting Properties and then the Tools tab. Click Check Now to start the Program or access it by clicking the Start button and choosing Programs, Accessories, System Tools, ScanDisk. (Other programs for hard disk maintenance can be found in System Tools too.) Although some versions of Windows check your hard disk for errors automatically when you restart it after a crash, you should still run the ScanDisk program yourself every month or so.

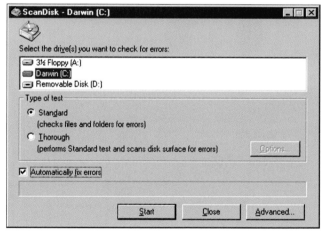

2 ScanDisk has two options. The Standard test checks your files and folders for errors. Run this option regularly. The Thorough test checks every part of your hard disk to make sure it is capable of storing data reliably. This test takes a long time. If you have a new PC there is no reason to run it.

Even the standard ScanDisk can take time. To make it faster, close other programs, and disable your screensaver while you run it.

Jargon buster

Defragmentation Data is stored in small blocks called clusters. As files are deleted, clusters are free to be used by other files. The free clusters may not all be close to each other on the disk, so files get spread all over the disk. The Defrag utility reorganizes clusters so all the bits that make up each file are next to one another. This increases speed.

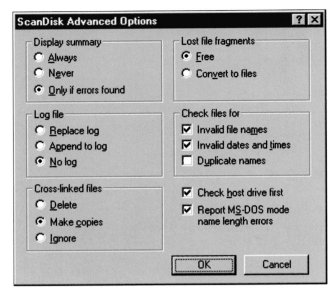

3 ScanDisk's Advanced Options dialogue box gives you some control over what the tool does. Cross-linked files are where two or more files apparently use the same block of data. The data can be correct for one file only. ScanDisk can copy the data so each file has its own copy, but one of the files will be corrupt. Alternatively it can delete both files. Ignoring the problem is not recommended. ScanDisk can convert lost file fragments into files so you can look at them. You might be able to recover lost data from these files, but usually they contain nothing of any use, so it's usually best just to free them.

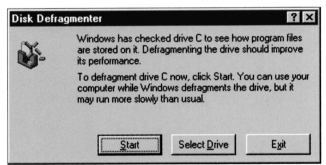

4 Running the Disk Defragmenter (also in System Tools) is less important than running ScanDisk. The Defragmenter's job is to make disk access more efficient by reorganizing the blocks of data in which your files are stored. The only penalty for not running it is that your PC will run slower. With a modern PC, however, the difference won't be that noticeable. It's unlikely to be worth defragmenting your hard disk more often than every couple of months. When you choose Defragment Now, Windows checks your hard disk to see how fragmented it is. It will then display a message telling you whether it is worthwhile to defragment it.

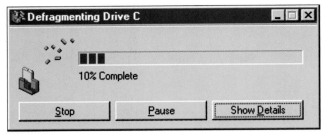

5 If you choose to start defragmenting your hard disk, Windows will display a progress indicator to show how far it has got. The job can take several minutes or hours, depending on the size of the disk. As with checking for errors, the Defragmenter has to redo some of its work every time a change is made to the data on the disk, so the task will be carried out more rapidly if you close down all your other programs and don't use the PC until it has finished.

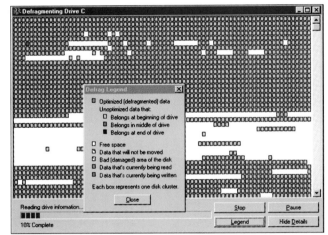

6 If you click on Show Details, Windows displays this map of the blocks of data on your hard disk, so you can monitor what Defragmenter is doing. You can see the key to the map by clicking the Legend button. White space is free space: it is this space that is used by new files. Some blocks have to stay in a particular location on the disk. They are marked with a red square in one corner.

If you see any blocks with a red diagonal line through them, these are damaged blocks. If there are many of these, your hard disk could be starting to fail. In this case, it would be worthwhile running ScanDisk's Thorough check at regular intervals and keeping an eye on the results to see if the number of bad blocks increases.

Deleting files

Getting rid of old, unwanted files and accessories can free up space and improve your PC's performance.

The chances are that the copy of Windows on your computer was installed by the manufacturer. There may be files and accessories that you neither want nor need. If your PC is short of hard disk space, you could recover several megabytes by cleaning out these unwanted files.

It is good practice to make efficient use of your PC's disk space. Be warned, however, that some cleaning

tasks involve deleting files from Windows' own folders using tools such as Windows Explorer. It's all too easy to delete a file that Windows still needs. So don't try to clean up Windows unless you really need the extra space. If you do, back up your system before starting, and don't empty your Recycle Bin until you are sure that none of the files in it are going to be missed.

How to clean up Windows

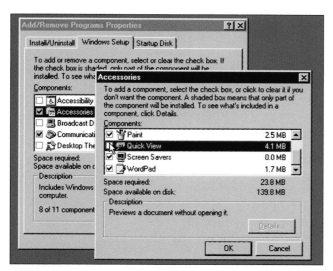

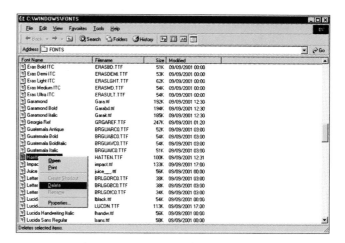

1 You can make big space savings by removing Windows components and accessories you don't use. This is one of the easiest cleaning tasks to do. Open the Windows Control Panel, click on Add/Remove Programs and click the Windows Setup tab. Wait while Windows looks to see what is installed.

Go through the list of options. If the Details button is enabled, click it to see the options in a category, and clear the check mark that appears alongside any items you don't want. Desktop themes take quite a lot of space because of the image and sound files they use. When you have checked them all, close the dialogue boxes by clicking OK. Windows will remove the items from your system.

2 Many software packages install fonts on to your system. If you are not interested in typography, most of these fonts will never be used. As they can take up a lot of space, it can be worthwhile to delete any fonts that you don't want.

Open the Fonts folder using Explorer, go to the Control Panel, and select the Details view. This will display the modification date of each font file, which will allow you to identify the fonts that were installed with Windows. Fonts which have the same date and time stamp as Arial, Courier New and Times New Roman are standard Windows fonts, and should not be deleted.

Any other font is a candidate for deletion, although there is a small risk that an application installed a font for an important reason. If you don't empty the Recycle Bin you can restore any font that you later find that you need. Open a font file to see what the font looks like before deciding whether or not to delete it.

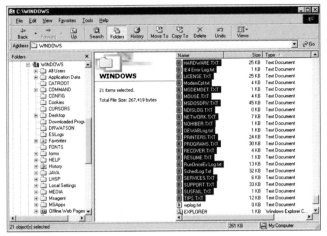

3 The Windows folder lists several text files, most of which contain technical information not included in the Windows documentation. Some of this information may be useful, but a lot will only make sense to an expert with a technical background. A substantial amount of space can be recovered by deleting these text files.

Select the Windows folder in Explorer, and sort the files into file type order by clicking on the Type header on the right-hand column. Select all the text files by holding down the Shift key while you click on the first, and then the last file. If you are concerned about deleting files that might later become useful, consider copying them to a floppy disk. Then delete the files.

Note: some Windows applications such as the Task Scheduler keep an event log in a text file. If this file is open, Windows won't let you delete it, and it will abort the delete operation. If this happens, deselect the open file by holding down Ctrl and clicking on the file name, then try the delete again.

5 Some of the Application files in the Windows folder may never be used, and can be deleted if you are really short of space. Arp, Dosinet, Ftp, NetStat, Ping, Route, Telnet and Tracert are all technical Internet utilities which you won't need if you aren't online, and you probably won't use even if you are. Net, Netdde and the file Net.msg won't be needed if your computer isn't on a network, and even then they may never be used.

Welcome is the Welcome to Windows program which you probably won't ever want to run again. Winfile, Progman and Taskman are the Windows 3.1 File Manager, Program Manager and Task Manager, and are there only for those who prefer to use them. Drwatson is a program debugging tool that you're unlikely to want. Directcc and Filexfer are needed only if you want to connect two computers using a cable.

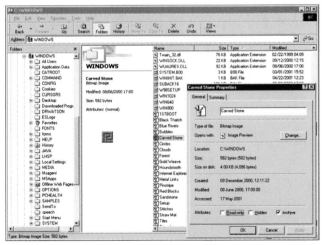

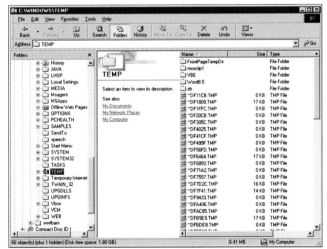

4 The bitmap files in the Windows folder are used for wallpaper backgrounds. If you are never going to use them you might as well delete them. The same goes for screensavers. In the Windows Help folder you can delete Help and CNT files for Windows accessories you don't want or don't need help with. Unused files in the Media folder can waste a lot of space.

If you are unsure whether or not a file is used, right-click its icon and select Properties. The Accessed date tells you when the file was last accessed. If it is the same as the Created date, the file has never been used. However, if a file has not been accessed, you should be cautious about deleting it if you don't know what it does. Some files may be needed for features of Windows that you have not yet used.

6 One place where you will often find large numbers of unwanted and unused files is the Windows Temp folder. This folder is used by applications that want to store information temporarily—hence its name. The trouble is that these applications don't always remember to delete the temporary files when they have finished using them. If the application or Windows crashes then it will not even get the chance. So, over a period of time, a large number of redundant files and folders can accumulate in this location.

For details of clearing temporary files, see pages 33–34.

Temporary files

Track down and delete any unnecessary temporary files from your hard disk to keep it working efficiently.

A degree of hard disk housekeeping is required to keep Windows in order. You could conceivably leave your computer's hard disk untouched for all of its working life. But powerful as it is, Windows requires occasional intervention from you to prevent it from drowning in a sea of superfluous files of its own making.

This section examines how to identify and remove temporary files. Fortunately, there are many useful housekeeping tools that deal with the problem of extraneous file generation and wasted hard disk space. These tools are a part of Windows itself, so you probably won't need to buy any extra software.

Getting rid of unwanted files

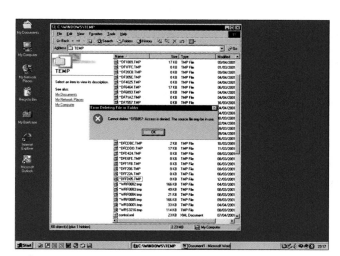

1 In the normal course of events a host of temporary files are created while you're working on a document or an image. You aren't notified that they've been created, but there's no need, as they'll be deleted when you quit that application.

The problem with temporary files arises if the application or Windows crashes before you've had a chance to quit. The end result is the temporary files don't get deleted and turn into permanent files, slowly wasting more and more disk space. As these files are never meant to be retained, they can be deleted.

How do you identify them and where are they stored? The last part is the easiest to answer because temporary files reside in a folder called Temp. This can be in the root (C:\Temp) or in the Windows folder (C:\Windows\Temp) or both. It's fairly safe to delete the files in this folder, but don't forget to quit any applications before you start; otherwise you'll try to delete a temporary file that's in use and you'll get an Access Denied error message.

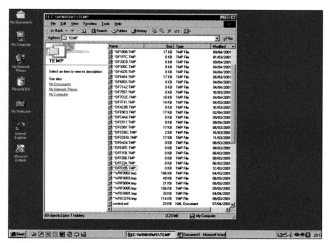

2 Identifying temporary files is simple if they generally have a .tmp or .bak file suffix. But temporary files don't always conform to the location and suffix rules. You won't necessarily locate them all simply by looking in the Temp folder; nor do all temporary files have a .tmp or .bak suffix. Sometimes they are also identified by having a tilde (~) as their first character. An example of this is the autosave file created by Word which has an .asd suffix but obligingly uses a leading tilde.

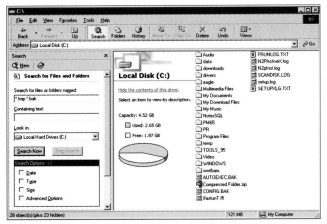

3 The best way to track down temporary files is to use Search in the Start menu. You can search for multiple file types such as .tmp and .bak in one hit by entering them in the Search for Files or Folders Named box; and if you want it to look in every drive, select Local Hard Drives in the Look in box.

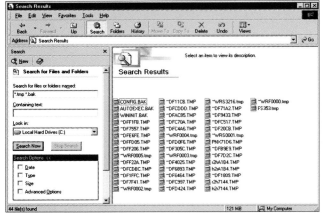

4 You can then delete files directly from the list presented. Exercise some caution. Don't just delete them all, or at the very least drag them over to the Recycle Bin so they can be recovered if you mess up. Leave files like System.bak alone.

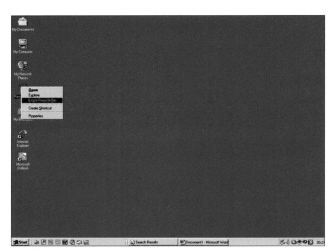

5 Deleted files can be rescued from the Recycle Bin if you make a mistake, but you should empty your Recycle Bin from time to time. To empty the Recycle Bin, right-click the icon and select Empty Recycle Bin. You can wade through the trash and pick the files you want to keep and the ones you never want to see again. Double-click on the Recycle Bin icon to open it. To delete a file, click on it, then click on the X button on the toolbar.

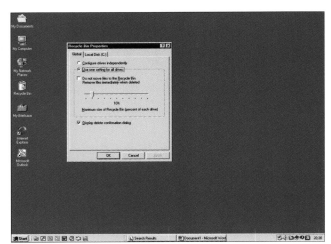

6 Windows sets aside an area of your hard disk to hold deleted files. If space is tight, you need to reduce this. Right-click the Recycle Bin and select Properties. Move the slider that controls the amount of space devoted to deleted files. This is defined as a percentage of the hard disk, so if you have a 10GB disk, the default 10% setting is 1000MB. Set it to 1% or 2% and click on the OK button.

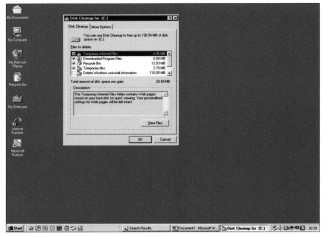

7 Windows Me and 98 come with the Disk Cleanup Wizard in the Accessories, System Tools menu. This can be set to remove a whole range of surplus files automatically.

8 Windows Me and 98 also come with the Scheduled Tasks utility (in the Accessories, System Tools menu) which lets you schedule housekeeping tasks to be performed at predefined intervals, such as during your lunch hour or after work. So you can set it to run the Disk Cleanup Wizard, ScanDisk and Disk Defragmenter every week. Windows 95 doesn't have the Disk Cleanup Wizard, nor does it have the Scheduled Tasks utility. But if you have the Plus! add-on for Windows 95, you have the System Agent, which is almost identical to Scheduled Tasks.

Removing software

If you discard old software properly, you can free hard disk space and speed up your computer.

One of the best things about having a PC is the amount of software available. Some of this software is free. Many other software packages are distributed as shareware or as demos. This is great, because it lets you try the software to see if it does what you want before you buy it. But it also makes it easy to fill your hard disk with programs you don't need.

To avoid this problem, always uninstall software that you decide you aren't going to use; and do it before you forget about it. However, there's a right way and a wrong way to uninstall software. Doing it the wrong way, such as simply deleting it, can cause problems.

Uninstalling programs

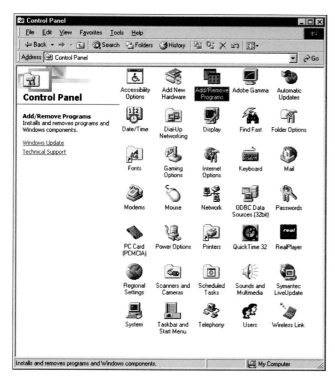

1 Uninstall a program using the uninstaller provided by the software developer. This program notes the files installed when you ran Setup and won't delete anything else. The software you want to remove must not be running. From the Start Menu click on Settings then Control Panel. The icon you want is labeled Add/Remove Programs. This is used to install and remove optional components of Windows.

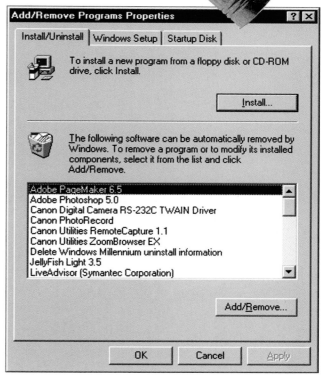

2 When you double-click on Add/Remove Programs, you'll see the Add/Remove Programs Properties dialogue box. Click the Install/Uninstall tab and use this page to add or remove applications. The lower half of the page will show a list of the programs. Select the program you want to get rid of and click Add/Remove. If the program you want to remove isn't listed here, it is either an old DOS program or a Windows program that was written before it was usual to provide an uninstaller. There's no easy way to remove such programs except by using a good commercial uninstaller utility like CleanSweep or Uninstaller.

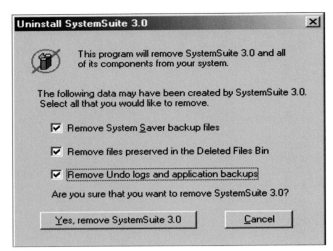

3 What you see after clicking on Add/Remove depends on the program you are removing. At this point you are running a program for adding or removing parts or all of the software. Some uninstall programs may display a wizard like the one shown above, which lets you choose what to remove. Others assume that you want to remove the whole program. If you see a wizard, read its instructions carefully, make your choices, and click Next until you come to the last page. Then click Finish.

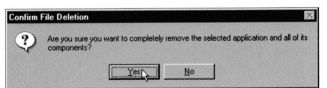

4 Whether or not your uninstaller includes a wizard, you will probably be asked to confirm that you really do want to remove the application you selected. Programmers can never understand why anyone might want to uninstall the program they have slaved for months to write. If you have a fit of remorse this will be your last chance. If you do want to remove it, click Yes.

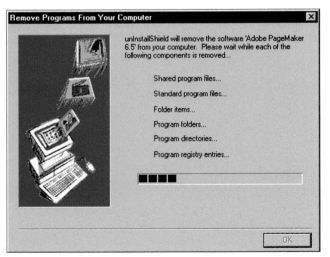

5 The uninstaller will display a window showing progress of the removal of the application. The one shown here is displayed by unInstallShield, one of the most popular programs used by software developers. The uninstaller removes software components from your hard disk, removes shortcuts and menu items that relate to it, and undoes changes that were made to your system's configuration files.

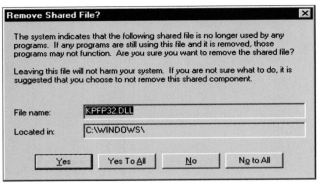

6 Most Windows applications share files with other applications, usually in the folder C:\Windows or C:\Windows\System. Only remove a shared file if no other application uses it. Programs don't record shared files, so you can't be sure if it is safe to remove a file. If the uninstaller asks if you want to remove a shared file, answer No. If you answer Yes and the file is needed, other programs, and possibly Windows, will not run.

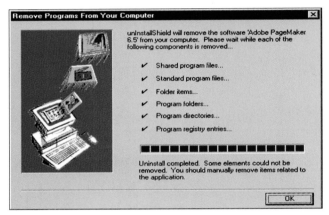

7 The uninstaller starts removing files and folders and deleting references to the program in the registry. You will see its progress by the dotted blue line at the bottom and a check will appear beside each task as it is finished. When the uninstaller has finished you may be asked if you want to restart Windows. The uninstaller may not be able to delete some files if they are still in use. Configuration file changes may not come into effect until Windows restarts. For the uninstaller to complete its task, restart Windows.

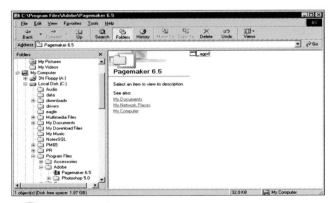

8 Files and folders created by the unwanted application may remain on the hard disk. Many uninstallers only remove files installed by Setup program: files created using the application will not be removed. Uninstaller files may also be left. Use Windows Explorer to find the folder in which the application was installed. If there's nothing you want to keep, delete the folder.

On time

You can use Windows' Task Scheduler to carry out regular chores automatically.

Some PC chores need to be done on a regular basis. Examples are running maintenance tools such as ScanDisk, Disk Defragmenter and a virus scanner. If you are a more advanced user you could create processes using a macro language or Visual Basic for Applications that, when run, would automatically perform certain tasks such as producing a monthly report.

If you have to run these tasks manually, the chances are you'll forget. Fortunately, you don't have to. Windows Me and 98 include a Task Scheduler that will initiate tasks automatically at the times and dates you specify. The Task Scheduler replaces the System Agent for Windows 95 which was included in Microsoft Plus!

Using Windows' Task Scheduler

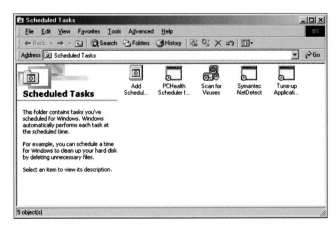

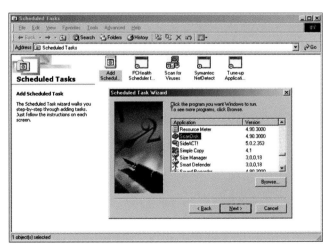

1 You can add, change and remove tasks to be run by the Task Scheduler from the Scheduled Tasks window. To open this, go to the Start menu; you will find it under Programs, Accessories, System Tools. The list of tasks is shown in an Explorer window. The list shows the name of the task, the time it is scheduled, the last time it ran and the time it is next due. If the scheduled item is disabled, the task's icon has a red cross by it instead of a small clock.

2 To add a new task to the list of those to be run, double-click on Add Scheduled Task at the top of the Scheduled Tasks window. This will launch the Scheduled Task Wizard. Click Next, and after a pause of a few seconds you will be presented with a list of programs that you may choose to run. This list is taken from the programs in your Start menu. If you want to schedule a program that isn't on the list, click Browse and use the Select Program to Schedule dialogue box to locate it.

Scheduling tips

If you edit the task's advanced properties (see step 5), you can use command line switches to get a program to run automatically. To run ScanDisk automatically on all drives you should add /A /N after the program name. Make sure there's a space between the name and the first slash. For Defragmenter you should add the switches /all /noprompt.

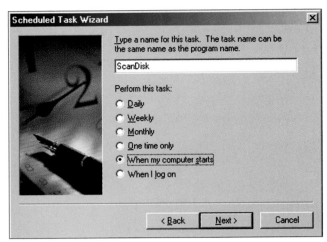

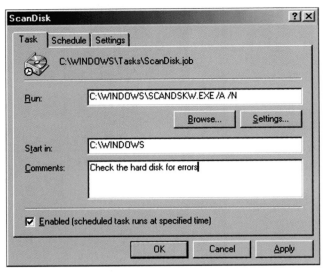

3 The next step is to specify when you want the program you selected to run. You can run it every day, once a week, monthly, or just once on a specific date and time. If you choose one of these options then your computer has to be running at the date and time in the schedule or the task won't be run. The scheduler doesn't warn you if a task wasn't run because the computer was off at the time.

Instead of specifying a set time you can have tasks run when the computer starts, or when you log on. The former is equivalent to adding a program to the Startup program group on your Start menu. The latter is useful if you have enabled user profiles on your PC and only want the task to start when you are using it.

5 On the final page of the wizard is a check box which you should check if you want to edit the advanced properties for the scheduled task. Do this if you want to specify any command line parameters (see Scheduling tips on page 37) or change the startup folder for the program when it runs. You can do it at any time by right-clicking on the appropriate entry in the Scheduled Tasks list and selecting Properties. To remove a task from the list, select it and then press Delete. To prevent a task from running without deleting the entry (so that you can restore it without re-creating it using the wizard), open the task's property page and uncheck the Enabled box in the bottom left-hand corner.

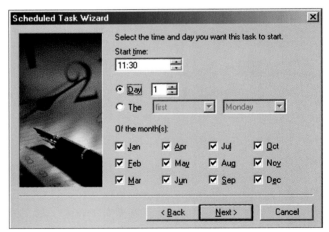

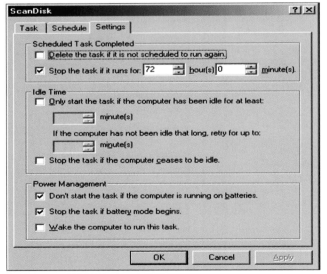

4 On the next page of the wizard you can specify exactly when you want the new task to run. The options you are offered depend on how frequently the task is to be run. If you want it to run daily, you will need to specify the time only. If you want it to run at startup or when you log on, you won't see this page at all.

If you chose the Monthly option in the previous step, you can have the task run every month, on alternate months or in specific months. You can select which months you want the task to run by clicking on the relevant box. You can have a monthly task run on a particular day in the month—which is not much use for a work computer if that day falls on a weekend—or on a particular day of a specific week, for example the first Wednesday of the month.

6 The Settings property page has some advanced options which cannot be set using the wizard. For example, you can choose not to have a task start if a laptop computer is running on batteries. You could do this for disk maintenance tasks where constant hard disk activity would drain the batteries.

Using the Idle Time options you can specify that a task should start only if the PC is idle, or that it should stop when the PC starts being used. This is useful for maintenance tasks that make the PC respond slowly when they are being run. If you use these options, you should schedule the task to run often. If the computer is always busy when the time comes, the task will never be run.

You can get the scheduler to delete a one-off task from the list after it has run. You can also set a time limit for tasks to prevent automated Internet activities from taking too long, for example.

2

Quick customizing

Custom PC

Alter the way Windows works to suit your taste and the way that you work.

Windows is a highly configurable operating system. This means you can change almost every aspect of its look and feel—from the patterns or pictures on the desktop, to the sounds that play when specific events occur. You can alter the responsiveness of the mouse and the keyboard, and even change the mouse pointers if you prefer different ones.

Some of the things you can change in Windows, such as the desktop theme, are purely cosmetic. But others can help you work quicker and more effectively. Therefore, it's worth making the effort to customize Windows to suit your own preferences.

Altering your PC's look and feel

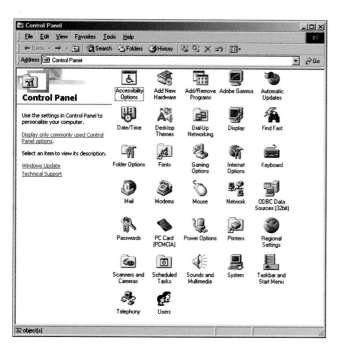

Most Windows custom options can be found in the Control Panel. You can open this from the Start Menu by clicking Settings, Control Panel, or you can open My Computer on the Desktop, and then double-click the Control Panel folder. The objects in the Control Panel folder are either folders or little programs that let you adjust various settings. Sometimes the programs are called applets, a word Microsoft invented to describe little applications.

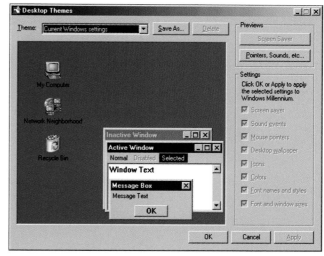

The wallpaper on your desktop, the frames of your windows and even your mouse pointer can all be based on a theme. Several themes are packaged with Windows, such as Jungle, Leonardo da Vinci, Space or the moody view of a train station in Travel. Each theme has its relevant sounds that you can attach to events in Windows (such as Start Up or a dialogue box opening, etc.). But you can mix and match elements from a theme to create your own customized version. To do so, go to **Desktop Themes** in the control panel, click on the theme you like from the Theme list and clear the checkboxes against any items you don't want. Use the Save As button to save your changes under a new name.

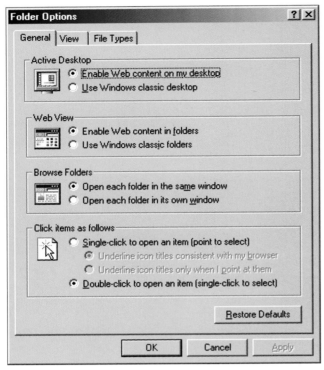

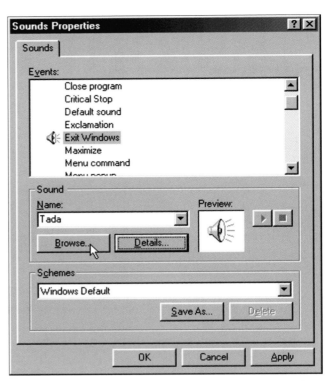

On the desktop a single-click selects an item and a double-click launches a program. However, you can set up single-click opening. Open the **Folder Options** control panel and select the single-click option on the General tab. Then choose either Underline Icon Titles Consistent with my Browser to show links under all icons and file names, or Underline Icon Titles Only when I Point at them which makes things a bit neater.

To change the sounds played when events occur use the **Sounds and Multimedia** applet. Windows comes with several different sound schemes, but they aren't installed by default. If the only scheme you can select is Windows Default, use Add/Remove Programs to install other schemes. You can make your own schemes by associating different sounds with events. Pick an event from the list, then pick a sound to play when it occurs.

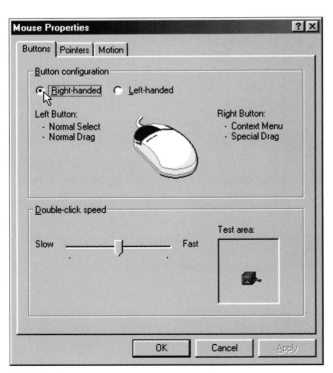

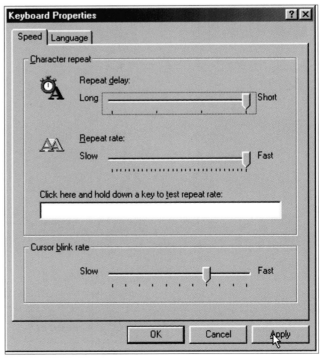

The **Mouse** applet lets you customize the way your mouse works. If you find your double-clicks are interpreted as two single-clicks, increase the interval Windows allows for a double-click by moving the double-click speed slider toward Slow. The Motion page lets you adjust the sensitivity of the mouse, and choose whether the moving pointer should leave a trail.

Keyboard lets you adjust the speed of the keyboard's auto-repeat. The Repeat delay slider sets the length of the interval between the first key-press and the auto-repeat starting. If you find keys repeating inadvertently you should move this toward Long. The Repeat rate slider controls how rapidly the keys repeat once the auto-repeat has started.

On display

The display is a vital part of your PC, especially if you stare at it all day long.

By altering the display of your PC, you can reduce eye strain. For example, you can change the resolution, wallpaper patterns and the colors and the size of elements on screen. This is very important if you are using your computer for long periods of time.

There are also settings that can make things easier for your PC. Using a screensaver can extend the life of your monitor. And you can help the environment by using the power management features to blank the screen when the PC is turned on but not being used.

Experiment with different settings to find the right combination, but remember that what is ideal for you is not necessarily ideal for someone else.

Altering your PC's display

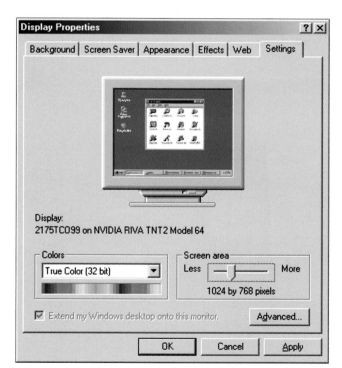

 The **Settings** page controls important attributes of your display. The Screen Area slider sets the resolution. The minimum is 640 x 480 pixels; the maximum depends on your monitor and graphics card. Don't choose too high a resolution. If you do, text will be too small.

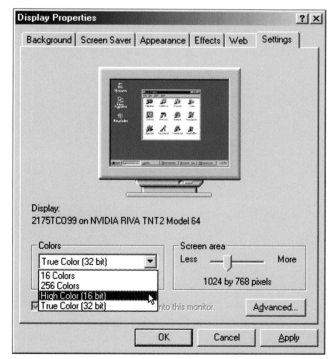

 The **Colors** determines how many different shades of color can be displayed at a time. This affects the quality of photographic images. The more colors you use, the better images look. However, more colors use more memory and more processing power. Some PCs may limit the number of colors you can use at high-screen resolutions because the graphics card isn't powerful enough or doesn't have sufficient memory.

Click Advanced, and under the General tab check the Show Settings Icon on Task Bar box to show a Display Properties icon on the taskbar. You can use this to switch display resolutions quickly and to call up the Display Properties dialogue box when you need it.

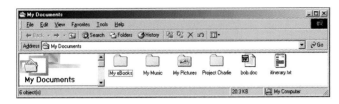

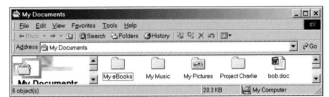

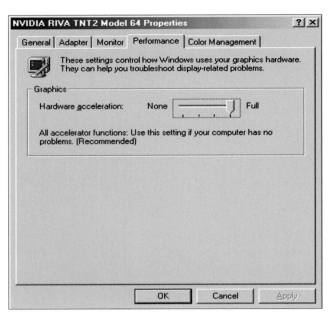

 Font size lets you change the size of the fonts used in windows and dialogue boxes and for icon captions. If you want to use a high-display resolution but find text hard to read, click the Font size dropdown list and choose Large Fonts. This will make the text 25 percent larger. The two screen shots illustrate the difference. You can also choose Other…from the dropdown list. Windows will then display the Custom Font Size dialogue box to let you choose the size of text to use. Don't use this unless you have to, because many programs don't cope well with non-standard font sizes and you may find text and captions they display are truncated.

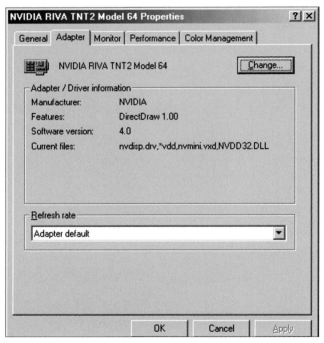

Also under **Advanced** you'll find other settings for your display. You are unlikely ever to have to change anything here except on the advice of a support hotline when troubleshooting a problem. However, it's worth checking the Monitor and Adapter pages to make sure Windows is using the correct drivers. If your monitor is not shown as the correct type, Windows may not be using its full capabilities. You can install the correct driver by clicking Change, then Show All Devices on the Select Device box that appears, and then locating the maker and model. If your monitor isn't listed your PC vendor may be able to help you. If you change your display hardware and Windows doesn't detect it you can use this dialogue box instead of the Add New Hardware Wizard to install the drivers for it.

The **Performance page** of Advanced Display Properties is one you need touch only if you are experiencing display problems. Graphics card drivers use various tricks to speed up display performance. These tricks are sometimes incompatible with certain programs. If things are not being displayed as you think they should, try reducing the Hardware Acceleration slider. This will disable some of the tricks and may cure the fault.

You may need to change the Compatibility settings on the General page if you often use Display Properties to change the color settings for Windows. Under Windows Me and 98, unlike Windows 95, you don't have to restart the PC after changing these settings. But, older programs may not be able to cope with these changes while they are running. One solution would be to close these programs before making the changes and restart them afterward so you can have Windows display a warning. But if you prefer you can force Windows to restart before making the changes.

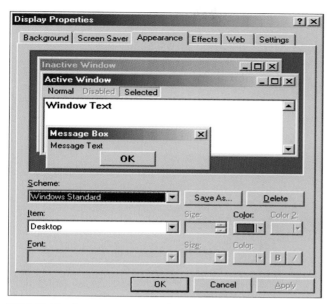

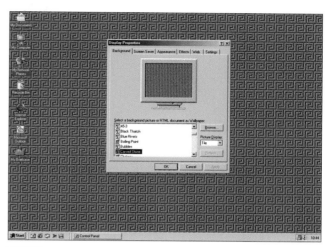

 The **Appearance page** of Display Properties lets you change the colors and fonts used by windows, dialogue boxes and the Desktop. You can choose from one of a number of pre-defined color schemes by picking them from the Scheme dropdown list. The window above shows you what the selected scheme looks like. To apply the scheme click Apply or OK.

You can also design your own schemes. Select an item by clicking on it in the preview window or picking it from the Item dropdown list. You can then set the background color and, if appropriate, the font and the color of the text. If you don't like the graduated color fill that Windows Me and 98 use for window title bars, set Color 1 and Color 2 to be the same. After you have changed a scheme, click Save As and save it with a new name.

 Background patterns are similar to wallpaper tiles, except that they don't contain color information. They also don't use as much memory as wallpaper. Patterns are like masks or stencils and the Desktop color shows through the holes in the mask. To change the color of the pattern you must change the Desktop color from the Appearance property page.

To use a pattern choose one from the dropdown list. The effect is previewed—though too small to see clearly—in the screen at the top of the page. To see the pattern on the Desktop click Apply.

If you want, you can alter the background patterns. If you click Edit Pattern the Pattern Editor will appear showing an enlarged copy of the mask. You can toggle holes in the mask on and off by clicking on the pattern with the mouse. When you close the Pattern Editor, Windows will ask whether or not you want to save the changes you have made.

 The Appearance page lets you set the color of the Windows Desktop, but if you don't want a plain desktop use the **Background page** to apply a pattern to it or cover it with wallpaper. Wallpaper can be a tile pattern or a photo. Most wallpaper files supplied with Windows are tiles. When you use one of these files, click the Tile radio button so that the pattern fills the screen. For larger wallpaper images such as photographs, click Center so that you see a single copy of the image positioned centrally on the screen. Wallpaper images use memory that could otherwise be used by your software. If your PC has limited memory of 16MB or less, wallpaper could adversely affect its performance.

 The **Effects page** of Display Properties lets you customize your system even further by changing the icons used by Windows. Select the icon you want to change and click the Change Icon button. You will then see the Change Icon dialogue box. Using this you can scroll through the alternative icons that are available. When you see an icon you like, select it and click OK. To restore the default icon, click the Default Icon button.

If you don't find any suitable alternative icons use the Browse… button to locate other files that contain icons. Two files that contain a number of icons are Shell32.dll in the Windows System folder and Moricons.dll in the Windows folder.

If you have a high-resolution display, and have chosen to use large fonts you might want to check the Use Large Icons option. This causes Windows to use larger 48 x 48 icons instead of the standard size which is 32 x 32 pixels.

Jargon buster

Resolution Screen images are made up of dots of color called pixels. The number of pixels across and down the screen is called the resolution. Common screen resolutions are 640 x 480, 800 x 600 and 1,024 x 768.

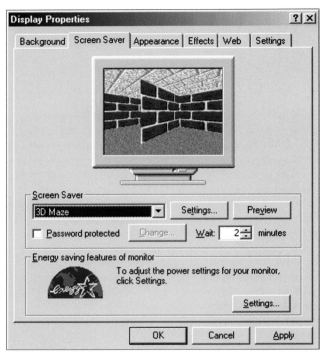

 On the **Screen Saver** page you can choose an animation to be displayed on the screen if your computer is left idle for a few minutes. The purpose of the animation is to prevent a static image from becoming imprinted on the screen, which might happen if it was left for many hours. With modern color monitors, however, there isn't much risk of this happening and most people install screensavers just for fun.

You choose a screensaver from the dropdown list. If you click Preview, you will see the screensaver running in the screen above. Click Settings to customize the screensaver. The settings you can change will vary from one screensaver to another but will typically control things such as the speed of the animation.

You can set how long the computer must be idle before the screensaver starts. If you check the Password Protected box Windows will require you to enter a password to return to your Desktop after the screensaver has started. To set the password click the Change... button. If you work in an office setting a short wait interval and using a password will deter people from tampering with your unattended computer.

Display tip

If gradated shades appear to be banded rather than smooth, it could be due to the particular combination of the color depth and screen resolution that your system is using. For example, if you're using 256 colors, try increasing this if your system and monitor will allow it.

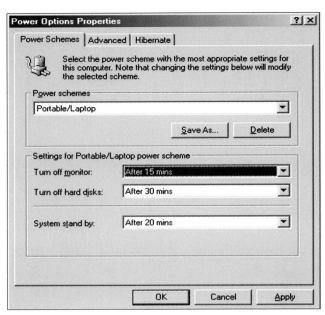

 If you have an energy-saving monitor you can access the power management settings from the Screen Saver properties page. Click Settings under Energy Saving Features of Monitor and the **Power Options Properties** dialogue box will appear. From this you can specify that the monitor should turn itself off if the computer is left idle for a specified period. Using power management will save electricity, but don't specify too short a period before the power turns off. Constantly turning the power on and off stresses the monitor components and can shorten its life. It can also be annoying when you return to your computer to have to wait for the screen to warm up before you can see a picture.

 Unless it is important to you that the colors shown on the screen are as accurate a reflection of the original image as can be, you won't need to worry about the **Color Management** page of Display Properties, accessed by clicking Advanced on the Settings page. Color management lets Windows control the color balance instead of using the color controls provided on the monitor. This enables you to get more consistent colors between different display devices. To use color management, monitor profiles must be provided by the monitor manufacturer. From this property page you can install monitor profiles, switch between them and specify the default.

Startup folder

Automatically launch the programs you always use when Windows starts up.

There are probably a small number of programs on your PC that you want to run from the moment that Windows starts up. These may include virus checkers, crash monitors or a scheduler which can automatically run other tasks at set times.

Windows has more than one way of running programs at startup. If you use your PC for word processing, for example, you could have your word processor start up ready for you to

use every time you turn the PC on.

However, there is a downside to having programs start automatically at startup. It can take a long time to start lots of programs at once, and until they are all started the PC is too busy to do anything else. Some applications install programs that run automatically at startup whether you want them to or not. So it's useful to know how to remove programs from the startup list.

Altering Windows' startup

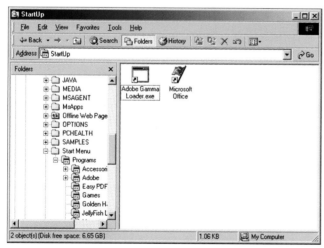

1 The method for launching programs automatically at startup that most people are familiar with is the StartUp Folder. You can see the contents of this folder by clicking on the Start button and opening Programs, StartUp. The items here—usually shortcuts to a program, but they could be shortcuts to files that you want opened automatically—will be run whenever Windows starts in the normal way.

Items in the StartUp folder aren't run when Windows starts in Safe Mode. Windows may start in Safe Mode if there has been a problem during the previous startup. The purpose of Safe Mode is to allow you to correct startup problems, so Windows ignores the StartUp folder in Safe Mode in case one of the programs there is the cause of the startup problem.

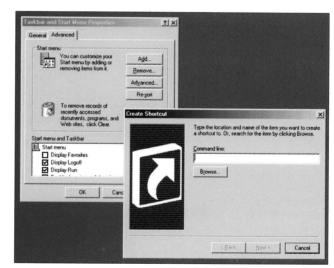

2 To add an item to the StartUp folder, click Start, Settings, Taskbar and Start Menu to open the Taskbar and Start Menu Properties box. Click on the Advanced tab. Click Add, then click Browse on the Create Shortcut dialogue box that appears and locate the program you want to run automatically at startup. When you have found the program, click OK so its name appears in the Command Line field.

Startup tip

To prevent programs in the StartUp folder running during a normal startup, hold down the Shift key until Windows has finished loading.

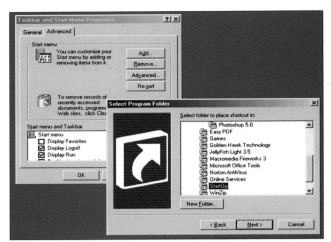

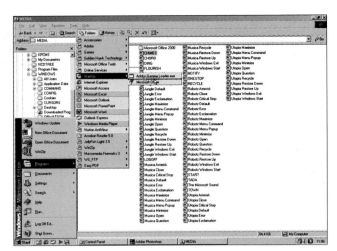

3 Click Next, so that the Select Program Folder dialogue box appears. Scroll down the list of menu folders. Under Programs you should see the StartUp folder. Select it and click Next again. Enter a name for the program that you have selected, or accept the default, then click Finish. The program has now been added to your StartUp folder and will be run automatically the next time you start Windows.

5 In Windows Me and 98 there is an easier way to add items to your StartUp folder. Locate the program you wish to add using Explorer. Click and drag it to the Start button on the Taskbar. If your Taskbar is set to auto-hide, drag the program to the screen edge, wait for the Taskbar to appear and then drag it to the Start button.

Keep the mouse button down and the Start menu will appear. Drag the program to the Programs item on the menu. Don't release the mouse button. Wait, and Programs appears. Drag the program to the StartUp item. The StartUp menu appears. Move the program to the StartUp menu (a line will show where it will be inserted) and release the button. A new shortcut will be inserted. To remove an item from the StartUp menu right-click it and select Delete.

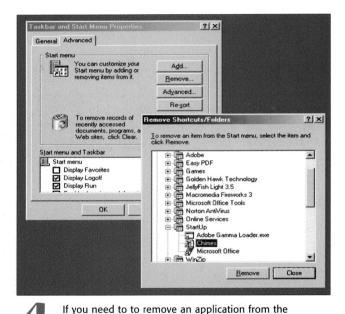

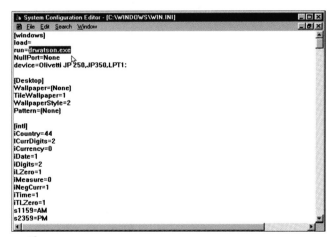

4 If you need to to remove an application from the Windows StartUp folder, click on Start, Settings, Taskbar and Start Menu Properties and then click on the Advanced tab. Next click on Remove. The Remove Shortcuts/Folders dialogue box should appear. Scroll down the list of menu folders shown in this dialogue box until you see the one named StartUp. Click on the plus sign alongside it to expand the folder and show its contents. Select the item you want to remove from the StartUp folder and click Remove. Click Close to close the Remove Shortcuts/Folders dialogue box, and OK to close the Taskbar and Start Menu Properties.

Most programs are run automatically at startup for a good reason, so be careful when removing items from the StartUp folder. It may be difficult to locate the program again so that you can add it back to the folder later. The removed item will be in your Recycle Bin. If you find when you restart Windows that the program you removed performed an essential function you can quickly restore it by opening the Recycle Bin, locating the shortcut you removed, right-clicking it and selecting Restore.

6 Windows has another method of specifying programs that are to be run automatically at startup, inherited from older versions of Windows. This method uses entries in the configuration file Win.ini. You might use this method instead of placing a shortcut in the StartUp folder to make it harder for others who use your PC to remove a program from the startup list.

To edit Win.ini, open the System Configuration Editor by going to Start, Run and then typing "Sysedit" in the open box. Select the Win.ini window. On the line that starts run= below the line that says [windows] type the full name (including location) of the program you want to run. If there is more than one program name on the line, the names should be separated by spaces and should be the MS-DOS short name, not a long Windows file name. The load= line has a similar effect, but is meant to load the program minimized as an icon. Many programs ignore this setting and load with the same result as if they were run using the run= line.

Final touches

Perfect the way the Windows interface works with a few special tweaks.

The earlier pages of this chapter dealt with customizing the way Windows works. There are many more options that can be altered using software rather than options in the standard user interface.

Microsoft probably decided there were enough customizing options already, and that adding more would just confuse people. So it created a special Control Panel accessory called Tweak UI for the extra options. This isn't part of Windows 98; it isn't even an option you can add from Add/Remove Programs. But it does come on some versions of the Windows 98 CD. Other users, including Me users, can get it from download sites, such as www.zdnet.com. It's very handy and you'll certainly find a use for it.

Understanding Tweak UI

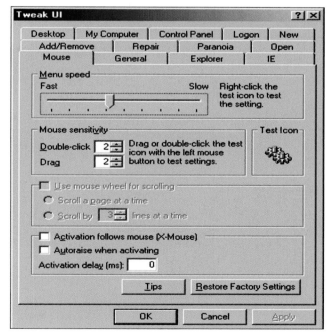

 Since **Tweak UI** isn't a standard Windows accessory you've got to install it before you can use it. Once you've downloaded the file double-click the tweakui.exe file. Make a note of the folder where the files will be unzipped to and click Unzip. Use Explorer to go to the folder. In the right-hand Explorer panel you'll see several files called tweakui. Right-click on tweakui.inf and select Install from the context menu. This action will install the Tweak UI accessory to your Windows Control Panel.

Tweak UI tip

 Use the What's This? help facility for an explanation of any Tweak UI option. Click the question mark button on the title bar, then click the setting you're interested in.

Tweak UI takes the form of a tabbed dialogue box with a different page for each option. The **Mouse page** lets you change settings that affect the responsiveness of the mouse. Menu Speed controls how quickly sub-menus appear. Double-click Sensitivity determines how far (in pixels) the mouse may move between clicks. If double-clicks don't register because you move the mouse slightly, increase this value. Drag sensitivity determines how far the pointer must move with a button held down to be treated as a move operation.

This page includes options for using the wheel, if your mouse has one. The X-Mouse activation option is a more radical change to the interface and may take some getting used to. It lets you make a window active—in other words, able to accept keyboard input—just by moving the pointer over it. There's no need to click it.

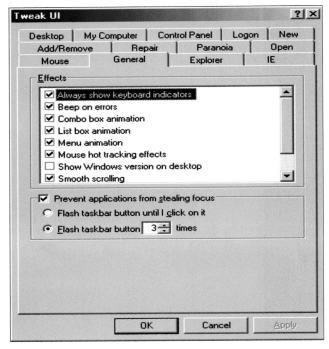

The **General page** contains many different options. Animation of windows, menus and dropdown lists can be annoying or make a system seem slow. Smooth text scrolling may not be to your liking either. These options can be enabled or disabled from the Effects list on this page.

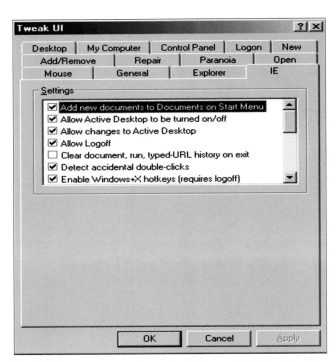

The **IE page** contains a list similar to the Effects list on the General page. Here you can enable or disable settings that relate to Internet Explorer, and decide whether you want the Documents or Favorites items to appear on the Start Menu.

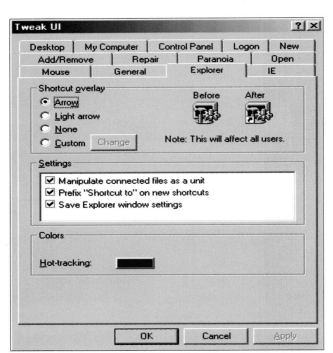

There are useful settings on the **Explorer page**. Under Shortcut Overlay you can specify whether you want the arrow on a white background, a subtle arrow or no arrow at all in the lower left corner of shortcut icons. Under Settings you can choose to prefix the words Shortcut To to the names of new shortcuts. Also under Settings, you can choose whether you want Explorer to remember the View type and icon display order used to display a folder, and to open at startup the folders that were open when you last shut down. Manipulate Connected Files as a Unit means that anything done to a file of one type (such as HTML) will also be done to related files.

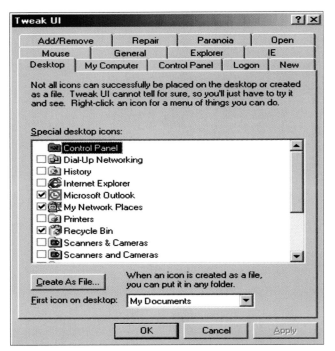

On the **Desktop page** you can choose whether you want certain special icons such as the Internet, Network Places or the Recycle Bin to appear on your Desktop. This is the only way to get rid of some special icons that Windows won't let you delete. If you select an item from this list and click Create As File... Tweak UI will create a file which will cause the selected item to be opened when you double-click it. You can save this file into any folder. You can use this option to create Desktop icons for things like the Printers folder or the Control Panel. Just save the file to your Desktop.

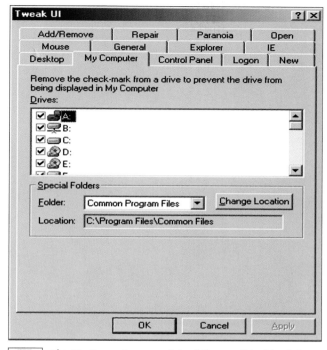

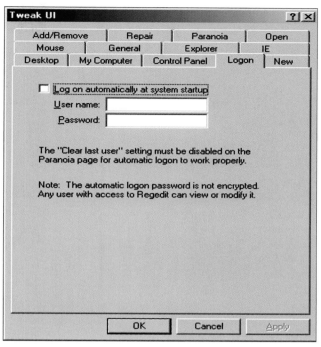

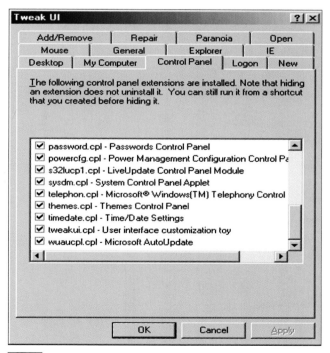

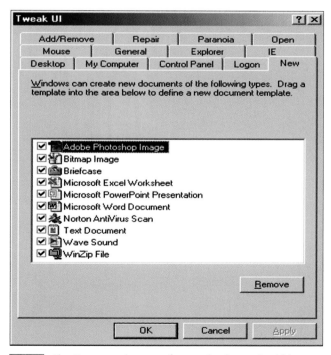

 The **My Computer page** lists all the possible drive letters on your computer. If you uncheck the box against a drive letter, that drive won't appear in My Computer or in Explorer. You could do this to hide a drive from other users. The Special Folders panel lets you change the location of vital system folders such as the one that holds Start Menu shortcuts. But it's best not to alter locations as this might have serious consequences.

On the **Logon page** you can enter your network user name and password and have Windows log on to the network automatically for you at startup. As the note warns, the password isn't encrypted so this option shouldn't be used in an environment where security matters.

The **Control Panel page** lets you choose icons to appear in the Control Panel. It contains a scrollable list with the names of the programs that run each Control Panel item and in most cases a description. You can remove an icon you don't use by unchecking the box beside its name. This won't do any harm: the file isn't uninstalled so if you decide you need it at a later date you can easily reinstate it.

The **New page** lets you choose what items should be listed in the cascading menu that appears when you right-click a folder and select New. This menu normally contains a list of file types. Choosing one of them creates an empty file of that type which you can rename and then open for editing in the appropriate application. Entries in this menu are added when you install applications. To remove entries you don't want, uncheck the box beside the file type in this list.

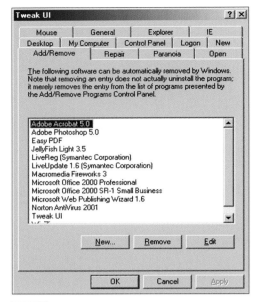

 If you have items in Control Panel's Add/Remove Programs list that no longer exist because you've uninstalled them, the **Add/Remove page** lets you remove these redundant items. Normally, items are removed from the list when you uninstall them. You should only use Tweak UI to remove entries where the program has been uninstalled and for some reason its Add/Remove entry was left behind. To remove an entry, select it and click Remove. You can also edit entries and create new ones, but unless you're a technical expert you're unlikely to need to.

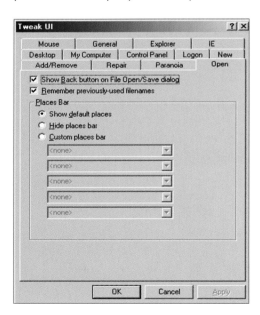

 The **Open page** features work with the Open page in Windows Me and Windows 2000 only. The first option, Show Back Button on File Open/Save Dialog, makes it easier to navigate back to the previous directory you were in. By selecting the Remember Previously-used Filenames option you can get a list of the names or files you've most recently opened or saved. To do so click the arrow beside the File Name box. This is useful if you've saved a file with a complicated name. The main feature of the Open page is the Places Bar which has links to five areas where you are most likely to find the file you are looking for. Using Tweak UI you can reinstate the default folders that include My Documents, the Desktop and Favorites. Alternatively, you can hide the Places Bar (in fact the bar remains, only the linked folders disappear) or customize it with your own list of folders.

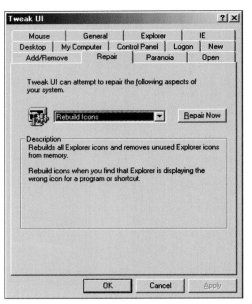

 The **Repair page** is one of Tweak UI's most useful features. It fixes a number of common Windows problems by resetting various items to the installed defaults. If some of the icons that are being displayed are wrong, select Rebuild Icons and click Repair Now. Choose Repair Associations if you lose the ability to open certain files or if options on the context menu for a file type disappear. Repair System Files can fix problems with missing or overwritten files, although Windows Me has its own System Restore process that is more thorough.

If the Fonts folder, the Temporary Internet Files folder or the URL History folder appear to be treated like normal folders instead of special folders, their special status can also be restored from here.

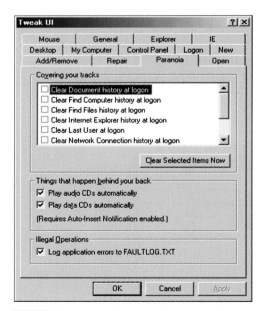

 The **Paranoia page** will appeal to the paranoid among you. If you worry that family, friends or Big Brother can see what you've been doing on the Internet or on your PC generally, options you can select here will cause various history lists to be cleared at login. You can also control whether audio or data CDs are started automatically—assuming that your CD-ROM drive supports auto-insert notification and that it is enabled.

If you aren't paranoid but merely persecuted by application errors, check Log Application Errors To FAULTLOG.TXT. Windows will then log details of every software crash to this file which you can then print out or e-mail to the vendor of the offending application.

Word power

Customizing Microsoft Word is easy. Here you will discover several ways of using it more efficiently.

Word can be customized as easily as any Windows program in terms of changing its colors, fonts and toolbars, but on the following pages you'll see how customizing Word can change the way you work and help you get things done more easily.

A different view

Switching between Word's four views means more than being able to display documents at different zoom levels or with greater or lesser fidelity to their printed appearance. Outline, Web Layout and Print Layout views all include tools and features that are not found in any of the other views, so being in the right mode changes both the way you work and the tasks you can tackle. In Outline mode, for example, you can structure and rearrange documents by manipulating paragraph headings. Also you can index or check the spelling of a group of files as if they were a single document.

Templates and tables

By customizing the templates supplied with Word you can create your own combinations of styles, toolbars and macros to suit the types of documents you want to create. You may also design new templates from scratch, or create them by borrowing features from existing templates. And because templates can contain any type of text or object, you can make them even more versatile by embedding pre-formatted tables to simplify the creation of tabulated lists.

Detailed information on using views, templates and tables is provided in the form of step-by-step examples. Try these out; then get to work customizing your own version of Word.

You will need

ESSENTIAL

Software Windows 98 or Windows Me and a copy of Microsoft Word. Word 2000 is used here, but earlier versions will also work.
Hardware 486 PC or better with 8MB of RAM.

Which software?

Any good word processor offers templates, styles, tables and alternative views. Versions of **Word** prior to Word 2000 are no exception, and although older copies of Word may not have exactly the same options as Word 2000, the differences are insignificant.

Corel WordPerfect and **Lotus Word Pro** users can duplicate the Word features here, but techniques may vary. Templates in Word Pro are called SmartMasters, and in WordPerfect there's no Outline view. Instead, it has an Outline/Bullets & Numbering command on its Insert menu. This adds a structured list to the document, which is less convenient than a separate outline view.

Lotus Word Pro adopts a similar approach but has a Show/Hide option in its View menu to switch between outline and layout views.

View review

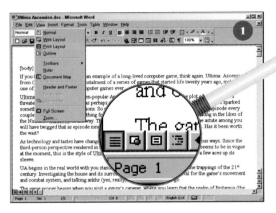

The **View menu** isn't the only way of choosing a screen display. At the left of the horizontal scroll bar are four buttons corresponding to the first four options on the View menu.

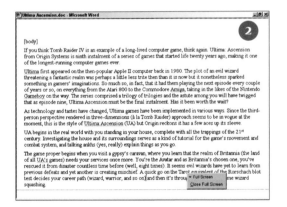

The standard menus and toolbars are not displayed in **Full Screen** mode. But floating toolbars appear when you select objects that require them.

Print Preview tip

Print Preview is the view in Microsoft Word that users often forget because it is found on the File menu and not the View menu. Its primary function is to show how a document will print, including headers, footers and page breaks. It can also be used for editing. When Print Preview is activated the left mouse button acts as a zoom control, but click on the magnifying glass icon on the toolbar and the magnifier is replaced by a standard editing cursor. You can then edit, type, use menus and click toolbars, just as if you were in any of the standard views.

Changing the way you view your documents in Word could change the way that you work.

A glance at Word's View menu seems to indicate there are four ways of viewing a document: Normal, Web Layout, Print Layout, and Outline. This fails to take account of the Full Screen and Zoom options at the bottom of the menu, which can be used to modify the primary views (1).

If Word is running in a window, selecting Full Screen temporarily expands it to fill the screen and displays the currently selected view without the clutter of tool, menu and status bars (2). The Zoom option scales a document to a fixed percentage. It can also shrink or expand a document to fit the screen and display several pages at once (3). Since the Full Screen and Zoom options can be applied to any of the primary views, the user can tailor the appearance of Word's screen for almost any task.

Main views

Word's default view is Normal. Here the layout of a page is simplified to make it easier to add and edit text. Columns, headers and footers are not shown; dotted lines show page breaks; and graphics do not appear in the positions in which they will print (4).

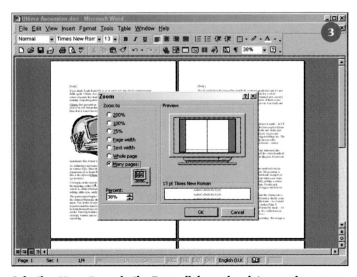

Selecting **Many Pages** in the Zoom dialogue box lets you view more than one page at a time. The setting in the **Percent** box determines how many pages will fit on a single screen.

A better view for most purposes is Print Layout, which represents the printed page. This has the disadvantage that the PC has to work hard to reformat a document while you type, which can slow older PCs to a crawl. For this reason, Normal view is set as the default mode. But if your computer can cope with the processing overhead of Print Layout there is no reason not to use it.

Supplementary views

Web Layout view is for documents destined to be seen online. In it, text wraps to suit the width of the window and normal page breaks are ignored. Pictures appear as they would in a browser. By selecting the Document Map navigation panel you have a fast way of jumping from one part of a document to another (5). (For more details, see pages 67–70.)

Outline view is for planning and restructuring. It displays blocks of text in the form of headings that can be copied or reorganized. Once the structure of a document has been modified it's usual to switch back to Normal or Print Layout view for editing (6).

The Outline view menu makes it easier to work with master documents. You can view related files, such as the chapters of a book or the sections of a report, as if they were a single document.

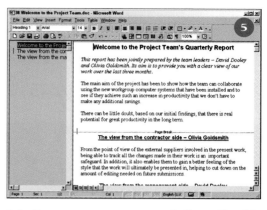

Selecting **Document Map** automatically enables this facility. Notice how the lines in the main part of the document have wrapped to suit the narrow margins while preserving the centered layout of the page.

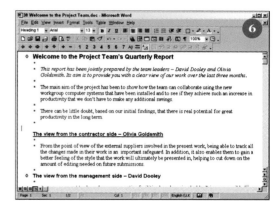

In **Outline view**, blocks of text can be collapsed to show nothing but their headings. The Outline toolbar determines which heading levels should be shown and which ones should be collapsed, and also provides additional tools to promote, demote and move headings.

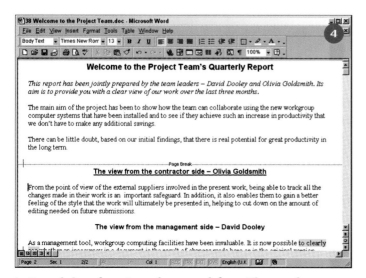

In **Normal view**, character and paragraph formatting are shown on screen as they'll print, as demonstrated by the underlining and centering above, but breaks between pages are marked by non-printing dotted lines and page headers are not shown at all.

Zoom tips

● The Zoom control on the Word toolbar allows you to choose whether to display a single page or two pages at once. But if you select Zoom from the View menu you can use the more versatile Zoom dialogue box instead to display multiple pages in thumbnail format.

● Intellimouse users can zoom interactively by holding down Control on the keyboard while rotating the wheel button on the mouse. Rotate the wheel forwards to zoom in and backwards to zoom out.

● You can set different zoom levels for each view in Normal, Web Layout and Page Layout modes but the Outline view always has the same zoom level.

Word templates

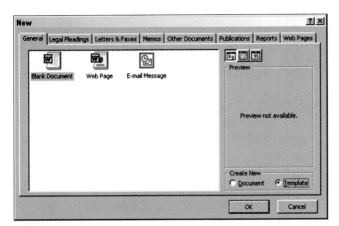

1 Create a new template by clicking New on the File menu. Click on Blank Document and select the Template radio button in the bottom right-hand corner. Click OK.

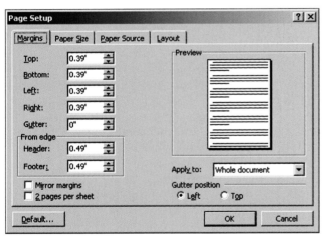

2 This is to be a template for a newsletter so set up narrow margins using Page Setup on the File menu. Click Margins and set the margins to 1cm. Save it as News.dot.

Template tips

● Changes made to Normal.dot affect every document based on it. If you have saved unwelcome changes to Normal.dot you can revert to the original version by closing Word, moving Normal.dot from the Templates folder and restarting Word. This rebuilds Normal.dot from scratch, which means that any modifications you've made are lost.

● You can use your favorite template as the default template by renaming it as Normal.dot. Move the original Normal.dot out of the Templates folder and copy your own file in its place. Keep a copy of the original file in case you change your mind.

Templates make it easy to create personalized documents that have a consistent style and layout.

All Word documents are based on templates. Word has a standard template, Normal.dot, which it uses by default. It appears in the New Document dialogue box as Blank Document.

What's in a template?

All visible information stored in a template falls into one of three categories. The most basic type is fixed data, such as company addresses, logos and other unchanging items. These appear in every document based on the template.

A second type of information is blocks of text, headings and pictures that always appear in the same place, but whose contents vary. This type of replaceable data is called a placeholder. Once a new document has been created, the author replaces the words and pictures in placeholders.

The third type of information in a template is generated by fields. Typically these are used for dates, times and page numbers. They differ from fixed information, which never changes, and placeholder information, which the user changes manually, as fields are updated automatically.

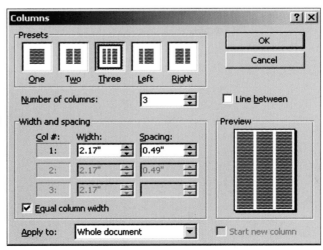

3 Turn on the display of text boundaries if they are not already on (Tools, Options, View, Text Boundaries) and select a three-column layout in the Columns dialogue box, accessed from the Format menu. Click OK.

Some templates contain no visible components. What they do contain is formatting data that determines a document's appearance. Templates store the margins and page layout options selected under Page Setup, the paragraph styles defined using the Format menu, macros and Visual Basic programs, Autotext entries, and all the customized toolbars, shortcuts and menus.

6 Create a text box below the title with the same wrapping options as the title. This will act as a spacer between the title and the text. Type or paste some text into the page.

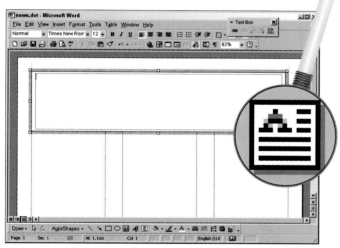

4 The title of the newsletter won't change from month to month so it goes in a text box. To create it, open the Drawing toolbar by clicking the Drawing button, click the Text Box icon and drag out a box shape at the top of the page.

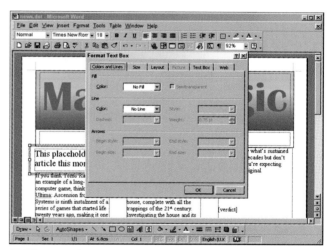

7 Draw a text box to contain the title of the first article. It should span the first two columns. Set the text wrapping as for the title, and use Colors and Lines to set the line color to No Lines and the fill color to No Fill. Type in some text.

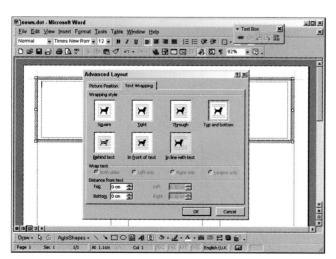

5 Right-click on the edge of the text box, select Format Text Box, click the Layout tab, then the Advanced button and then the Text Wrapping tab. Select Top and Bottom and click OK. This stops text in the main columns overwriting the title. Click OK, then type the title into the text box and format it.

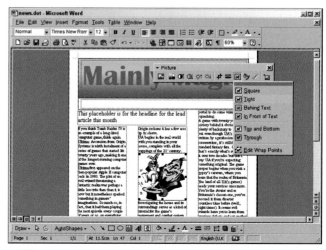

8 Click Insert, Picture, Clip Art. Double-click on any piece of clip art to insert it, then move and size the picture in Page Layout mode. Finally, click the Text Wrapping icon on the Picture toolbar and select Tight wrapping. Save the template.

Template changes

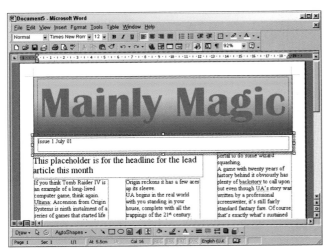

1 Load the News.dot template. An obvious improvement is to make better use of the empty box that is separating the title from the text below. Type Issue 1 and July 01, with a tab space separating them. Format the new text as 12pt Arial Bold.

2 Click twice on the tab control at the left of the ruler to change the left tab to a right tab. Click anywhere on the ruler to create a right tab, then drag it over the right margin marker. This should force July 01 up against the right margin. Because the template will be used in other months and years change Issue 1 to Issue No and July 01 to Month/Year.

Template tip

Always use styles instead of font and paragraph formatting. This makes it easy for a user to add new material to a document and format it to match the layout and appearance of the existing text.

Once you've made a working template it's easy to modify it if your needs ever change.

Before you can use the News.dot template you must put a copy of it in Word's templates folder. Click Options on the View menu, then the File Locations tab. The entry in the User Templates box indicates where Word expects to find its templates and you should use Windows Explorer to copy the News.dot template into this folder.

Once the template is in place, click New on the File menu. Make sure the Create New Document radio button is selected, highlight News.dot and click OK. The newsletter will appear, not as a template but as a new document, so any changes you make to the newsletter won't affect the stored template.

Using your newsletter template

The title doesn't need changing because it's the same every month, but the lead headline should be changed by highlighting the placeholder text and over-typing it with a new headline. New body text can be typed or pasted into the running columns in the same way.

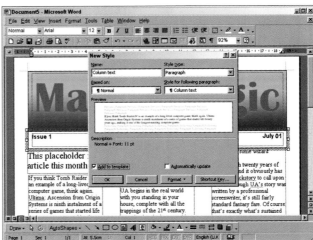

3 The text in the body columns is too small and too tightly packed. Create a style for column text that can be used in the future. Place the cursor anywhere in the first column and click Style on the Format menu. Click New and name the new style Column text. Check the Add to template box.

For the template to be useful it has to contain more than a title and headline. The best way to improve a template is to load it, make changes and then save it. It's also possible to save any document as a template if you decide that it could be useful. The only proviso is that when you save the document it can't have the same name as the template on which it was based.

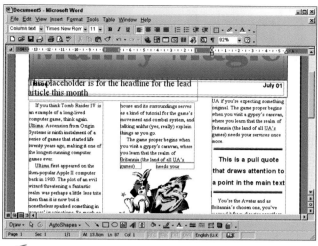

6 A really useful style for a newsletter is the pull quote, which is a way of drawing attention to an important point in the main text. To use it you copy a short block of text and apply a specially designed pull-quote style. This one uses a bold Arial font. The double-spaced lines are centered and the top and bottom borders are mirror images of each other.

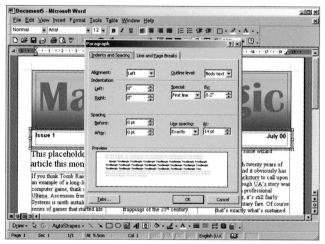

4 Click Format, Font and set the text to 11pt Times New Roman. Click OK to return to the New Style dialogue box. Click Format, Paragraph and use the settings shown above—Indent first line = 0.2" and Line spacing = exactly 14pt. Click OK twice, then click Apply to see the effect of the changes.

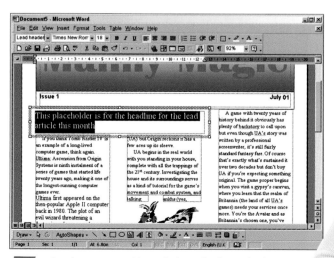

5 Another way to add a style is to duplicate the format of existing text. To create a style from the headline of the lead article, highlight the text and click in the Style box on the toolbar. Type in a style name.

Copy between templates

Being able to copy elements of one template for use in another saves you a lot of time. Even better, it lets you use good bits from existing templates, such as those installed with Word. More templates can be found in the Office 2000 CD-ROM and Internet users can download others from Microsoft's Web site. Just open the Help menu, point to Office on the Web and click on Template Gallery.

The items that can be transferred between templates are styles, macros, custom toolbars and AutoText entries. To copy any of them, open the Tools menu and click Templates and Add-Ins, Organizer. You are presented with two identical template panels between which files may be copied in either direction. If the templates you want to use are not already displayed, click the Close File buttons to clear the existing templates. When all the templates are closed, the Close File buttons change to Open File buttons and you can load the templates you want to use.

Once you've got the right files loaded, highlight the items you want to copy in one panel and click the Copy button to duplicate them on the other side. Items in either panel can be renamed if their names conflict. Note that there is no Cancel button in Organizer so always make copies of your existing templates before attempting to change them.

Table templates

1 Many people are under doctor's instructions to keep a record of what they eat, and anyone trying to lose weight would do well to keep an accurate record of intake. A grid or table for this purpose is easy to make and easy to use. Create a new file, set the page orientation to landscape and set all the margins to 1cm.

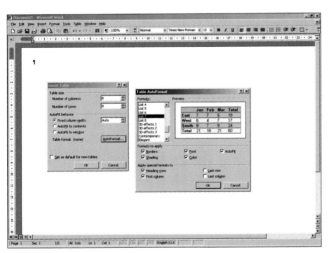

2 Open the Table menu and click Insert Table. In the Insert Table dialogue box set the number of rows and columns to 8, then click the AutoFormat button. There is no perfect pre-designed format for this purpose but List 7 is the closest. Click OK twice to create the table.

Watch out!

When clearing the contents of a table before saving it as a template do not use the Delete Cells command on the Table menu. This deletes the rows and columns containing the cells as well as the cell contents.

Tables can't be saved as styles, but there are ways you can save them so they can be used again.

If you have data to be presented in a tabular format, inserting a Word table makes a lot more sense than setting tabs and formatting paragraphs. One big advantage of using tables is that the cells in a table shrink and grow as text is added or deleted, preserving the layout.

Tables are created by clicking Insert Table on the Table menu or by clicking the Insert Table icon on the toolbar. The first task is to decide how many rows and columns are required. Once these are in place, the grid can be filled by keying in data or pasting it from elsewhere.

Custom tables

A table can be customized by highlighting groups of cells and applying selected effects or by choosing one of the 40 AutoFormat styles. AutoFormat styles can be modified by selecting or deselecting options, but there are limitations. While you can, for example, choose not to display green border lines, you can't choose to keep the border lines but change their color.

3 Save the table as a Word document. In the View menu click Toolbars, then Tables and Borders to display the Tables and Borders toolbar. Type row and column headings into the table. Rest your mouse pointer over the table until the table move handle (a cross within a square) appears. Select the entire table by clicking on this and use the border button to add black dividing lines.

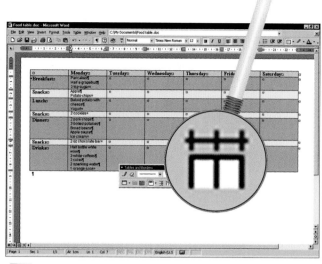

This type of customization has to be done manually by adjusting the table after automatic formatting. Such changes cannot be saved as styles for use in other documents so it's worth saving a copy of a complicated table in the form of a document template. If the table you want to reuse is part of a longer document, save the document in the usual way, delete everything except the table and save it as a template.

Using table templates

Table templates work like other templates. You create a new document from the template and then modify its contents. A better idea is to delete the contents of a table before saving it as a template. This doesn't affect the underlying format of the table, which is preserved in the empty cells, so you can work with an apparently blank table while keeping a customized format.

Another way of reusing a customized table is to make a copy of it as an AutoCorrect entry. When an AutoCorrect entry is created it's assigned a unique name. It can then be inserted in new documents simply by typing its name. This method is best reserved for simple grids. AutoCorrect entries are stored in Normal.dot, which could soon become unwieldy if used as a regular substitute for standard templates.

5 Change the color of the top row by selecting it and picking a color from the Tables and Borders toolbox. Manually adjust the width of the leftmost column so that it's just wide enough for the labels, then select the remaining columns and click the Distribute Columns Evenly button to make best use of the available space.

6 Save the document as a precaution and highlight all the cells apart from the row and column headings. Press Delete on the keyboard to remove the text from the cells. Save the empty table as a template that can be used for future food charts.

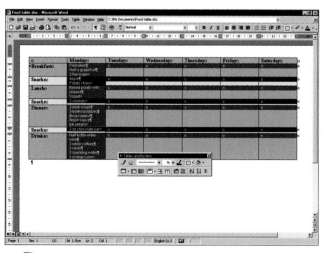

4 Type in some sample data for Monday. It will probably be in too large a font to make a manageable table so use the mouse to highlight every cell in the table, apart from the row and column headings, and set the font to 9pt Arial. The row and column headings are set to 12pt Times New Roman.

Custom toolbars

If you find that customizing toolbars by dragging tools and icons between them is too limiting, scroll down the list of categories in the Customize box and you'll find fonts, macros and styles, all of which may be added to your toolbars.

Custom tips

● To change the location where templates are stored, click Options on the Tools menu. In the Options dialogue box select the File Locations tab and double-click on User Templates. You can then pick a new location for your templates.

● Instead of storing Word's templates in their default location in the Program Files folder, put them in your My Documents folder. Then you can back up your custom templates at the same time as your Word files.

Find out how to make personalized changes to Microsoft Word's workspace menus and tools.

Before you tinker with Word's toolbars you have to make the most far-reaching decision of all: which screen resolution to use. The higher the resolution, the more tools you can fit on a toolbar and the more toolbars you can view simultaneously. In standard mode, using more than two toolbars crowds the screen, while at higher resolutions you can work with four or more. Higher resolutions will need a 17in or larger monitor.

Tooling around

Toolbars are customized through the Customize option on the Tools menu. New commands can be dragged from the Commands section of the Customize dialogue box and then deposited on toolbars that are docked at the top of the screen or floating within it. You may also drag toolbar icons from one bar to another, or drag them off a toolbar if you want to delete them.

Everybody has certain tools which they use frequently and others they never think of using. It makes sense to replace the ones you don't use with others that might be more useful. You can also remove the tools for actions that have easy shortcuts (Cut, Copy and Paste for example) and replace them with tools for which no shortcuts exist, such as case changing, style selection and envelope printing.

Optional extras

The Customize dialogue box isn't the only way of customizing Word. The Tools menu provides further possibilities via its Options dialogue box. This has 10 tabs including Edit, where you can change how Drag and Drop works; the View tab, which provides settings to create screen space by hiding the ruler, status and scroll bars from view; and the Compatibility tab, where Word 2000 can be set to emulate the features of earlier versions of Word. This is invaluable if you need to share documents with other people.

Find and Replace

Find missing files easily with Word's Find and Replace features.

Whether you're working with several documents or just a few large ones, one key to success is organization. For example, it is important to put items in the right folders on your hard disk, and to make sure you know how your long documents are laid out so you can navigate through them easily.

Not everyone is well organized. Many people spend unnecessary time looking for things that they ought to be able to find instantly. Even if you're not naturally organized, with the help of Word's Find and Replace features, you will certainly be able to retrieve things, no matter where they are located. What's particularly useful about these features is that they don't just work inside individual documents, but can be used to find files.

Like Windows Me's Search function, Word's Find and Replace can find words within a file or within the properties of a folder, as well as by a file's name.

You will need

Software A copy of Microsoft Windows 98 or Me and Word 2000 or Word for Windows 97.
Hardware Any PC capable of running Windows 95 or above.

Using Find and Replace functions

1 Start Word in the usual way and then load a long document so you'll have something to search. Since you won't have the document used in this project you'll have to use words other than those in these examples. Go to the Edit menu and choose Find. There's the dialogue box. Type in the word you're looking for and Word will find it. Now click on the Replace tab at the top of the box and you'll see the dialogue box now contains the Replace with: option. Here "back grounds" is going to be replaced with "backgrounds" and Word gives the option of replacing them all automatically, or one at a time.

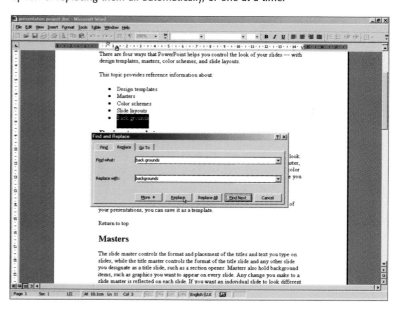

You will learn

- How to search for and replace words in a document.
- How to search for and replace special characters and different formats.
- How to find Word documents you've lost.
- How to save your document searches so you can use them again.

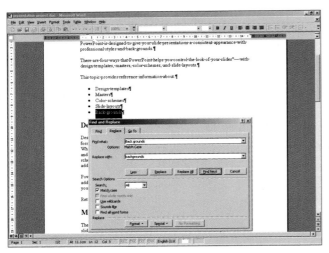

2 Stay in the Replace part of the dialogue box and click on the More button. You'll now see a new selection of options. In the Find What: section, "Back grounds" with a capital B is typed and then, by clicking on the empty box next to Match Case, you can search only for instances where the B is capitalized. Click on Find Next to start the search.

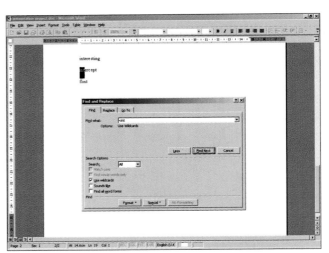

4 The two options underneath Find Whole Words Only are more arcane, but they can be useful. Use Wildcards lets you perform database-style searches on documents. Using this option, looking for "<int" will find words that begin with "int" like "interlude" but not words that contain "int" like "flint". Looking for Sounds Like words is a bit more hit and miss. For example searching for "socks" should highlight words like "box" but doesn't. This is a less useful feature.

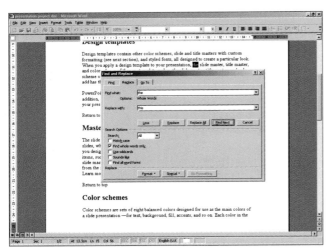

3 The list of options under Match Case can be extremely useful. Uncheck Match Case by clicking on the tick next to it, and then click in the empty box next to Find Whole Words Only. Here "the" is typed in. Start a search by clicking the Find Next button. As you can see from the screen shot, Word has found "the" while ignoring the same three letters as they appear in the word "other" two lines above it.

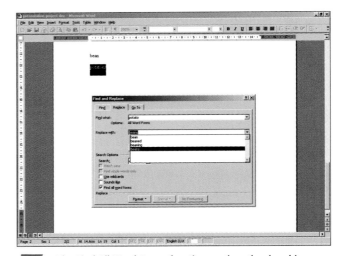

5 The Find All Word Forms function on the other hand is brilliant. As its name suggests, it can find and replace different forms of a word, for example, both singular and plural. In this example, all references to "potato" are to be replaced with "bean" and by clicking on the box next to Find All Word Forms, you can see that Word has replaced "potato" with "bean" and is now highlighting "potatoes" and suggesting that it be replaced by "beans."

Find tip

You can use the Find and Replace dialogue box to reformat entire documents quickly, or just sections of a document. Open up Word's Replace dialogue box and click on the More button. Make sure that the cursor is in the Find What: part of the box and click once on the Format button.

From here you can choose the font, paragraph style or entire style sheet that you want to replace. Having selected it, simply click on the Replace With: box and then choose the font, paragraph

style, or style sheet that you want to replace it with.

For example, you could replace all text that's in the 12pt Lydian typeface, which isn't bold or italic but which is blue, with text in the 10pt bold, italic Book Antiqua typeface. You'll see the selection made underneath the Find What: and Replace With: parts of the dialogue box. Because no words were entered to be found and replaced, Word will replace every word that has the specified formatting.

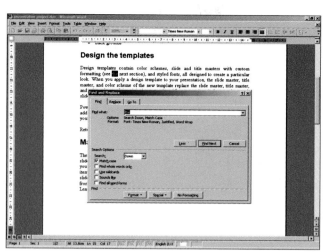

Find tips

● In the Find and Replace dialogue box, there's a dropdown list that allows you to tell Word whether you want to search up or down from the cursor position, or through all the document.

● In the File Find section, if you don't know the name of the document and can't remember what's in it, maybe you can remember when you wrote it. If so, the dropdown list called Last Modified allows you to specify time periods such as today, last week, last month and so on.

● You can use the Find dialogue box to navigate your way around long documents by clicking on the Go To tab at the top.

6 Clear all the checks from Match case and the other check boxes, and click on the Special button. This search trick helps you deal with some awkward situations—for example, if someone gives you a document where instead of letting Word handle all the line endings automatically, they've pressed the Return key at the end of each line and the formatting is a mess. With the Special button you can search for characters such as hard returns that affect formatting, but don't print out and aren't visible on screen. You can also search for sections of text that conform to a certain layout by clicking on the Format button. Here, Word is looking for "the" but only if it's in Times New Roman and in a justified paragraph. Format is extremely useful.

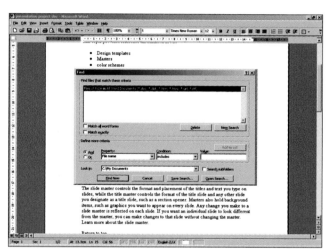

8 If you know the document's name, but it's in a huge folder filled with other documents, go to the Define more criteria section. Under Property, select File Name, under Condition select Includes, and in Value write the name. Click Add to List and Find Now. Here Word is looking for a document called "Ted" and, as you can see, Word highlights it and doesn't display any of the other documents in the folder. They haven't come to any harm, they're just not displayed.

7 Word isn't just good at finding items hidden in documents. It can also find the documents themselves. Close any open dialogue boxes and go to the File menu. Choose Open. If you know where the document is and what it's called, there's no problem. But what if you can't remember? That's where the Find Files section is useful. To access it, click on Tools and select Find.

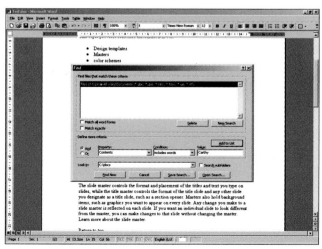

Jargon buster

Hard return Word processors automatically wrap text around when they reach the end of a line. But you can choose to press the Return key when you reach the end of a line as at the end of a paragraph. This is called a hard return.

9 Maybe you can't remember the name of the document, but you know what it's about. Here Word is looking in a specific folder for documents that mention the name "Carthy" which was typed into the Value: box.

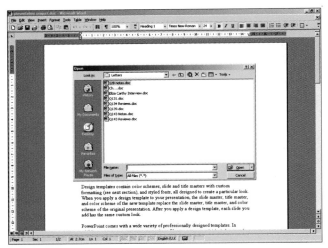

10 Click on the Find Now button and Word displays a list of documents in that folder that include the word "Carthy." In this example, you might have been able to find one of them from its title, but the others would have been much harder to track down.

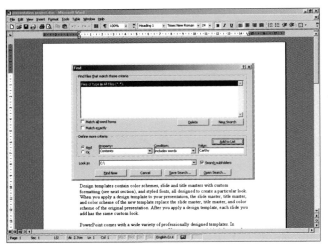

11 That's fine for searching in a single folder, but if you want to search for a document (or words in a document) that may be in a folder that's hidden inside another folder, you'll have to search the subfolders. If you're not already there, go to the File menu again, open Tools and Find. In the Look In box, select the topmost folder where you think the document is (here the whole of the drive C: is searched) and then check the option called Search Subfolders.

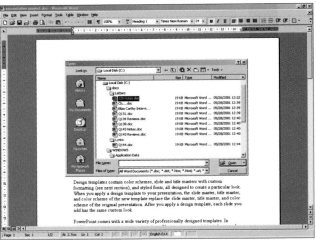

12 Click on the Find Now button and Word will search through all the folders on drive C:, looking for documents that contain the phrase searched for. Here's what the display looks like.

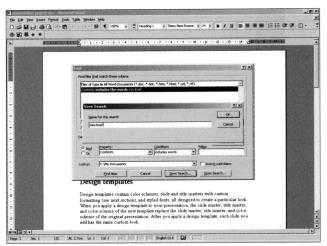

13 It's worth saving the details of a search so that you can use it again. To do so, click on Save Search at the bottom of the window. Give it a name that makes sense to you. Here it is called "mini brief."

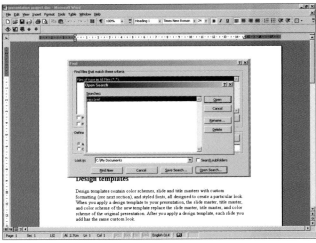

14 When you want to use it again, choose Open from the File menu, click Tools and Find, then click on the **Open Search** button.

Tackling long documents

Find your way around a long or complex document with Document Map.

Word processors such as Microsoft Word can handle anything from a two-line label to a 2,000 page treatise. Getting around short documents is always simple: you just scroll or page up or down. But navigating lengthy and complex documents is different.

Happily, Word has some useful features that help enormously, such as indexing and footnotes. Another great tool is the Document Map, first introduced in Word 97. This lets you display a structured list of topics in a special pane at the left of the screen. By simply clicking on one of these, Word takes you straight to it. You can also compress details or expand summaries for new perspectives.

To capitalize on this facility some solid preparatory effort is essential. In particular, you need to structure your document. You'll get more out of this project if you work with a long document, but experiment with a shorter one first if you prefer.

You will need

Software Microsoft Word 2000 or Word 97.
Hardware A Pentium PC or better, running Windows Me or 98, with at least 16MB RAM.

Using Word's Document Map

1 Although it's daunting to plan your structure when faced with a blank page, Word's Outline View can help. Open a new document and click the Outline View icon on the horizontal scroll bar or click Outline from View in Word's View menu. A blank document is displayed in Outline View. Type in the main section or chapter headings, finishing each with Return (Enter). Don't worry about sequence or structure, just try to capture all the subjects. By default, Word formats these entries with its built-in heading style, Heading 1. This style has an Outline Level of 1, which means it sits at the top of your structure. There are nine levels, more than enough for all but the most complicated pieces of work.

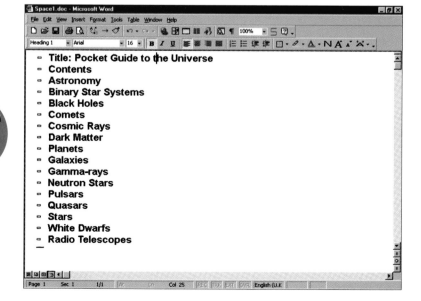

You will learn

● What the Document Map is and how it works.
● How to use Outline View to organize the structure of your document.
● How to use heading styles and Outline levels to optimum effect.
● How to find specific topics quickly in large and complex Word documents.

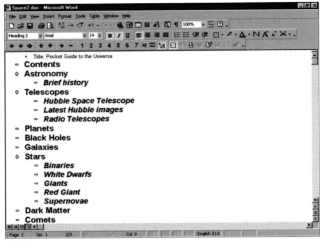

2 To work in this view, display the Outlining toolbar by clicking on Toolbars in the View menu. Click the button with two right-pointing arrows to demote your title to the Body Text style. You can format it later, but now you're concerned with structure only. Add other chapters and topics. For example, place the cursor to the right of Astronomy, and press Enter. Type Brief History on the blank line that Word creates. Do the same to add more topics for Telescopes and Stars. Position the new entries below the parent subject, ready to demote them. To move an entry, repeatedly click on the move tool, drag the symbol or use the shortcut Alt+Shift+Up/Down arrow keys.

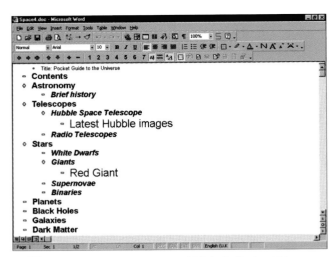

4 There are now two topics which logically should be further demoted, under Hubble Space Telescope and Giants. After demoting them to Level 3 you see that Heading Style 3 uses a rather large font by default in this demonstration. This is inappropriate if you want each successive font to be visually subordinate to its parent, so you'll need to change it. In your version of Word the heading styles may be different, as they depend on previous Word template settings.

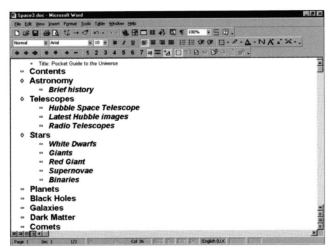

3 Word indents each heading according to its level. These indentations appear only in Outline View. Now make Brief History subordinate to Astronomy by demoting it, in one of three ways. You can place the cursor anywhere in the heading and click the Demote button, the right arrow second from left, or just press Tab. Alternatively, move your mouse cursor over the outline symbol on the left of the heading (like a minus sign), until it turns into four arrows, and drag right. A vertical line appears when you reach each of the eight possible positions. Release the mouse at Level 2. Make similar demotions to Telescopes and Stars.

Jargon buster

● **Outline symbols** The symbol to the left of each heading which looks like a minus sign for those without sub-text, and a plus sign for those with sub-text. Double-click the plus symbol to expand it into its components.

Outlining tips

● You will probably want to keep some visual contrast between Outline levels, but if you find character formatting such as large fonts or italics distracting, you can display the outline as plain text. On the Outlining toolbar, just click Show Formatting to toggle it on or off.

● The tab key is a shortcut for demoting a paragraph in Outline View, but to insert a real tab character you can press Ctrl+Tab.

● To see the true formatting of a document while you work in Outline View, you can split the document window. Work in Outline View in one pane and in Print Layout View or Normal View in the other pane. Any changes you make to the document in Outline View are visible in the second pane.

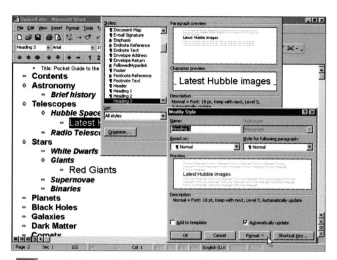

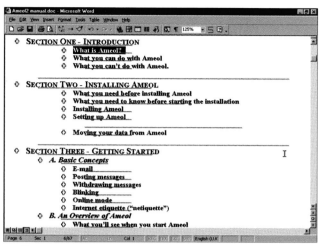

5 Select Latest Hubble Images and in the Format menu click Styles and then the Modify button. From there click Format, Font and then change the Heading 3 Style to Arial 12 Regular. Click OK to return to the Modify Style dialogue box. If you want Word to redefine this style every time you make any manual formatting changes to it, check the Automatically Update box, and click OK, then Apply or Close. Note that paragraph formatting doesn't appear in Outline View, and paragraph formatting commands are not available in the Format menu. This is because the focus here is on structure, not appearance.

What's the difference?

The Document Map feature was introduced in Word 97, so users of Word 95 or earlier versions will unfortunately have to sit this one out. Word 2000, is used for this project. The approach in Word 97 is very similar, and differs only in minor details.

Jargon buster

● **Outline View** This shows the document's structure. The indentations and symbols in Outline View do not affect the way your document looks in Normal View and do not print.

● **Demote** To make a heading subordinate to another. To demote a heading to a lower level, drag its outline symbol to the right (or press Tab).

● **Promote** To make a heading senior to another. To promote a heading to a higher level, drag the outline symbol to the left (or press Shift+Tab).

● **Heading style** Formatting applied to a heading. Word has nine different heading styles, Heading 1 to Heading 9. Each one has an associated outline level, so using Word's built-in heading styles ensures that your document is structured.

6 When you're satisfied with how the structure is developing, switch to Normal or Print Layout View to add detailed body text, graphics, tables, fields and other formatting (such as for your main title). For a long document such as this you would probably also want to add a Table of Contents section at the front, and an Index at the back. Return whenever necessary to the Outline View to make structural changes and additions. Within a long and complicated document, perhaps running into scores or hundreds of pages, these are much easier to achieve in Outline View than elsewhere. This example is the user guide document for AMEOL, the CIX online communications package. Such examples of well-planned structure can be fruitful sources for developing your outlining skills.

7 The Document Map can be displayed at any stage after the document is suitably outlined. You don't have to wait until every last detail is perfect. Choose the view you want to use, such as Normal View or Print Layout. Then either click the Document Map tool in the Standard Toolbar or go to the View menu and choose Document Map.

Watch out!

It's useful to select a number of lines in Outline View and move them up or down using the move tools. But be careful about moving them, because Word doesn't warn you if you slip into another structured section.

Outlining tips

● It's always important to save your document regularly, but especially when you're about to make make major changes to its outline structure or styles. Not all operations can be easily reversed with Word's Undo menu, so it makes sense to err on the safe side.

● You can use Outline levels when you want to apply levels but don't want to change the appearance of your text by applying the built-in heading styles. They still apply specific formatting, but the Outline levels can apply a sort of invisible format to distinguish the heading's level. To achieve this, switch to Print Layout View and select the tailor-made paragraph. On the Format menu click on Paragraph, then the Indents and Spacing tab, and then in the Outline Level box, click on the level that you want.

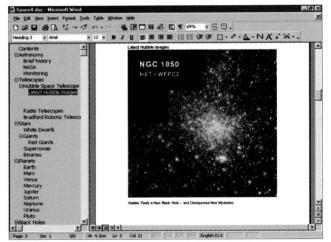

8   The Map opens in a pane on the left, which can be varied in width by dragging its border. It gives you a simultaneous combination of the Outline View and the Main View. Clicking on any entry takes you straight to that part of your document—the Latest Hubble Images in this case.

Jargon buster

● **Outline level** A paragraph formatting option which you can use to assign one of up to nine hierarchical levels to selected paragraphs in your document. You must assign a level, either through the built-in styles or separately, if you want to display the paragraphs in Outline View or the Document Map.

Watch out!

Although it's not consistent behavior, you'll sometimes find that on changing views, say from Print Layout to Normal or vice versa, the Document Map will disappear and have to be reactivated.

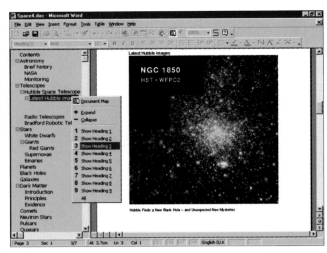

9   A right-click on the Document Map displays this dialogue box, which you can use to perform some Outlining toolbar operations. For example, from the pop-up menu click on 3 to show all levels up to and including Level 3. An individual line can be expanded or collapsed with the respective button.

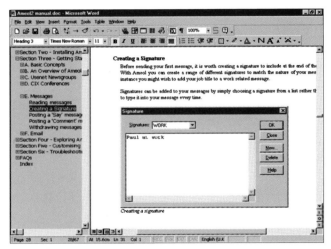

10   Try these Map operations with any other suitable long Word document, from whatever source you have available. Here the CIX Ameol User Guide is loaded again. From Print Layout View, click the Document Map tool, then right-click and show all Level 1 headings, in this case chapters. Expand this by successively clicking the outline symbols for Section Three and then Messages. Finally, home in on Creating a Signature by clicking that heading. No matter how large or intricate the document, you can reach any part of it faster than you can blink.

Document tips

Many of the projects in this book use small files that are easily created during the project itself. This project is rather different because the Document Map is most useful with a large file. If you want to follow the steps but don't have a suitable document, search your hard drive, including Web downloads, user guides and so on. From the desktop, use Start/Search For Files or Folders...and enter *.doc as your target. Sort the resulting hits in descending order of size and open possible files until you find a suitable one.

Easy spreadsheets

Learn all the tricks of the trade to make creating complex spreadsheets a quick and easy operation.

You can become productive with a spreadsheet program within hours of seeing one for the first time. The basic concepts are easy to understand because they have a close correspondence to the paper-based systems people use every day. If you understand how your bank statement works you already know the principles of spreadsheeting.

Productivity

Because spreadsheets are so easy to grasp there's a tendency for users to ignore the advanced features they provide. And while there's no point changing the way you work just for the sake of it, it's worth looking at how you might be able to use your existing worksheets more productively.

On the following pages you can see the advantages of splitting big spreadsheets into separate worksheets that are easier to handle, and how to arrange them on screen, and load and save them as a group. By turning on the revision tracking features of your spreadsheet you can keep a log of changes you make and recover from situations where your data has apparently been lost.

Time savers

Another option is to turn worksheets into templates that can be used for similar sheets in the future, saving you the trouble of reconstructing formats, fonts, column widths and other options you've already defined. And if you think your spreadsheet already has too many commands and settings to remember, why not customize its toolbars and menus to reflect only the ones that are useful to you? You might even devise macros to turn more complicated procedures into one-click operations.

You will need

ESSENTIAL
Software A spreadsheet program. Excel 2000 has been used for the examples on the following pages but the features described are found in other mainstream spreadsheets such as Lotus 1-2-3 and Quattro Pro.
Hardware A Windows PC, preferably one with Windows Me or 98 installed.

Jargon buster

Active worksheet The sheet of a workbook that you're currently working on. The name tab of the active worksheet is bold.

Hidden worksheet A workbook sheet whose existence is hidden from other users and whose name tab does not appear alongside the others.

Using workbooks

Creating and viewing a workbook

The budget planner used in the following exercise was chosen purely to illustrate the principles involved. You could easily follow the steps without creating a budget planner just by entering dummy data on each worksheet. Alternatively, you could copy and paste data from your existing spreadsheets or the examples on the Office and Excel CD-ROMs.

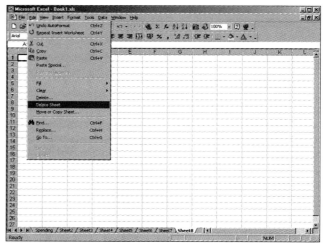

1 New Excel workbooks can be set to contain anything from one to 255 sheets. Two sheets are visible at the bottom of this workbook. If you want to see more tabs, drag the dividing bar (between the tabs and the horizontal scroll bar) to the right.

2 The tabs for sheets 1 to 8 have now been made visible and Sheet 1 has been renamed Spending. To rename a sheet, double-click its tab and type the new name. Notice that this does not affect the file name of the workbook itself, which is still called Book1.xls.

The workbook system means you can divide complex spreadsheets into easily manageable chunks.

Early spreadsheets were little more than grids for manipulating data. While simple in concept, they became difficult to work with as sheets grew to huge sizes with hundreds or thousands of rows and columns. Users needed some way of reducing big spreadsheets to a more manageable size. They would then be able to navigate with just a few keystrokes instead of scrolling endlessly in search of the required information.

Divide and conquer

The solution was the introduction of workbooks. A workbook is a collection of smaller sheets that can be loaded and saved as a single file. Under MS-DOS this solution was only partly successful: switching from one sheet in a workbook to another was tedious and it wasn't easy making cross references to other sheets. The arrival of Windows changed that and now all good spreadsheet programs have adopted a system of workbooks with tabs to identify sheets. Switching between sheets is as simple as clicking the appropriate tab.

3 Give sheets 2–6 descriptive names in the same way. Delete the extra two worksheets. To delete a sheet, click on its tab and choose Delete Sheet from the Edit menu. Multiple sheets can be selected for deletion by pressing Shift while clicking.

The name tabs appear in a line along the top or bottom of the worksheets, but it's convenient to think of sheets stacked one behind the other rather than side by side. This is because you can calculate through a stack of sheets. For example, if each sheet in a workbook has details of one year's income in the same cell, say B20, you can find a cumulative total using the Sum function to add the contents of that cell to all the sheets and insert the answer in the current sheet.

For your eyes only

Sheets in a workbook can be hidden to reduce screen clutter; or if you have a large monitor you can choose to see several views of the same workbook or sheet. This is useful when you're making changes to a sheet and want to see what effect they are having elsewhere. Instead of having to scroll back and forth, you can keep your totals visible in a separate window.

What's the difference?

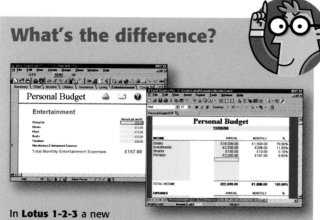

In **Lotus 1-2-3** a new workbook contains a single sheet identified by the letter A. Additional sheets can be added by selecting Sheet from the Create menu. Multiple sheets can be added at the same time and these may be placed before or after the current sheet. If you add two sheets before sheet A, these will become A and B and the original sheet A is renamed C. To avoid confusion it's a good idea to change the letters to names before adding new sheets. Simply double-click on a sheet's letter and type in an appropriate description.

Quattro Pro, the spreadsheet in Corel WordPerfect Office, also uses tabbed worksheets stored in a single workbook but its terminology is slightly different. A workbook is called a notebook and by default each new notebook contains 255 sheets. As in Excel and Lotus 1-2-3, sheets may be renamed by double-clicking them and typing a descriptive name.

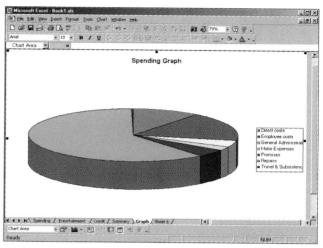

4 The fifth worksheet contains a graph created from data from the summary worksheet. To see the graph at the same time as the data, select New Window on the Window menu.

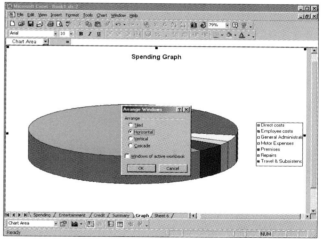

5 To stack the windows, click Arrange on the Window menu and then Horizontal in the dialogue box. Now two windows are visible, both showing the same graph sheet that was active in step 4.

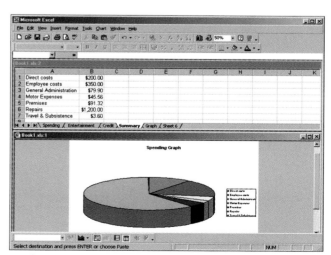

6 By selecting the Summary tab in the top window you can view the expenditure costs at the same time as the graph. If this is a view you'd like to use often, save it by choosing Save Workspace from the File menu. When you reload it, the windows will be arranged in the same way.

Using templates

Save yourself time and effort by creating a template for the basic formatting in your spreadsheets.

Any workbook can be saved as a template by choosing Save As from the File menu. Simply change the file type from Excel Workbook to Template and store it in the Templates folder. This is a sub-folder of the Excel or Office directories, depending on whether you installed Excel on its own or as part of Microsoft Office.

Using templates

To use a stored template click New on the File menu and double-click the name of the template from the list that appears. A new workbook will be created and its name will be the same as the template, with the digit 1 appended. When you save the workbook you can change its name to something more appropriate.

Changing every worksheet

If all your spreadsheets tend to be alike and you always use the same fonts, number formats and page layouts, there are two Excel templates you should know about: Book.xlt and Sheet.xlt. These must be stored in the Xlstart folder or in

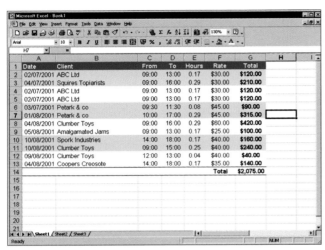

1 The easiest way to create a template is to start with an existing worksheet, remove the data you don't need and store the skeleton for future use. The example here is a billing calculator for time spent working on clients' accounts.

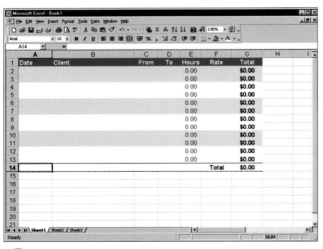

2 The hours spent working for each client (column E) and the amount to be billed (column G) are calculated by formulas, which are left in place. The other columns are blanked by selecting the data and pressing the Delete key.

Template tips

● If when you create a new workbook you're not offered a list of templates it's because you haven't created any. Once you've saved a template the list appears.

● When creating a default worksheet with the name Sheet.xlt, remove all other worksheets from the workbook. If you don't, instead of inserting a worksheet you'll insert a workbook full.

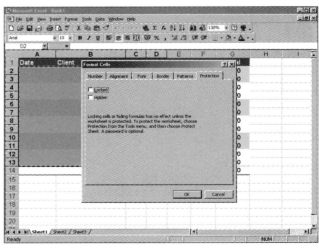

3 Users will need to enter data into columns A, B, C, D and F of the worksheet template so these should be unlocked. To do this, highlight the cells, select Format Cells and remove the tick from the Locked box in the Format Cells dialogue box.

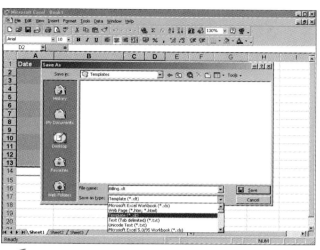

an alternative folder you can select by choosing Tools, Options, General and filling in the Alternative Startup File Location box.

Book.xlt and Sheet.xlt store default settings for new workbooks and sheets. When you start Excel it looks for Book.xlt and creates a blank workbook based on it. If you insert a new sheet into a workbook Excel looks for the Sheet.xlt template. The inserted sheet is based on it.

6 Save the template by clicking Save As on the File menu. In the Save As dialogue box select Template as the file type and enter a suitably descriptive file name. The file may be saved in the main Templates folder or any of its sub-folders.

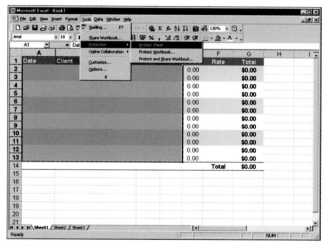

4 The worksheet can be protected by selecting Protection, Protect Sheet from the Tools menu. Click OK in the dialogue box. You can also protect the workbook as well as the worksheet. This stops users adding or removing sheets.

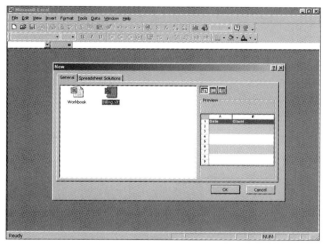

7 To use the billing template click New on the File menu and highlight the template in the dialogue box. If you checked the preview box in step 5, you'll be able to see a thumbnail representation of the template on the right. Click OK to use it.

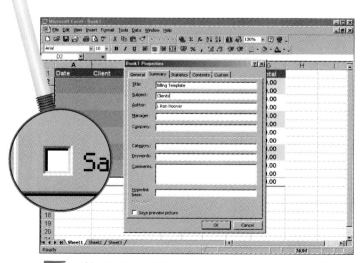

5 This step is useful if you want to be able to preview the appearance of a template when loading it. Click Properties on the File menu and select the Summary tab. Enter anything you like in the information panels but be sure to check the box labeled Save Preview Picture. Click OK.

Custom setup

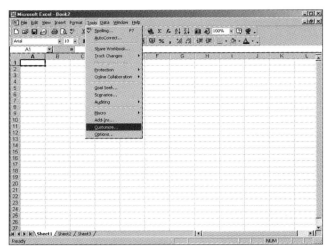

1 The plan is to create a customized toolbar containing the most useful options from the standard and formatting bars plus a macro button. The new toolbar will then replace the two existing bars. Click Tools, Customize to get started.

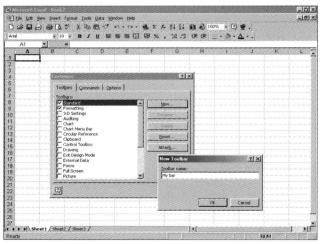

2 Select the Toolbars tab and click on the New button. In the New Toolbar dialogue box type a name for your toolbar and click on OK. When the empty toolbar appears, drag it into an unused area of the spreadsheet.

You can customize spreadsheets in several ways to suit your taste and the way that you work.

Customizing a spreadsheet is not only a fun task but has practical benefits too. These depend on the way you use spreadsheets and the equipment you run them on. If you have a small monitor you may find the default view of 100 percent doesn't let you see enough of your worksheets. And if you're the sort of person who works the mouse hard, clicking on icons and menus instead of using the keyboard, you could put the commands you use most often on the standard toolbar. You could even create a toolbar of your own, featuring your favorite commands.

A question of taste

Some types of customization are a matter of personal preference, such as whether you want the cursor to move down or across when you press Enter, or whether you want to see the dividing lines between cells. Other modifications may be called for by your employer. It's common for companies to insist on a house style governing issues like the formatting of dates and the font styles to be used in documents.

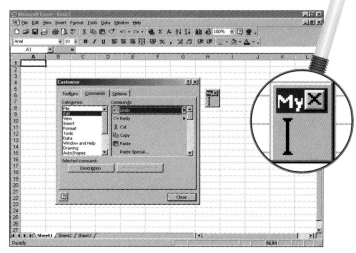

3 To assign icons to the new toolbar, click on the Commands tab. Select one of the categories on the left, which are grouped according to function, and drag the commands in the right-hand pane over to your new toolbar. The screenshot shows the Undo command ready to be dragged to the toolbar.

Many such choices can be made in the eight tabbed section of the Options dialogue box, which is in the Tools menu. The General tab is where you can set the preferred font for your worksheets and choose how many blank worksheets you'd like each new workbook to have. From the View tab you could choose to make more space for your worksheets by turning off the formula and status bars, and removing the vertical scroll bar.

Easy labels

If you often find yourself typing the same set of labels into a worksheet, why not define them permanently on the Custom Lists tab? Then you only have to type the first name in the list and drag it across or down to create the others.

Toolbar tip

Instead of creating a toolbar by selecting commands from the Customize dialogue box you can drag them from existing toolbars. This is faster and easier, but when you've finished, the toolbars from which you dragged the command icons will be incomplete. To rectify this, select the Toolbar tab in the Customize dialogue box and highlight each incomplete toolbar in turn, pressing Reset after each one.

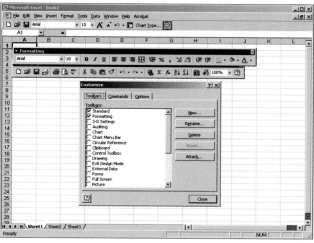

5 Position the mouse to the left of the standard toolbar and drag it out of the way. Repeat with the formatting toolbar, then drag your new toolbar into position below the menu bar. Finally, remove the checks from the standard and formatting toolbars in the Customize dialogue box. This makes them disappear from the screen, but they are not deleted permanently.

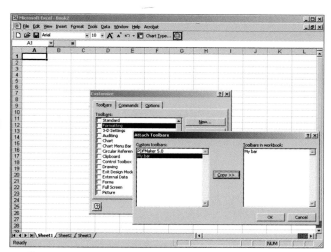

6 Your new custom toolbar will be available when you use Excel on your own PC, but if you want it to be available when using this workbook on other PCs, attach the toolbar to the workbook. Click the Attach button and in the Attach Toolbars dialogue box, highlight My Bar, click the Copy button then click OK.

Watch out!

While the Customize dialogue box is open you can modify the dropdown menus by dragging commands off and on to them. This increases the risk of accidentally removing the Tools menu command from the menu bar. If this happens, the Customize dialogue box cannot be accessed in the usual way to rectify the situation.

There is a solution, which is to right-click on any toolbar. This brings up a context-sensitive menu with a Customize option. Click this to open the Customize dialogue box and highlight Built-in Menus in the Categories list. Drag the Tools menu from the Commands list back into position between the Format and Data menus.

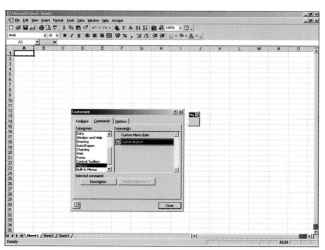

4 Most of the required commands have been dragged onto the new toolbar. There's just room on the end for a Custom button which can later be used to launch one of your own macros.

Macro maker

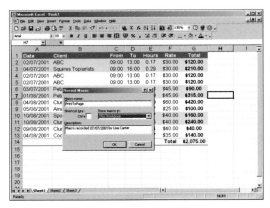

Selecting Tools, Macro, Record New Macro brings up the above dialogue box. Call your macro anything you like but don't use spaces. If you type a letter into the Shortcut key box you'll be able to run the macro by pressing Control at the same time as the designated key. As soon as you click on OK everything you do will be recorded.

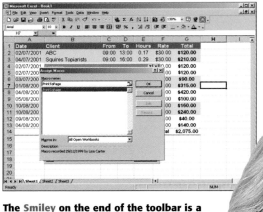

The Smiley on the end of the toolbar is a Custom Macro button placed there when the toolbar was created. Clicking on the Smiley brings up the Assign Macro dialogue box in which you can choose a macro to attach to the button. Just highlight it and click OK. Now when you click on the Smiley the Macro will run automatically. To change the Smiley to something more meaningful right-click it, select Customize, then right-click the Smiley again.

Make creating spreadsheets even easier for yourself by using macros for repetitive tasks.

If you've ever carried out a procedure in a spreadsheet and been tempted to write down what you did for future reference, macros are for you. In Excel, as in Lotus 1-2-3 and Quattro Pro, keystrokes can be recorded and played back when you need to perform the same action. Where an activity requires you to set several options in dialogue boxes or use multiple menu selections, a macro will save both time and effort.

Printing made easy

Print jobs are good candidates for macros. Worksheets often need to be printed in different ways for different audiences. While you might prefer a full-sized landscape printout in a bold font on multiple sheets for day-to-day reference, you may be required to produce a monthly headed summary compressed to just two portrait pages.

Switching between the two print styles involves changing the font, setting the number of pages, changing margins and so on. By recording these options on two separate macros and putting them on a toolbar you can switch between them at will.

Recording studio

To record a macro use the Tools menu and select Macro, Record New Macro. Give the macro a name and carry out all the actions you want to record. When you've finished, press Stop Recording to save a record of your activities. The macro can be replayed from the Tools menu by selecting Macro, Macros and picking it from a list, or you can assign the macro to a toolbar icon and start it with a click.

3

Easy upgrades

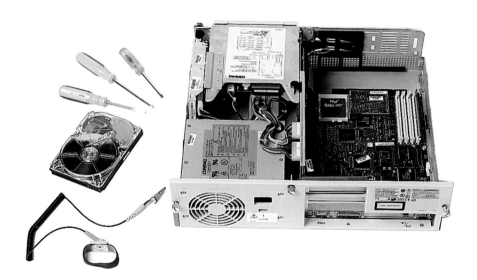

Improving hardware

There's no need to be nervous about taking the lid off your computer and fiddling about with its insides.

Upgrading old equipment is an alien notion to most of us. Very few people would attempt to upgrade a washing machine with a faster motor and nobody would even dream of converting a black-and-white TV to color. When household equipment becomes outdated you either put up with what you've got or you save up for something new.

Computers are different because, unlike other electrical appliances, they're built from standard components which are generally interchangeable. You can't pop into a department store and buy a better tape unit for your radio cassette player, but there's usually no problem buying better and faster CD-ROM drives, hard disks, graphics cards, and modems that will work in any PC.

No skill required

It's not only easy to buy new parts for a computer, it should be easy to install them too. Of course, if you're the type of person who's nervous about changing a plug or a lightbulb you shouldn't consider upgrading your own computer. But if you're able to replace a fuse and wire up a plug you probably already have all the tools and expertise needed to tackle a computer upgrade.

The pace of development in computer technology is as rapid as ever and last year's top-of-the-range computer probably looks pretty tame compared with what's in the stores today. The good news is that judiciously upgrading your old PC needn't cost a fortune and could extend your computer's life by many years.

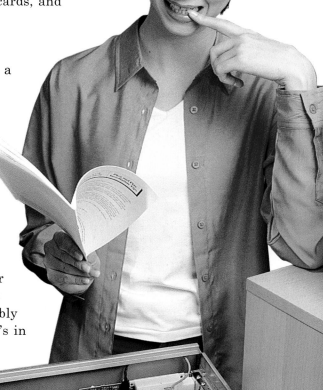

You will need

ESSENTIAL
Hardware Very few tools are needed. You can get by with just two medium-sized screwdrivers: one cross head and one flat-head. Some smaller screwdrivers might come in handy, as will a roll of masking tape and a marker pen for labeling cables. What you must have is a pencil and paper for keeping notes and making diagrams as you work.

RECOMMENDED
Hardware An anti-static wristband is useful but not essential.

Upgrade and add

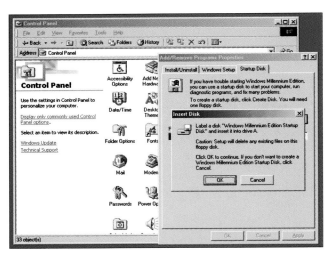

1 Before attempting any upgrade, make copies of important data files and store them on a removable disk. If you use Windows Me or 98, make a Startup disk by clicking Add/Remove Programs in the Control Panel, and then clicking the Startup Disk tab.

It makes good sense to upgrade the components in your PC rather than shell out for a new one.

There are many reasons for upgrading a PC. High on the list is the problem of hard disks filling up with data. Not so long ago hard disks smaller than 1GB were common, but software titles now demand a huge amount of storage. The inexpensive solution is to delete programs that you no longer use from your hard disk (see pages 35–36.) You can gain even more space by transferring out-of-date or unused data to removable disks, but there comes a point where you have to bite the bullet and fit a new hard disk or stop installing new programs.

Better than new

Another reason for upgrading is to add features such as a modem, sound system, DVD drive, or joystick. These are popular because they extend the capabilities of a PC and make it more fun to use; and because the components are additions, not replacements, nothing has to be thrown away.

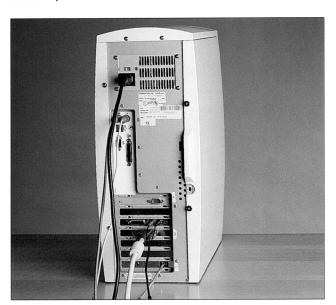

2 Turn off your PC and then disconnect all the cables from the back. To make it easier to reassemble them, stick a loop of masking tape around each cable and write on it where the cable came from. If you don't mind writing on the back of your PC you could match cables to their sockets using numbers.

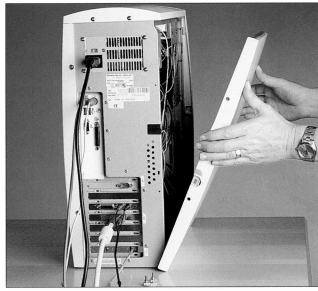

3 Remove the cover of your PC. In this case two screws retain a side panel but there are hundreds of different case styles. Keep the screws in a safe place and label them.

Keeping up with the Gateses

If there's a new piece of software you simply must have, you might be forced into upgrading your PC to run it. New software is written to take advantage of the higher processing speeds and advanced features of the latest PCs.

While the system requirements printed on the box might lead you into thinking that your PC can run a new piece of software, the reality could be that without extra memory or a faster processor it does not so much run as hobble.

The need for speed

Speeding up your computer could involve adding memory, or fitting a more powerful processor, a faster graphics card, or a more efficient hard disk. All have a bearing on the speed of a computer and just one weak link could hold back the entire system.

If your reason for upgrading is to have a faster PC, it might be less costly to buy a new one instead. However, if you can pinpoint the component that's slowing down your system, especially if it's something as simple as insufficient memory, an upgrade is worthwhile.

5 If your PC is in a tower case, lay it on its side for easier access. Familiarize yourself with its internal layout and make a rough sketch of the positions of the expansion cards (rear left) and any cables attached to them.

6 Before touching anything inside the PC, earth yourself by touching a metal pipe or radiator to dissipate static electricity. If you have an anti-static wrist strap, wear it. The picture shows an expansion slot blanking plate being removed prior to fitting a new expansion card.

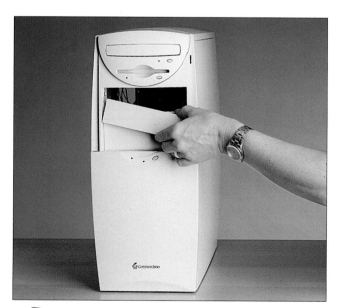

4 If you're about to add a new CD-ROM or removable drive, push out the drive blanking plate from inside the case. These are made of plastic but there may be another metal plate behind. This can be pried out with a flat-bladed screwdriver.

Processors

The **Intel Celeron** processor was produced as an inexpensive but fast processor for budget PCs. Originally designed to fit on a Pentium II motherboard, it now requires a completely different type of board—a Socket 370.

Fact File

● **Clock speed** The internal speed at which a processor runs. This is almost always faster than the bus speed (see Fact File, page 86), sometimes by a factor of six or seven.

● **CPU** Central Processing Unit. This is the same as a processor.

● **Dip switches** Miniature switches usually mounted in banks of four or eight on the motherboard of a PC. They are used singly or in combination to set processor, clock, and bus speeds.

● **Slot 1** A type of processor socket introduced by Intel for the Pentium II and still used for Pentium III processors.

● **Socket 370** The type of socket used for the latest, fastest Intel Celeron processors.

● **Socket 7** The socket type of the original Pentium processor. Intel abandoned Socket 7 with the introduction of the Pentium II but other manufacturers persevered. An updated format called Super Socket 7 has a 100MHz bus enabling AMD processors to deliver the same high speeds as Pentium III chips.

You can dramatically improve the performance of an older PC simply by upgrading its processor.

The big name in PC processors is Intel, but rival company AMD is a major player and VIA produces low-cost chips. Evergreen doesn't make chips, but it has developed a lucrative niche market adapting AMD processors for use in a variety of systems.

Suppliers

What all chip manufacturers have in common is a reluctance to deal with the public, preferring to sell their processors in batches of thousands to system builders and distributors. So it's no good telephoning Intel or AMD and asking them to sell you a processor directly. Instead, you have to buy your processor from a company that specializes in components—five top suppliers are listed on the opposite page. If you need after-sales support, this is also the responsibility of the vendor rather than the manufacturer.

This **AMD Super Socket 7** processor requires a separate heat sink and fan without which it would soon overheat and be damaged.

Techniques

It really isn't worth upgrading older PCs fitted with Intel 286, 386, and 486 chips, but there are upgrade options for every other type of machine. Even though Intel has stopped making the original Pentium processor, Evergreen produces Pentium compatible processors by putting AMD chips onto circuit boards that take care of differing speed and voltage requirements.

As long as the processor in your PC is still in production, the simplest way of upgrading it is to buy a faster one of the same type. All you have to do is take the old one out of its socket, put in a new one, and set a few Dip switches to let your computer know the speed of the new chip. Simple as this sounds, it is essential that you have a manual to tell you what sort of processor socket is inside your PC and how to set the speed switches on the motherboard. Without these it is not advisable to try upgrading a processor yourself.

Expert advice

To buy the right sort of replacement processor you need to know more than just its name. When the Intel Celeron was introduced it was designed to fit onto a Pentium II motherboard, but the current Celeron requires a Socket 370 board, which is completely different. Other such anomalies abound, so when buying a new processor it makes sense to discuss your needs with potential suppliers who have up-to-date knowledge of compatibility issues and can help you choose the right product. Here are the things they'll want to know: the type of socket in your PC (Super Socket 7, Slot 1, Socket 370); the speed of the memory (66MHz, 100MHz, etc.); and the maximum bus multiplication factor (5x, 5.5x, 6x, and so on). All this information should be in your computer's motherboard manual.

Watch out!

There's a limit to how many times you can multiply the speed of the system bus to create ever faster processors. A computer cannot run efficiently if the processor spews out data faster than it can be distributed, which is why a 750MHz processor on a 100MHz bus runs faster than a 750MHz processor on a 66MHz bus.

Most PCs can be set to run at 66MHz or 100MHz or more, but there is a catch to using the higher speed: if you switch your motherboard into 100MHz mode you must ensure that the system memory is rated at the same speed. If it isn't, you'll have to fork out for new memory as well as a new processor.

Buying tips

● The constant introduction of faster chips means prices of older processors are always falling, but it does pay to look around because some vendors drop their prices sooner than others.

● A fast processor is expensive and might account for half the price of a new computer. A good rule of thumb to keep costs down without compromising too much on quality is to buy the third fastest processor in a range. At the time of writing the fastest available Pentium 4 processor (1.8GHz plus) costs around $675.

● Powerful processors need the support of fast disks and accelerated graphics cards, so don't blow all your savings on a processor that will outrun the other components in your system.

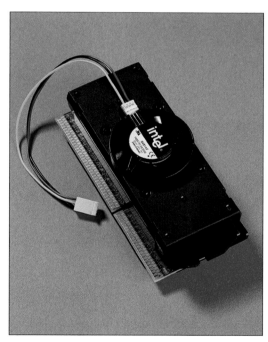

This Intel Pentium III processor with integral fan can be used to upgrade a machine equipped with a 100MHz bus and 100MHz memory.

Top suppliers

● **CWD** www.cwd.com
● **Comp-U-Plus** www.compuplus.com
● **PC Connection** www.pcconnection.com
● **MicroWarehouse** www.warehouse.com
● **Computers4Sure** www.computers4sure.com

Motherboards

Fact file

● **AGP** Stands for Advanced Graphics Port and has taken over from PCI as the standard socket for graphics adapters.

● **Bus speed** The speed at which the processor communicates with other devices on the motherboard. This is always less than the actual speed of the processor. Many recent processors require a 100MHz bus rather than the once-standard 66MHz.

● **ISA** The older of the two types of expansion sockets found on motherboards. It stands for Industry Standard Architecture, which is ironic because ISA slots are being superseded by PCI and AGP.

● **PCI** The type of motherboard socket for which most expansion cards are made. PCI cards will not fit into ISA sockets.

● **PS/2** Stands for Personal System/2, which was once a range of IBM computers, but now refers almost exclusively to the small (8mm diameter) round connectors used for mice and keyboards.

● **USB ports** Flat connectors, usually mounted in pairs, into which printers, cameras, and other serial devices can be plugged.

If you want to upgrade your PC, you may need a new motherboard to accommodate the chips and cards.

The motherboard inside a PC is the main circuit board to which all the other components are connected. The design of a motherboard determines which processors can be used and with how much memory, as well as which accessories can be plugged into the PC's external ports and sockets.

Unless it breaks down, there is little need to think about the motherboard until you want to upgrade, at which time it is usually the desire for a faster processor that forces the upgrade. You can't, for example, replace an old Pentium MMX with a Pentium III or Pentium 4 without a new board.

Motherboard transplants

Replacing a motherboard doesn't require any skills or special tools, but it is a major undertaking if you've never opened up your PC. Before you can remove the old board, you have to disconnect the power cables from it and remove the adapter cards, data cables, and any wires leading to lights and indicators. It's usually possible to release some retaining screws and lift out the motherboard complete with its processor and memory. These can be transferred to the new board which is installed in the PC by reversing the procedures described.

AGP slot **for the graphics adapter.**

ISA slots **for expansion cards.**

PCI slots **for expansion cards.**

The motherboard mounting holes **must match the pre-drilled holes inside the case.**

Output ports **for PS/2, USB, parallel, and serial devices.**

Power connector **(AT or ATX).**

Socket for Intel or AMD processor.

RAM sockets **for memory modules.**

Know your needs

Motherboards vary greatly in price with the expensive ones costing ten times as much as the inexpensive. Fortunately, most ordinary PCs work fine with motherboards from the lower priced makes. The expensive boards are for network servers requiring special features such as being able to run two processors at the same time or work with ultra-fast SCSI hard disks.

When buying a motherboard for a standard PC, the most important consideration is to match it to the processor. Classic Pentium and Pentium MMX processors worked on Socket 7 boards, but K6-2 and K6-3 processors from AMD need Super Socket 7 boards fitted with fast 100MHz memory.

Intel Pentium II and Pentium III processors demand a Slot 1 motherboard, which is unsuitable for any other type of processor, and there's another special board, aptly called Socket 370, which is solely for Intel's 370 Celeron processor.

Form factor

Having found out which boards are suitable for the processor you want to use, the next consideration is which form factor to buy. This is not simply a question of size. Form factor determines the shape of a board, its mounting points, and the type of power supply it requires. The AT form factor is for older machines and the ATX for newer ones. There are also the slightly smaller Micro-ATX and Felx-ATX motherboards. As a rule of thumb, if a motherboard has PS/2 sockets for the mouse and keyboard and USB for peripherals, it's probably ATX. There are so-called baby versions of each type of board for use in smaller tower and desktop cases.

Motherboard manufacturers do not sell direct to the public but leading names to look out for are Asus, Elite, Gigabyte, Intel, and Supermicro. Budget motherboards are available from Abit, PC Chips, and TMC.

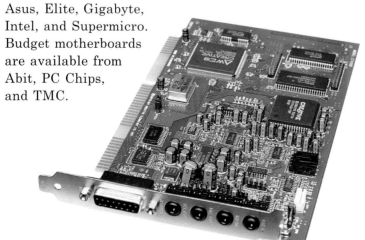

When a soundcard like this is mounted in an ISA slot (see page 86), the audio connectors and joystick port are accessible from the back of the PC.

Buying tips

● Motherboards and processors are sometimes packaged together at discounted prices. You can even buy motherboards and processors pre-assembled in a suitable system case.

● Make certain a motherboard has enough slots of the right types (ISA or PCI) for the expansion cards in your computer. Typically, you need slots for a modem, soundcard, and graphics adapter, but some computers have additional cards for special features such as TV tuners and networking.

● If money is tight, choose a motherboard that can be used with your existing memory chips until you can afford new ones. Such combination boards have sockets for older 72-pin and newer 168-pin RAM modules.

● For the sake of political correctness some manufacturers use the term mainboard as an alternative to motherboard. There is no difference in the products.

Watch out!

Some motherboards have built-in AGP graphics, saving the expense of buying a separate graphics card. The drawback is that for technical reasons these boards are manufactured without a separate AGP slot and therefore can't be upgraded in line with new technology. The same isn't true of integrated sound chips, which can usually be disabled in favor of a separate soundcard.

The radically different designs of the Pentium MMX (right) and Pentium III processors show how important it is to select the right kind of motherboard.

Top brands

● **ABIT Computer** www.abit-usa.com
● **AMD** www.amd.com
● **ASUSTek** www.asus.com
● **Intel** www.intel.com
● **Tyan** www.tyan.com

Soundcards

1 After releasing its retaining screw, the existing FM soundcard is withdrawn from its PCI slot.

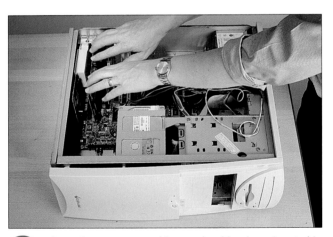

2 The replacement wavetable soundcard has been inserted in its ISA slot and is being firmly pressed into place. The next task is to connect the internal audio cable between the soundcard and CD-ROM drive.

3 The external connections are to a microphone, line input, (in this case a cassette deck) and speakers. The large connector on the left is for a joystick or MIDI cable.

The ability to record and play back sound greatly enhances the versatility of your PC.

If your PC hasn't got a soundcard, an upgrade is almost obligatory. Inexpensive soundcards are readily available and even with speakers powered by household current, the bill won't be more than you'd pay for one software item.

If you've already got a soundcard but yearn for something better, consider what sort of sound you want to improve. If you want to hear the higher quality playback of audio CDs, a new soundcard is unlikely to help. You'd be better off buying a superior set of amplified speakers.

Recording

Wave files store speech, short clips of music, and recordings from real life. Most soundcards play these at CD quality but might be able to record at telephone or radio quality only. To make your own recordings in CD quality you need a card with a 44KHz sampling rate.

The best reason for upgrading a soundcard is to play MIDI files. For high-quality playback you need a soundcard with wavetable synthesis. These incorporate samples of real musical instruments to create more authentic music.

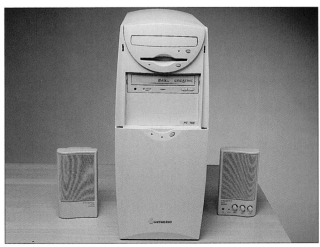

4 These compact speakers are typical of those provided in a multimedia upgrade kit along with a soundcard and CD-ROM drive.

Graphics cards

Take control of the images you see on screen and speed up your PC's display with a graphics card.

Computers have come a long way since the time when the only readout you could get was a row of blinking lights. Today, information is fed to a screen via graphics controllers mounted on a plug-in card. Your monitor creates the image you see, but it is the graphics controller that interprets information from the PC's processor through the operating system and sends it to the monitor.

Graphics for all

As computing becomes more reliant upon graphics, a greater demand is placed on graphics controllers. This is something that affects everyone who uses a PC, from business people to those who use their PC mainly for games. The ability of a graphics controller to process basic information, such as the Windows interface, affects overall system performance. Upgrading the graphics card can often make an apparently slow PC much faster.

Taking the strain

At the core of the controller hardware on one of these cards sits a chip. This takes much of the strain from the PC's CPU, freeing it for more important tasks. Graphics cards are generally rated according to the bit size of the processor, usually 64-bit or 128-bit. Theoretically, a 128-bit graphics card should be much faster than a 64-bit. It will enable Windows to open faster on-screen, and a text document to scroll more quickly, for example, although other factors and components have an effect on speed too.

Rich color

One such factor is the speed and the video memory on the card itself. The greater the amount of video memory, the richer the color that can be produced and the higher the resolution possible. Typically, graphics cards come with a minimum of 4MB of memory, and can come with up to 64MB for greater flexibility and better performance.

Buying tips

● Specify how much video memory you want on a new graphics card. You'll find that 4MB is an acceptable minimum for business software on a 14in monitor, but if you want to play games, run paint programs or use a 17in monitor, consider 16MB, 32MB, or 64MB.

● Instead of upgrading an aging PC with a new graphics card plus a 3D add-on device, you may find it cheaper to buy a combined 2D/3D card.

● When buying a dedicated 3D accelerator card, find out which ones are supported by the most games.

● Make sure that any graphics card you buy supports Microsoft's DirectX 5. DirectX support is required by many Windows Me and 98 games and without it you won't be able to play them.

● Some home PCs incorporate the graphics hardware on the motherboard. In most cases, you can still add a new card, but check your PC manual to see how to disable the motherboard's graphics controller first.

● Some combined 2D/3D AGP cards are just as good as the dedicated PCI 3D accelerator cards, so if your computer has an AGP slot, think carefully before you buy a new 3D card.

Top brands

● **ATI** www.ati.com
● **Creative Labs** www.americas.creative.com
● **Guillemot** www.guillemot.com
● **3dfx** www.3dfx.com
● **VisionTek** www.visiontek.com

Fact file

● **CAD** Stands for Computer-Aided Design. CAD software is used to create engineering, architectural, or scientific models on screen. Applications can create 20 or 30 models, and some programs can rotate or resize the models and show interiors.

● **Color depth** The variety of colors each screen pixel can display at any given resolution, usually measured in binary bits; 8-bit color depth allows 256 color variants, 16-bit allows 65,536, and 24-bit allows 16.7 million.

● **DirectX** Microsoft's accelerated operating system interface between software programs and PC graphics hardware. DirectX includes DirectDraw and Direct3D for 3D graphics cards.

● **Pan** Many graphics cards allow you to work in a virtual Desktop bigger than the pixel resolution actually shown on screen. Moving the mouse to the edge of the screen causes the on-screen image to shift (or pan) in that direction enabling you to see the rest of the Desktop.

● **TV-out** The TV-out port enables a PC to connect to a standard TV for display purposes.

● **Pixel** Picture element, a single identifiable dot on a PC screen, made up of convergent red, green, and blue points of light.

● **Resolution** The width and height of the image shown on screen, irrespective of screen size and measured in pixels.

● **VGA** Video Graphics Array, a PC graphics resolution of 640x480 pixels, used now only for games, DOS programs, and on notebook PCs with small screens. 800x600 and above is generally termed SuperVGA.

Another important factor is 3D capability, which allows 3D modeling packages and games to run faster, with higher quality images. You can buy a 3D add-on card which works with your existing graphics card, although many now come with 3D and 2D capability in one product. Unfortunately, there is no 3D standard for the industry yet; the PC market is split between two camps, Direct 30 and OpenGL. However, most games will run under both. For computer-aided design (CAD), go for an OpenGL-compliant card because most CAD software is written to comply with this.

What to look for

Most PCs have an AGP graphics card—the faster successor to PCI graphics cards. AGP was introduced in 1997, and the 2xAGP, which runs twice as fast as the original, is now the norm. Some high performance PCs will have the even faster 4xAGP cards.

Game playing with a regular graphics card—but see below.

This is the same game as above run on the same PC but with a Matrox m3D accelerator added to work alongside the existing graphics card.

Hard disks

Upgrading your hard disk will give you more space for storing your applications and documents.

It's easy to forget about your hard disk until it goes wrong, at which point you begin to think that it's the most important part of your PC. It stores your operating system, your programs, and your data. Without an operating system, such as Windows, you can't start your computer; without programs you can't do anything with your PC once it has started; and without a bank of data to draw on you have to type in everything from scratch.

Keep it sealed

Hard disks are among the few mechanical parts of a PC and you'd expect them to have a higher failure rate than purely electronic devices. In fact, they are very reliable. This is mainly due to the fastidious way in which they are made and tested. They are assembled in clean rooms in which the air is constantly filtered to remove particles. Before they're allowed out of the room their cases are sealed. Open a hard disk out of curiosity and you will ruin it, which is why they're usually smothered in warnings against tampering.

Inside a hard disk, data is stored on one or more platters. These are made of a hard magnetically sensitive material, which is how the disks get their name. A read/write head moves just above the

Fact file

● **EIDE** An enhanced version of IDE (see below). These days all hard disks are made to at least the EIDE standard but they can also be used in older PCs with ordinary IDE controllers. In this case they perform like ordinary IDE drives.

● **Gigabyte (GB)** A measure of how much data a hard disk can store. A gigabyte is a thousand megabytes (MB) so a disk described as 2GB stores 2,000MB of data.

● **IDE** Refers to both a type of hard disk and the controller that governs it. IDE, along with its two advanced variants called EIDE and Ultra DMA, is the most popular type of hard disk system in ordinary PCs.

● **SCSI** Refers to an alternative type of hard disk to IDE and to the controller that governs it. Mechanically, SCSI disks work in the same way as IDE disks but are governed by a SCSI controller which is able to transfer information very quickly. SCSI disks are usually found on advanced computers serving a network of PCs.

● **Ultra DMA** The third and latest variant of IDE. The performance of Ultra DMA hard disks can be as good as more expensive SCSI systems, but to use one you must have a PC and a controller specifically designed for the purpose. You can use an Ultra DMA disk with an IDE or EIDE controller but you won't reap any speed benefits.

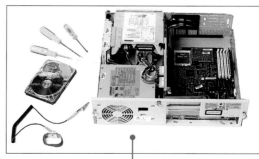

Before removing your hard disk, make certain you have all the tools you need for the job, including an antistatic wristband.

This is what's inside a hard disk, but don't open up yours to check! The disk platter spins at speeds up to 7,200rpm and the read/write head above it is controlled by a stepper motor on the bottom left.

Buying tips

● What is commonly called the size of a hard disk actually refers to its capacity, which is how much data it can store. Physically, PC hard disks are usually 3.5in wide but this is unrelated to their storage capacities.

● There are two ways of calculating the capacity of a hard disk, based on different interpretations of how many bytes there are in a megabyte. Hard disk manufacturers prefer to say there are 1,000,000 bytes in a megabyte because it makes their disks sound bigger than if they used the technical definition of 1,048,576 bytes. This is why a hard disk described as 528MB shows up in many software applications as 503MB.

● When choosing a hard disk you should make certain that it's big enough to store all your programs and data with room to spare. As a general rule you can't have enough disk space so buy the biggest disk you can afford.

● Don't worry too much about manufacturers' quoted speeds for their hard disks—they're all fast these days—but do ensure you buy the right type for your PC. If it can support Ultra DMA then don't buy a slower EIDE drive.

When you reconnect the power lead and ribbon cable to your new hard disk, make certain the ribbon cable is the right way around. A red line down the side of the cable should match up with pin 1—marked on the label on the drive.

Top brands

● **IBM** www.ibm.com
● **Castlewood ORB** www.castlewood.com
● **Maxtor** www.maxtor.com
● **Seagate** www.seagate.com
● **Western Digital** www.westerndigital.com

surface of the platters as they spin, either reading (loading) or writing (saving) data. Because hard disks store data magnetically they do not lose it if they are deprived of power. They can be safely removed from one computer and fitted to another.

Laying tracks

Before they can be used by your computer, new hard disks have to be formatted. This process consists of laying down a magnetic pattern of concentric tracks and then chopping these up into smaller sectors like pieces of a pie. Be careful: once information has been stored on a hard disk, formatting it again destroys all the data.

Slice it up

It should be necessary to format a hard disk just once in its life, and if you buy an off-the-shelf computer it will have been done for you already. But when you buy a new hard disk you have to format it yourself. At the same time you can partition the disk so that your PC treats it as several smaller disks. If you're using Windows 95 version A you must do this because it can't understand disks larger than 2GB. Some motherboards don't directly support drives larger than 32GB, so make certain yours can before investing in a large drive.

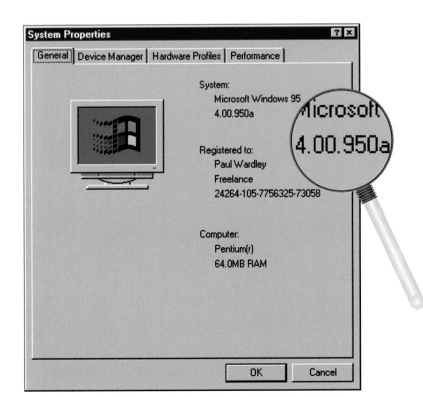

Early versions of Windows 95 (such as Version A, indicated by "a" above) imposed a 2GB limit on the size of hard disks, so larger disks have to be split into smaller partitions. To find out which version of Windows you have, right-click on My Computer and select Properties.

Storage space

When Windows warns that you're running out of disk space, it's time to decide on a new storage system.

When you try to install a new program or save your work, Windows will warn you if there's insufficient disk space. A new hard disk can be fitted as a replacement or as a second drive. In either case, buy the biggest you can afford so you don't have to upgrade again.

CD-ROM drives

You may decide you want a faster CD-ROM drive or a CD-recordable (CD-R) or CD-rewritable (CD-RW) drive so you can record (burn) your own CDs. You may want to have two drives so you can keep a reference CD or encyclopedia in one and use the second for installing new software and running other programs.

Other types of storage

Backing up is vital, but this is easier said than done if you don't have anywhere to store backups. Backing up a hard disk onto hundreds of floppies is out of the question. You need a form of removable storage with a much higher capacity. If backups are your sole concern the inexpensive option is to buy an internal tape drive. Backing up a big hard disk might take

Installing a second hard disk

1 The hard drive with IDE data cable on the left and power connector on the right. Its jumper blocks are just visible between the two. The red line on the IDE cable indicates pin 1 and should be aligned with pin 1 of the hard disk IDE connector.

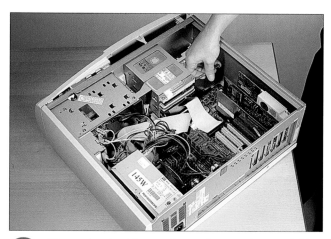

2 After setting the drives as slave and master (see Hard drive tips, page 94) the cables were removed from the old disk to allow the new one to be slipped into place. The new disk is firmly screwed into position. If access to screws is restricted, a short-handled screwdriver is invaluable. In some cases it's easier to remove the complete disk mounting cage before fitting a drive.

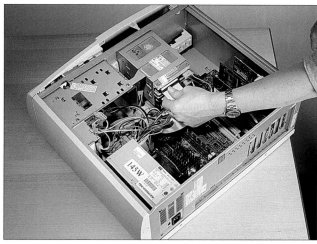

3 With the new drive in position and its IDE and power cables attached, the original drive is reconnected to the same cable, keeping the red stripe aligned with pin 1.

Jargon buster

Jumpers Contacts used to connect two metal pins. Placing a jumper over both pins completes a circuit and is regarded as On or Enabled. Removing a jumper or placing it on one pin breaks the circuit and is regarded as Off or Disabled.

Installing a CD-ROM drive

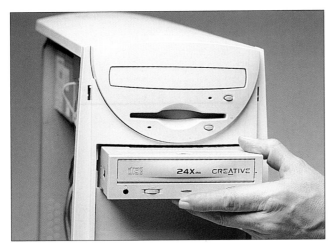

1 With the drive bay cover removed a new CD-ROM drive is being pushed into position from the outside of the case.

2 Because there's not enough space to reach the back of the drive when it is fully in position, it has been left protruding while its cables are fitted.

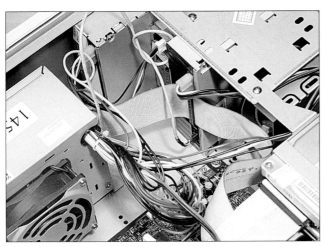

3 CD-ROM drives, like hard disks, have jumpers for setting them as master and slave. The cables are for power, IDE and connecting to the soundcard's CD audio input.

several hours but you can leave your PC to get on with it while you do something else.

Jaz and Zip drives

A more flexible alternative is a removable device such as a Jaz or Zip drive. These can run programs in the same way as conventional hard disks and you can make backups onto them. Jaz drives are as fast as fixed hard disks but because the 1GB and 2GB disks can be removed and replaced they offer potentially unlimited storage. Zip drives store only 250MB and aren't as fast as Jaz drives, but the disks are cheap.

Interfaces

There are two factors to weigh up when choosing a removable drive. Is there room for it inside your PC and what sort of connector does it use? If a drive uses a SCSI interface, make certain that a controller card is supplied and you've got a free expansion slot for it. An alternative for internally mounted drives is to buy one designed for the IDE interface. If you don't have space inside your PC, there are removable drives that can be plugged into the printer port.

Hard drive tips

● A second hard drive should be attached to the same IDE cable as the existing drive. Because you are connecting the two drives to the same cable, one has to be in control of the other. The primary drive is the master, which is in charge of the secondary drive, the slave. The task is accomplished by moving jumpers on the back of each drive. Your PC will regard the master drive as drive C.

● After fitting a new drive you may have to invoke your computer's setup program so it can detect the drive.

● If you fit a second hard drive and use it as a slave there are no problems, but if you're replacing an existing drive or want to boot from the new drive, things are more complicated. Simply copying all the files from the old disk to the new one doesn't work. One solution is to reinstall Windows and all your other software, then copy your data files from the old disk. The fast track is to buy a utility specifically designed for transferring one disk to another. PowerQuest's DriveCopy is a good choice.

Zip drives

It's easy to install an internal Zip drive to increase storage space.

With nineteen million users, the Iomega Zip drive is the world's favorite removable storage device. Although it's not compatible with other removable media, such as the 3.5in floppy, its ubiquity makes it a good choice as a medium of exchange.

It offers good storage capabilities, allowing you to store 100MB or 250MB on one disk. The performance of the Zip drive isn't bad either. It's not quite as fast as a hard disk but it's certainly much faster than the LS-120 SuperDisk. Speed is important if you want to copy a lot of data. Some PCs with the right BIOS will let you boot from a Zip drive.

Originally, the Zip was launched in parallel port external and SCSI internal and external versions. This

meant that if you wanted an internal Zip drive, you had to have a SCSI host adapter card installed in your PC. But Iomega released an internal ATAPI version that can be hooked up to your PC's hard disk interface. This tutorial shows you how to install one of these drives.

Before you install a Zip drive, take a few precautions. You should ground yourself and discharge any static charges you've built up before touching any components. You can do this by touching an unpainted metal part on the case of your PC or any metal device that's plugged in, such as a lamp. If you're feeling cautious, you could buy an anti-static wristband to wear when you're working with the insides of your computer.

Installing an Internal Zip drive

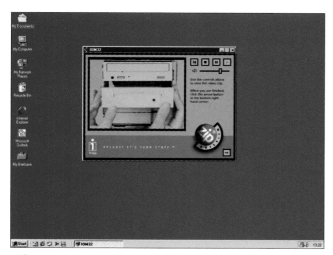

1 Insert the Iomega Toolbox CD-ROM in your PC. The install program should automatically run. Select English and then view the Hardware Installation video. This gives a good insight into the mechanics of physically installing the Zip drive. Then click Exit and remove the disc from the drive.

2 Follow the instructions on page 96 to install the Zip hardware. Power up your PC and load Windows, which should automatically detect the new drive—IDE devices don't require special device drivers as a rule. If you open My Computer, you'll see an extra drive, Removable Drive D:.

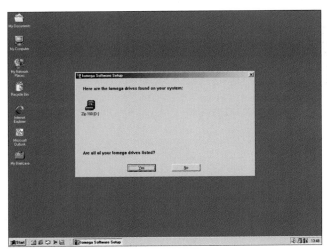

3 Next re-insert the Iomega Toolbox CD-ROM disc and install the Iomega Software.

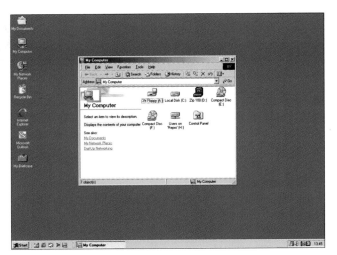

5 When you restart your PC, you'll see a shortcut on your Desktop, pointing at the Iomega utilities and the icon for the Zip drive will have changed to a blue picture of a Zip.

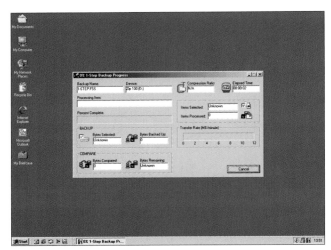

4 When you have installed the Zip software as well as drive utilities, you also get a simple backup program called 1-Step Backup, a Zip disk copying program called Copy Machine and a disk cataloging utility called FindIt.

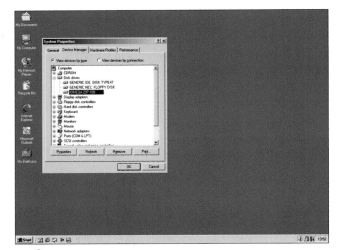

6 Right-click My Computer and select Properties. Select Device Manager and click the + sign next to Disk Drives. Select Iomega Zip 100 and click Properties. Then make certain the Device Status reads: This device is working properly.

Installing your Zip hardware

Shut down your PC, unplug it from the wall outlet and disconnect all other cables. Take the lid off the PC. It'll be held on by four or five self-tapping screws and you'll most likely need a Philips screwdriver to undo them. Put them in a safe place.

Decide where the Zip drive is going to go. It's a 3.5in device so it can go in a 3.5-in drive bay—you just have to remove the 5.25in mounting frame it comes in first—or it can go in a spare 5.25in bay. Try to choose the drive bay next to your CD-ROM drive. Make certain you have the right mounting hardware—things like bolts or rails. The Zip comes with its own mounting bolts so use them.

If your PC has one hard disk and a CD-ROM there should be no need to alter any jumpers on the Zip drive. Most PCs have two IDE channels and you can fit two IDE devices to each, one a master, the other a slave. Whether a drive is a master or slave is determined by a set of jumpers. Typically, your hard disk will be a master on the primary IDE channel; the CD-ROM a master on the

secondary IDE channel. The Zip drive is factory-set as a slave, so it can be connected to either IDE channel. For best performance, you should put it on the same IDE channel as the CD-ROM drive. If you need to make the Zip drive a master, a diagram on the drive case shows you which jumpers to move.

Install the Zip drive in the drive bay. Slide it in and tighten the bolts, then attach the power cable and the ribbon cable at the rear. Trace the gray ribbon cable from the rear of the CD-ROM drive and look for a spare connector. Plug this in to the socket at the rear of the Zip drive. Some ribbon cables are polarized with a little notch so they can't be fitted wrongly. If yours isn't, make certain the colored stripe on the ribbon goes to the first pin of the connector on the drive, next to the power connector. If the CD-ROM cable lacks a second connector, a spare data cable is supplied with the drive. The power cable plug is also polarized. If you don't have a spare power connector, a Y-splitter cable is included in the box.

DVD-ROM drives

Upgrade your CD-ROM drive with a DVD-ROM and you will be able to play movies and the latest reference titles.

If you're thinking about upgrading an old CD-ROM drive, be sure to replace it with a DVD-ROM drive. DVD-ROM drives play all previous CD formats as well as the DVD movie, game, and edutainment titles.

The storage capacity of DVD-ROM is vast: a CD-ROM can hold 650MB, while the maximum capacity of a DVD-ROM will be 17GB. So if you have an eye on the future, this is another reason to upgrade. Game players will appreciate this vast capacity because it will mean more realistic graphics and better sound.

The arguments for upgrading your PC are compelling. DVD movies contain Dolby surround sound and MPEG-2 video, while reference titles on DVD-ROM discs require less disc swapping because of their high capacity. DVD-ROM drives and upgrade kits used to be expensive, but not so now. A complete upgrade kit, including an MPEG decoder, is reasonably priced.

There are three steps to installation. You have to install two pieces of hardware—the drive and the decoder card—and then the MPEG playback software. If your computer's processor is fast enough and you have the right sort of graphics card, you may need to purchase just a DVD-ROM drive and not a complete kit to play MPEG movies.

How to install a DVD-ROM drive

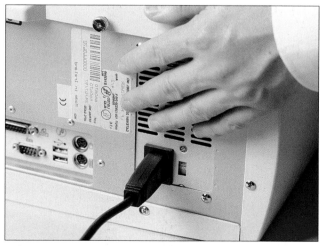

1 Take a few elementary precautions before starting work: ground yourself and discharge any static charges you've built up before touching any electronic components.

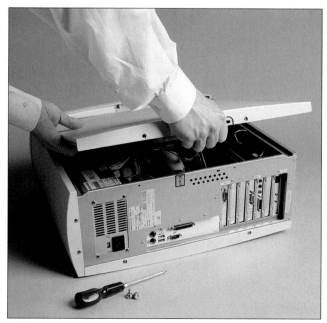

2 Switch off the PC, unplug it from the mains and disconnect all other leads. Take the lid off. It'll be held on by four or five self-tapping screws and you'll probably need a Philips screwdriver to undo them. Put them in a safe place.

3 Decide where the DVD-ROM drive is going to go. It's a 5.25in device so it has to go in an empty 5.25in drive bay, preferably one high enough to avoid obstructing the keyboard if you have a desktop system unit. Also, make certain you have the right mounting hardware—such as bolts or rails. It may come with its own mounting bolts, so use them. Tighten the mounting bolts but don't over-tighten them.

4 Most PCs have two IDE channels and you can fit two IDE devices to each, one a master, the other a slave. Normally, hard disks go on the primary IDE channel and slower devices, such as CD-ROM and DVD-ROM drives, go on the secondary IDE channel. Whether a drive is a master or slave is determined by a set of jumpers on each drive. For example, the Encore DVD-ROM drive is factory-set as a master. Typically, your hard disk will also be set as a master on the primary IDE channel, so if your PC has one hard disk and no CD-ROM, you'll attach the Encore drive as a master on the second IDE channel so there will be no need to alter its jumper settings.

If, however, your PC already has a CD-ROM (set as a master on the second IDE channel) and you want to keep it, then the DVD-ROM drive has to be set to a slave. A label on the rear of the drive shows you which jumper to move. Otherwise, remove the old CD-ROM and replace it with the DVD-ROM drive.

Jargon buster

DVD-ROM Officially, DVD-ROM is not an acronym but it used to stand for Digital Versatile or VideoDisc, Read Only Memory. It's a type of compact disc that can hold a minimum of 4.7GB and up to 17GB of data. DVD-ROM drives are backward compatible with CD-ROMs. This means DVD-ROM players can play CD-ROMs, CD-R and CD-RW disks, and video CDs as well as DVD-RAM discs, the rewritable version of DVD-ROM.

5 Connect the DVD-ROM to the IDE data cable: trace the gray ribbon cable from the secondary IDE channel on the PC motherboard and plug the connector at the end into the socket at the rear of the DVD-ROM drive. Some ribbon cable connectors are polarized with a little notch, so they can't be fitted the wrong way around. If yours isn't, make certain the colored stripe on the ribbon cable goes to pin 1 of the connector on the drive, next to the power connector. Plug in the power cable. This is also polarized to prevent incorrect insertion.

6 The DVD-ROM will come with a thin audio cable. Plug this into the audio output socket on the back of the drive and into the socket on the edge of your soundcard. This lets you play audio CDs through your soundcard. Switch on the PC and load Windows. Windows should detect the new drive. IDE devices don't require special device drivers. If you open My Computer, you'll see an extra drive, in this case Removable Drive D:.

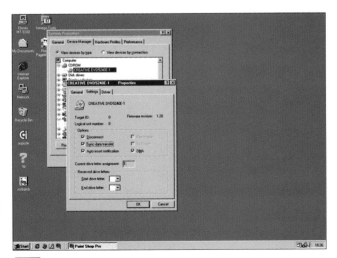

7 To make sure the installation is correct, right-click My Computer and select Properties from the pop-up menu. Select the Device Manager tab and click on the + sign next to CD-ROM Drives to expand that section. Select your DVD-ROM and click the Properties button. Under the General tab, make certain that the Device Status reads: This device is working properly.

Decoder cards

Complete your DVD-ROM drive installation with an MPEG decoder card and your DVD-ROM software.

On pages 97–98 you learned how to install a DVD-ROM kit. Upgrading to DVD enables you, among other things, to watch full-length movies on your computer or play amazingly realistic games. You have already installed the most important part, the drive. In this section you will learn how to install the MPEG decoder card and the DVD-ROM software.

Fitting an MPEG decoder

1 Refer to page 97 for instructions on how to remove the system unit cover. The Encore MPEG decoder is a PCI card, so it must go in a PCI expansion slot. These are normally white and about 3in long. Examine the motherboard and choose a free PCI slot. Undo the bolt securing the blanking plate at the end of the slot and remove the plate. Hold the card by its top edge and press the connector edge firmly into the expansion slot. This may be a tight fit and you may have to use a steady force. Tighten the bolt to stop the card from flapping around.

DVD-ROM tips

● If you're going to watch movies on your PC, be sure to turn off your screensaver. Screensavers monitor keyboard and mouse use and come on after a set interval, which you don't want to happen when you're watching a movie.

● Power Management can also shut down your PC when you haven't touched the keyboard or mouse for a while. To avoid this happening when you're watching a movie, open Control Panel, double-click the Power Option icon and in the Power Schemes dropdown list, choose Always On.

2 Unplug the audio cable that connects the DVD-ROM drive to your soundcard and plug it into one of the Audio In sockets on the top of the MPEG card. Plug the supplied audio cable into the Audio Out socket on the MPEG card and the other end back into the audio socket on your soundcard.

3 Unplug the video cable that connects your monitor to the graphics card and plug it into the lower of the two VGA sockets on the back of the MPEG card. A special VGA cable is provided. Plug one end into the VGA socket on the graphics card and the other into the upper VGA socket on the MPEG card. Put the system unit cover back, do up the screws and plug everything in. Plug in any speakers to the soundcard, plus any line connections. Switch the PC on and make certain everything is working.

4 The next step is to install the DVD-ROM player software, here the Creative Labs CD-ROM. Put it into the DVD-ROM drive and then close the tray. The Setup program should automatically start by itself. This doesn't take long.

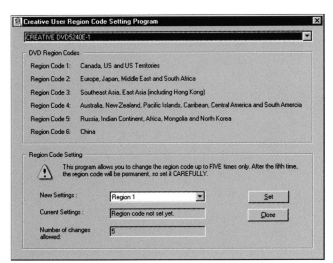

5 The most important thing to set here is your DVD region: the US is Region 1, Europe is Region 2. Discs from one region won't play in another, so if you're going to watch only imported European titles, select Region 2. Otherwise select Region 1. It is possible to swap back and forth, but no more than a total of five times. The PC then restarts. Before you can use your DVD-ROM drive to play back movies, your graphics card needs to be calibrated, which is done automatically.

Surround sound

DVD supports Dolby Digital 5.1 channel surround sound, which means that with the right hardware you can have sounds coming at you from all directions. This will, of course, entail connecting your existing home cinema AV amplifier to the MPEG decoder card, using a digital connection called SP/DIF. The Encore comes with a special cable, which has a phono-style plug at either end: just plug it in to the SP/DIF sockets on the MPEG card and your AV amplifier. Note the Encore DVD-ROM drive has a digital audio connector; this isn't required for Dolby Digital/AC3 presentations.

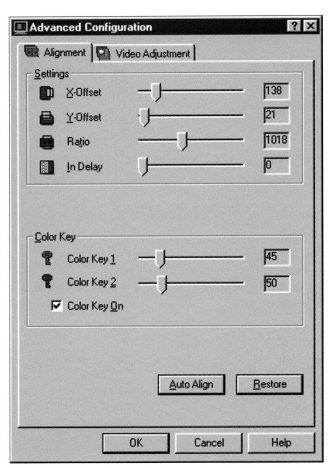

6 It will also be necessary to position the movie image to make it fit with the edges of the viewing window, similar to the horizontal and vertical hold on a TV. This can be handled automatically or you can fine-tune it manually.

If you want to watch your MPEG movies on a TV screen you can, providing it (or your VCR) has either a phono-style Video In socket or an S-Video socket. An S-Video cable comes bundled with Encore. Plug it into the S-Video socket on the MPEG decoder card and the other end into the appropriate socket on your TV or VCR.

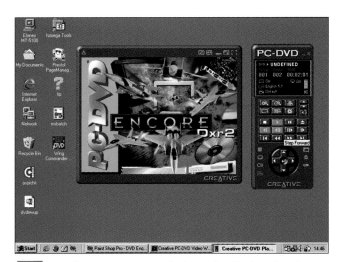

7 To play a DVD-ROM movie, insert the disc into the player. This will be detected and the player software will automatically load. The main control resembles the familiar TV remote control and you can do all the things you'd expect to do, such as start and stop the playback, jump to a particular chapter, adjust the volume and so on.

Memory upgrades

Adding more RAM is one of the easiest ways to pep up the performance of your PC.

The memory in your PC has an important job to do. It's where your programs are stored while they are being run. Data that is being worked on by the programs is also kept in random access memory (RAM). If you want to open several programs at the same time, or work with large data files, you need to make certain your PC has plenty of RAM.

Next to the capacity of its memory, the PCs most important attribute is its speed. The faster the processor in your PC, the faster the memory needs to be so the processor isn't kept waiting whenever it reads or writes data. For most systems, 128MB is fine, but 256MB or more is better.

The cache

Memory fast enough to keep up with the processor is expensive, so most PCs have a small amount of fast memory, called a cache. Data that is needed straightaway is kept in the cache. When it's full, data is moved back to the slower main memory, and new essential data is moved to the cache.

A cache is a bit like an office desk. You keep the files you are working on within easy reach to save having to go to the filing cabinet every time you want something. The bigger the desk, the more files you can keep on hand, and the more time you save.

Buying tips

Before attempting an upgrade, check that there are empty memory sockets in your PC. If this isn't mentioned in the manual, you will have to take off the cover and look inside. If there aren't any spare slots, you'll have to take out some of the existing memory chips and replace them with higher capacity modules. While you're looking, make a note of how many chips are on each module, whether chips are on one or both sides, and write down the numbers on the memory chips. This information will help a good supplier choose memory which matches what you already have.

Watch out!

When installing memory, be careful how you handle it. Static electricity from your fingers can damage the chips. Hold the modules by the edges only. Make certain the notched edge of the circuit board is on the same side as on the existing module. Slide the module into the empty socket, then press it upright until the retaining clips click into place.

Adding RAM is one of the easiest things you can do inside your PC. When you open it you will see a row of connectors. Most PCs today use the 16-pin DIMM cards, which install memory, one at a time, in different sizes. The memory also has to match the speed of your system's bus.

Wear an antistatic armband to make certain you don't damage your new chips or anything inside your PC.

Slide the memory module into the socket at an angle, checking that the notch is on the correct side. Rotate upright to click the retaining clips into place.

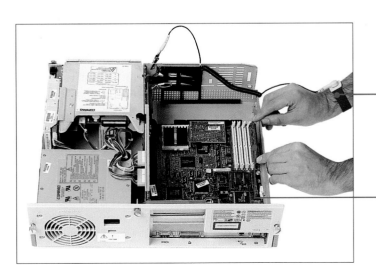

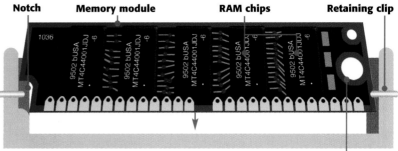

Notch   Memory module   RAM chips   Retaining clip

Locating hole

Carefully insert the memory module into the socket, making sure you hold it by the edges.

The upgrade chip should rotate smoothly into position and the retaining clips should click into place.

Jargon buster

● **RAM** Computer memory is called RAM. This stands for random access memory. It means that information within the memory can be accessed completely at random. RAM is volatile, which means it loses its data when the power is turned off.

● **CMOS** Stands for complementary metal oxide silicon. It's a type of memory chip that draws a low current. A small battery can provide enough power to retain the data. Your PC uses CMOS memory to store system details and options such as the type of hard disk installed.

● **DIMMS** Stands for dual inline memory modules. These standard memory modules are small circuit boards with RAM chips on both sides.

● **Video RAM** A PC's video board uses RAM to store the picture being displayed. The larger the screen resolution and the more colors that are used, the greater the memory needed.

● **Jumpers** Not every adjustment can be done using the setup software. Some motherboards, hard disks and cards need physical switching to make them work properly with the rest of your system.

Real switches would be too bulky, so PCs use small connectors called jumpers which clip into pins on the motherboard. When major parts such as the CPU are changed, you may have to move the position of the jumpers. Your instruction manual will tell you if this is necessary.

Top suppliers

● **CompuVest** www.compuvest.com
● **Kingston** www.kingston.com
● **PNY** www.pny.com
● **Simple** www.simpletech.com
● **Viking** www.vikingcomponents.com

Most PCs have two levels of cache. The first level, containing the fastest memory, is on the processor chip itself. The size of the cache depends on the processor. Ordinary Pentium processors have 16KB of cache, while MMX Pentiums have 32KB. This is small compared to the size of modern programs, so most PCs have a secondary 256KB cache installed on the motherboard.

Some PC manufacturers skimp on secondary cache to save money. If your PC has little or no cache, you could improve performance by up to 20 percent by installing 256KB of cache RAM. However, there are many different types of cache memory chips and almost as many ways of installing them, so it isn't an easy matter to buy the right parts and install them yourself. Leave this job to an engineer or the dealer who sold you the computer.

RAM raiding

Another good way to improve performance is to install more RAM. The minimum needed to run Windows and Windows applications is 64MB. You need 128MB to run them well. If you don't have enough RAM, Windows has to use your hard disk for 'virtual memory'—a storage area for information there isn't room for in RAM. It's much slower to access data from disk than from real memory, so this holds performance back. It's like having to store some of your office files in the basement because your filing cabinet is too small.

It's relatively easy to upgrade the main memory in a PC, and not too expensive. Most PCs use DIMMs. Newer ones might have the more expensive RDRAM which needs special RIMM slots on the motherboard. Laptops may require custom modules.

Adding peripherals

Installing new peripherals is easier than ever as Windows does all the hard work for you.

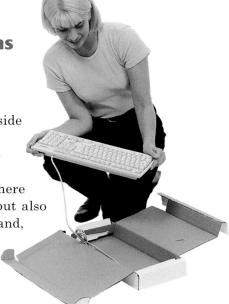

Adding new hardware is a daunting task if you are new to computers. However, Windows makes things as easy as possible. You still have to physically install the card or attach the cables, but Windows helps you install the software.

Most modern computers are "plug and play", which means that you no longer have to worry about tinkering with little switches inside the computer to get a new piece of hardware working.

The steps described here are for Windows Me, but also work for Windows 98 and, with the exception of steps 7 and 8, for Windows 95 as well.

How to add new hardware

1 The easiest hardware to install is plug and play hardware, as long as you have a plug and play computer. Once you have installed the hardware in the computer, turn the PC on and Windows will detect the new device. Have the driver disk that came with the device ready to insert in the drive if Windows asks for it.

If you have an older device or an older computer, Windows may not automatically detect the new hardware. In this case, you must run the Add New Hardware Wizard from the Windows Control Panel. This will guide you through the steps involved in installing software.

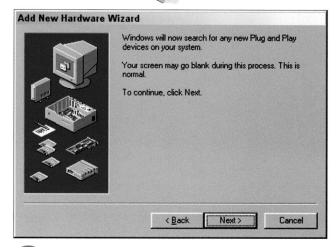

2 The Add New Hardware Wizard will ask if you want Windows to look for your new hardware. This is the best choice, as it simplifies the procedure. Click Next to start the detection process. Windows will take a couple of minutes to search for the new device. A progress indicator will show you how far Windows has got.

Plug and play

Plug and play devices and your PC talk to each other using **input/output (I/O) ports**, **interrupt requests (IRQs)** and **direct memory addressing (DMA)**. You don't need to understand these things, but it's important that no two devices share these channels. If they do, conflict results, and the affected devices may refuse to work. Plug and play devices have software which uses a special protocol to discover what options are available and configures the hardware automatically.

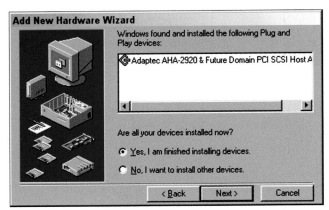

3 If Windows finds your new device, it will tell you it is ready to install software support for it. To install the software, click Finish. Windows may ask you for a driver disk which will have been supplied with the hardware, or to load the Windows CD-ROM. The wizard will ask if you have installed all the plug and play devices you wish. Click Yes and on completion, you may be asked to restart Windows.

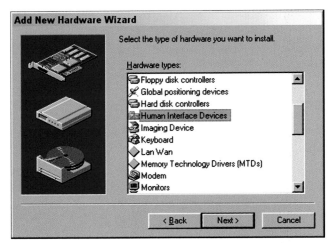

4 If Windows does not detect your new hardware, you need to tell it exactly what the new hardware is. Select the type of device, then click Next. On the next page that appears, choose the manufacturer from a list, and then the model of the device. Click Next again and Windows will load the driver software.

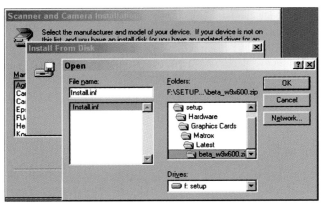

5 If your hardware manufacturer or model are not listed, click the Have Disk button. Insert the driver disk, then select the drive for the disk and use the Open dialogue box to locate the driver file, which will be called something like Oemsetup.inf. Click OK twice to get back to the Wizard. You should now see a list of names which will include your new hardware device. Select it, click OK and then Finish and Windows will install the software.

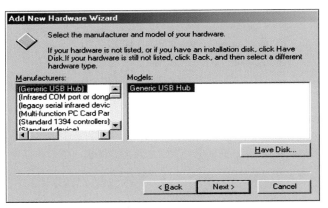

6 If you still can't find a driver, look at the list of devices that Windows recognizes by selecting Unknown Device. Scroll down the list to see if the maker of your device is listed. A list of models of that maker's hardware will appear. Your hardware may be compatible with an older model, in which case you may be able to use it by installing the driver for that model.

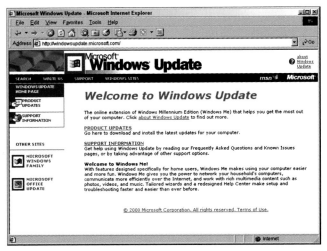

7 Windows Me and 98 have added an online update feature. If you have an Internet connection, clicking on the Start button, Settings, Windows Update takes you to a Web site for downloading updates for Windows and new drivers.

8 The Web site examines your computer to see if there are any updates available, and you can choose the ones you want from a list. When you click the Download button, the updates are downloaded from the Microsoft Web site and automatically installed on to your computer. (See pages 123–124.)

Express bus

The introduction of USB has made it easier than ever to install new hardware.

Although Windows has made PCs much easier to use, until recently you still had to take the lid off your system unit to install a new hardware device—something many users were reluctant to do. What was needed was a simple way of connecting devices to a PC that didn't require configuring, that let them install themselves and that would permit them to be installed and removed without having to shut down your PC.

The first step along the route to the sealed box PC is the Universal Serial Bus or USB. USB has been around for a while but initially had poor support from Windows and so didn't take off. However, with the release of Windows 98 and Me and the Apple iMac, USB is becoming more popular and USB devices are appearing on dealers' shelves in greater numbers.

USB was designed to replace the PC's parallel and serial ports. These ports, especially the parallel port, were increasingly being asked to do tasks they weren't designed for. The parallel port was designed as a simple printer port, but today you can fit all sorts of devices to it, including

Installing a USB device

1 The first thing to do is to check that your PC has USB ports. These are small rectangular sockets, about ¹/₂in by ¹/₄in. A pair of them will normally be located at the back of your PC, probably close to the keyboard and mouse sockets. Most Pentium and later PCs will have USB ports.

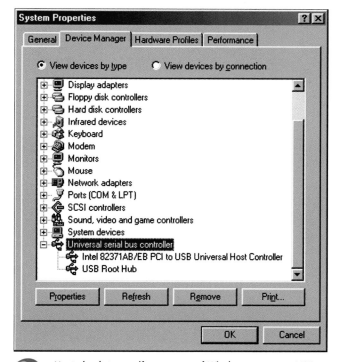

2 Next check to see if your copy of Windows supports USB. Windows Me and 98 do, but USB support wasn't standard with Windows 95. However, final versions were shipped with a supplementary floppy disk containing USB drivers. Right-click My Computer and select Properties. Click on the Device Manager tab and scroll down the device list to the end, where you should find Universal serial bus controller.

scanners and disk drives. This is fine if you just want to connect a scanner and a printer, but not if you want to attach more devices.

USB offers many advantages over the serial and parallel ports. Its maximum data speed of 12Mbps is about 100 times faster than a serial port. This makes USB ideal for tasks where a lot of data has to be transferred, as from scanners or digital cameras. USB ports also carry power, which means some devices don't need a power adaptor.

USB beats serial and parallel ports when it comes to numbers: you can link up to 127 USB devices to a single socket. It also makes it easy to install new devices. Windows Me and 98 automatically detect new USB devices and install the correct software for them without having to restart your PC. Finally, USB can eliminate the need for an interface card in some cases. This means, for example, that USB speakers don't require a soundcard and a USB video camera doesn't require a video capture card.

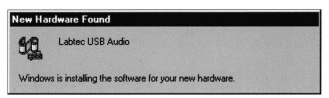

3 If your PC does have USB ports and they aren't listed in the Device Manager, open Control Panel and click on the Add New Hardware icon to run the hardware wizard to install them. Have your Windows installation disk or USB supplementary floppy disk ready to insert when Windows requests it.

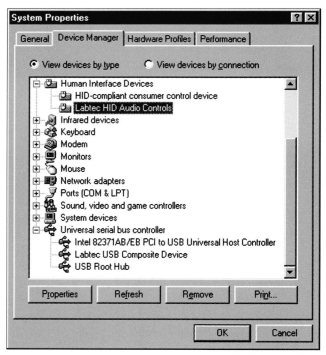

4 Assuming that your USB ports are listed in the Device Manager, installing a USB device is simply a matter of plugging it in. Here a pair of USB loudspeakers, the Labtec LCS-1040, are used as an example. Windows has drivers for these speakers already in its driver database and so requires no additional software; as soon as you insert the USB plug, Windows automatically detects it and will install the drivers for it, which takes a minute or two. When you unplug the speakers, the drivers are unloaded from memory. It's that simple.

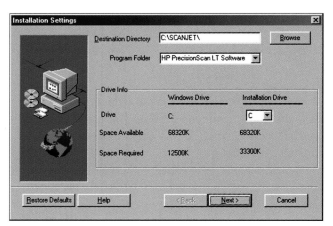

5 More sophisticated USB devices such as scanners require software installation prior to connection. For example, with the Hewlett-Packard ScanJet 4100C, you have to install the scanning software, PrecisionScan LT, first. Once this is completed and the PC rebooted, you plug in the scanner's USB cable. Windows automatically detects the new scanner and loads the appropriate drivers which have now been installed.

6 One benefit of USB is that you can initiate scans by pressing a button on the scanner, rather than loading the software first and starting the scan from your PC.

Adding USB support

You can buy adapters to convert your PC to USB. Many motherboards have USB headers or connectors but lack USB plugs. All you need is a blanking plate with USB ports that you can plug into the motherboard. If you have an older PC, it's possible to buy a PCI expansion card with USB ports. You can also buy a parallel to USB converter cable to make your printer USB-compatible.

Monitors

The right monitor can make your PC easier to use and save your eyesight. Here are all the options.

Many vendors of otherwise decent PCs provide cheap, poor-quality monitors to keep prices down. This is a false economy because the monitor is the only part of a computer you use all the time.

Using a monitor with a picture that's flickery, fuzzy or too small can damage your eyes. If this sounds familiar you should buy a better monitor right now. There are dozens of suppliers and each has a host of different models to choose from. The best way to start is by deciding what size you need.

The big picture

The cheapest monitors have 14in screens, and these are the ones that most people upgrade from. The screen image is made up of thousands of tiny colored dots, called pixels. The lower the resolution, the fewer the number of pixels used and the fuzzier the image. On a 15in monitor you can comfortably use 800 x 600 pixels; on a 17in monitor you can use 1,024 x 768 pixels and higher resolutions are more practicable. Monitor prices start to rocket after 17in so big screens tend to be bought by specialists in desktop publishing and design.

LCD displays are desirably flat, impressively high tech and they fit almost anywhere. Unfortunately, they cost more than conventional monitors.

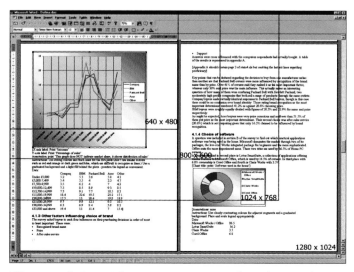

This screenshot was taken at 1,280 x 1,024. It shows how much more you can see on a large monitor running at a high resolution.

Fact file

● **Dot pitch** Monitor screens are coated on the inside with patterns of red, green, and blue phosphor dots. The dot pitch is the distance between two dots of the same color and serves as a rough guide to picture quality. Look for a dot pitch of 0.28mm or less.

● **FST** Stands for flatter, squarer tube. Only found on 15in and larger monitors.

● **Lifespan** Monitors don't last forever and tubes deteriorate over time. After ten years of normal use a tube will drop to half its original brightness. It should be replaced long before then.

● **MPRII** A Swedish standard to which most monitors adhere. It governs the emission of non-ionizing radiation. Some monitors satisfy the more rigorous conditions of TCO92, TCO95, and TCO99, also from Sweden.

● **OSD** Stands for on-screen display. A menu that appears on the screen to help you make adjustments to the picture.

● **Trinitron** A type of monitor invented by Sony. It uses a screen coated with stripes of phosphor instead of dots. A similar technology, called aperture grille, has been adopted by other manufacturers and such monitors are typified by their flat screens, high contrast, and good anti-reflective qualities. They are, however, more sensitive to vibrations.

Buying tips

- Don't buy a monitor with an etched screen. This method of reducing reflections also reduces the sharpness of the picture. Choose a silica or AR coating instead.

- LCD panels are emission-free. They have absolutely flat screens and require less space than conventional monitors. They're also more expensive than conventional monitors, although prices are falling.

- If you'd like a bigger monitor but you're short of space, buy a multimedia monitor and get rid of your desktop speakers.

- Monitors can be bulky and heavy. If you want to stand a monitor on top of your PC, make sure the system unit is big enough to take the strain.

- The official size of a monitor is actually the diagonal measurement of its picture tube. Some of the tube is always hidden by the frame of the monitor so when comparing screens you should consider visible diagonals, which may be considerably smaller than the physical ones.

Top brands

- **Acer** www.acercm.com
- **Compaq** www.compaq.com
- **Hewlett-Packard** www.hp.com
- **NEC** www.neccomp.com
- **Sony** www.sony.com

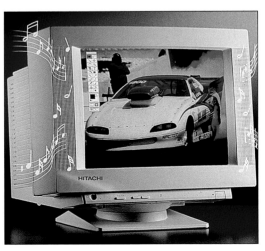

A multimedia monitor can save space on your desktop, but don't expect to get stereo-quality sound from its built-in speakers.

Going dotty

The point of all these extra dots is that instead of having each of your programs filling the entire screen, it's possible to run them side by side. This enables you to make full use of the drag-and-drop sharing facilities in Windows. Of course, you can also use a large-screen monitor at a low resolution to make everything appear bigger, which helps prevent eyestrain if you use your computer for long periods of time.

Refreshing news

Apart from size, monitors vary in how frequently they redraw the screen. The picture on a monitor is constantly updated many times per second and the more often a screen is redrawn, the less it seems to flicker. The frequency with which the screen is redrawn is called the refresh rate and is measured in Hertz (Hz). For most people a refresh rate of 75Hz looks fine, but some people are more sensitive to flicker and need higher refresh rates to avoid discomfort. When comparing refresh rates, make certain the figures quoted are non-interlaced. Interlaced refresh rates don't work so well.

Use your eyes

A monitor is the one part of a PC you should never buy without seeing it in action. Having picked one of an appropriate size and checked that it has high refresh rates at the resolutions you want to use, look closely at the surface of the screen. Make certain it doesn't reflect light from windows or ceiling fittings into your eyes. Look for distortion in the corners of the picture—which may be correctable—and for even illumination over the entire screen.

Obviously the picture should be sharp and flicker free, but also check that the brightness and contrast controls allow for a sufficient range of adjustment to suit different lighting conditions. Finally, check the price to see if you can afford it.

Watch out!

Buying a monitor with a high refresh rate doesn't necessarily solve the problem of flicker. A monitor depends on the graphics card inside a PC for its picture. If the graphics card can't generate the same high refresh rates as the monitor, the available refresh rates are limited to those on the graphics card. The only solution is to buy a new graphics card with the same capabilities as the monitor.

Modems

Make the most of e-mail and harness the potential of the World Wide Web with a modem upgrade.

There are two reasons you might want to upgrade your computer by installing a modem: one is that your existing modem is too slow and the other is that your PC hasn't got one at all. In the latter case, you're missing a lot because with a modem your computer can be used to send and receive faxes and e-mail, as a telephone answering machine and as your route onto the Internet.

Choosing a modem

There are just two decisions to make: how fast a modem to buy and whether to get one that fits inside your computer or one that plugs into the back of it. Improvements in modem design mean that these days it's almost impossible to buy one that's too slow. Most modems have a speed of 56,000bps. Bps stands for bits per second, but modems are often described as simply 56K. If you have an older 28.8K or 33.6K modem, it's time to upgrade.

Data speeds

The faster the modem the less time you will spend sending and receiving data. Faster modems mean lower phone bills. But before you dash out and buy a 56K modem you should be aware that they aren't always faster—at least not at the 56,000bps they claim. Under the old V.90 standard, modems send information at 33.6K only, but are able to receive it at faster speeds, although seldom at their theoretical limit of 56K.

However, the first modems conforming to the V.92 standard are appearing. Although the maximum download speed is still 56K, the upload speed—the speed you can send files to the Web—is faster at 48K. The modems also have a quick connect feature which can shave up to 10 seconds off the time it takes to get connected.

Internal modems don't need a separate power supply and don't tie up a serial port on the back of your PC. They also cost less. The sole advantage of an external modem is that you don't have to open up your computer to install it.

Here an **internal modem** is being fitted into the computer's **ISA** expansion slot.

This modem has a **single socket** for connection to a telephone line. If you want to connect a handset to the same line you need a Y-adapter for the wall socket. Some modems provide a separate socket for a telephone handset.

Fax tips

● Faster modems don't send faster faxes. They're transmitted at a maximum 14,400bps regardless of the speed of the modem.

● A modem can transmit faxes to other PCs and fax machines, but without a scanner you can only send faxes that have been typed into your PC.

● A modem can receive faxes from other computers and from ordinary fax machines.

Fast Internet access

Jargon buster

● **Analogue** The traditional type of phone service.

● **DOCSIS** A standard for cable modems. With this standard, you can use your cable even if you move and change cable company.

● **Ethernet** A type of network connection, often used to link a PC to a cable modem.

● **Backbone** The Internet backbone is made up of the largest fiber optic cables that connect the various service providers and countries on the Internet together.

● **Bandwidth** The amount of data that can be transmitted between two points in a fixed time, usually measured in bits per second (bps). In other words it measures how quickly information can be moved across any given medium.

● **Gigabyte/GB** A billion bytes of data, or 1,024MB if you prefer.

● **Terabyte/TB** This is 1,024GB.

You can dramatically speed up your access to the Internet using a broadband connection.

It's not surprising that the Internet is sometimes known as the World Wide Wait. With ever more complicated Web pages, and larger files to download, even the fastest modem can take an age to bring you the information that you want. There are speedier solutions in the form of broadband modems, such as cable or ADSL, and satellite connections. Cable modems connect to cable television systems, and can be around ten times the speed of modems that use telephone lines —and sometimes even faster. We'll look at them in more detail on pages 112–113.

DSL

Fast taking off for the small business and home user are DSL connections, of which the most common is ADSL (asymmetric digital subscriber line). Its great advantages are that it provides a quick, always on connection to the Internet. A web page with lots of graphics that would take minutes to download over a normal modem will appear in seconds. What's more, unlike cable, it doesn't need expensive, new fiber-optic cabling. It operates over your existing telephone lines. ADSL works at a higher frequency to normal voice traffic so you can use a phone or fax on the same line while you are connected to the Internet.

You still need to connect via a modem to an ISP who provides your gateway to the Internet. As most providers charge a fixed monthly price for unlimited usage you can stay connected to the Internet 24 hours a day and cut out any connection/disconnection delays.

ADSL is just one variant of a group of similar technologies grouped under the name xDSL. As it is asynchronous, that is it delivers data at a faster speed than it can upload it, it is also being used for "broadcasting" style services, such as the growing market for video on demand.

New symmetric ADSL services (SDSL) are emerging where the speed of data transfer is the same both to and from the Internet. This will be better for online gamers and video-conferencing.

Out of space

As ADSL services are not available in all areas, the only option for those in more remote areas who want a broadband connection is to head for space and get a satellite link.

To access the Internet you go through a standard Internet dial-up connection, but data is received in high-speed downloads of around 500Kbps from satellites orbiting the earth. As well as the cost of the monthly subscription you will have the additional cost of buying a satellite dish and its installation, typically around $300–$500.

Supersonic modems

ADSL allows modem connections at speeds of up to 1.5Mbps. This technology uses existing copper phone lines by exploiting a recent discovery that copper can carry data very quickly over short distances using a high frequency.

The only trouble is that the further the distance traveled, the slower the speed becomes. Having said that, 1.5Mbps is toward the low end of the scale. Over short distances speeds can reach 9Mbps. Like some satellite systems, this is a one-way data street; upload speeds vary from 64Kbps to a still impressive maximum of 640Kbps.

There are several Web sites that explain ADSL technology, particularly in the US where many homes and offices are equipped with a high-speed ASDL link. Try this one at www.dslreports.com for a good overview.

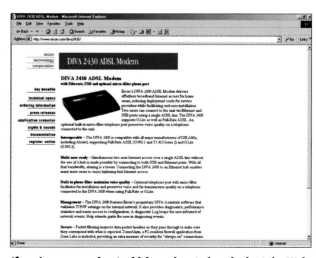

If you're unsure about which modem to buy, look at the Web sites of different manufacturers—for example, www.eicon.com.

Cable modems

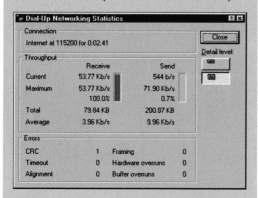
A network designed for an entirely different purpose provides quick Internet access.

Fiber-optic cable makes high-speed Internet access possible, but laying a new network that connects every household would be immensely expensive, not to say disruptive. Fortunately, such a network already exists, thanks to the efforts of cable TV companies over the last decade or so. Although the cable TV (CaTV) network was originally intended to deliver TV programs to homes, the fiber-optic cable it consists of can also handle computer data. All you need is a device that connects your PC to a CaTV point—a cable modem.

Why cable?

Internet access over the CaTV network has two big advantages over dial-up access using the phone network. The first is speed. A cable modem is capable of receiving and transmitting data at rates between 3Mbps and 30Mbps—dozens of times faster than a 56Kbps modem. Such speeds are not always achievable though. The CATV network is designed in such a way that whole neighborhoods share a single fiber-optic cable connection. This makes little difference to delivering television programs, but it does for Internet access. In a worst case scenario, up to 30 households can be sharing a 3Mbps connection and if they're all using the Internet at the same time, speed will drop significantly. Cable companies are aware of this and most will restrict the modem speed of each household to a constantly maintainable level, which is still much faster than an ordinary modem.

Ever ready

Another advantage is that cable modems are always on. Unlike a dial-up modem where you need to make a phone call when you want to be online, cable modems are permanently connected to the Internet. This means that to browse the Web, you just start up your browser.

Cable provides a permanent high-speed always on connection to the Internet, and it costs about twice as much as regular dial-up service. Most CaTV companies charge a flat monthly rate for unlimited Internet access. How cost effective this is depends on how much time you plan to spend online. You'll also have to pay a connection fee, plus you may have to buy a cable modem.

Cable for all?

If you've tried to subscribe to CaTV, you may have discovered that it's not available in all parts of the country. Different CaTV companies serve different areas and the easiest way to find out if you're covered is to consult your local phone book. Even if a CaTV company covers your area, that doesn't mean it offers a cable Internet service. Some companies are further ahead than others. Once you know whom your local cable company is, the best place to go for information is its Web site. On the NTL site, for example, you can see its plans for the rollout of its cable Internet service.

One final point: don't confuse a regular ISP service with a cable one. Since they provide telephone services as well as television, some CaTV companies, notably ATT, already offer dial-up Internet access. This is no different from that offered by any number of ISPs, including the free ones. Contact your CaTV division of the company for information specifically about its cable service.

Keep in touch

If you want to keep up-to-date with what's happening with cable modems, there's a useful Web site that you should bookmark. Cable-Modems.org covers the world of cable modems and high-speed communications. The first port of call for novices should be the cable modem tutorial, where there's a brief history of the technology and an explanation of the terminology. Other parts of the site include recommended reading and even a gallery of current modems.

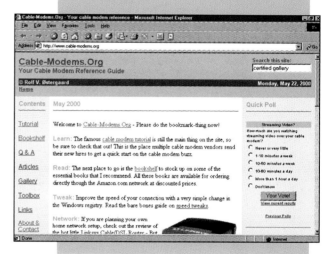

Connection tip

If you want to know more about the fast connection technologies available now, or being trialed, then the best starting point is your telephone services provider. After all, they provide the connection that you use with your modem even though your Internet service provider is a different company.

Jargon buster

● **XML** Stands for eXtensible Mark-up Language, a Web site technology that enables browsers to know what type of content is being loaded and display it accordingly. The same content can be displayed in different ways on different browser platforms such as a mobile phone screen, a desktop computer or an Internet-enabled television.

● **Artificial intelligence** This describes a method of programing software so that it learns to accomplish goals and learns from its mistakes, getting better as it learns more, rather than just doing exactly the same thing each time.

Buying tips

● If you opt for a cable modem connection, check to see what's included in the price. Is there a charge if you download more than a certain amount of information each month, for example?

● Find out how the cable or ADSL modem links to your computer. You might find you need a network card in your PC, for example.

Keyboards

Upgrade your keyboard and mouse to make using your computer as easy and comfortable as possible.

Fact file

● Some keyboards cost ten times as much as others. Prices vary due to their internal construction. The best keyboards have a separate switch under every key. They are described as clicky and are extremely durable. The cheapest keyboards have a one-piece rubber membrane that is pressed against a sandwich of printed electrical contacts when you hit a key.

● Infrared and radio-controlled mice and keyboards have to be powered by batteries. The most power-hungry models can eat a set of batteries every few days.

● Some ergonomically styled mice are sold in left-handed and right-handed versions. Others can be used in either hand.

● Left-handed users can switch the operation of the left and right mouse buttons from within Windows. No special hardware is necessary.

● You can buy flexible, transparent keyboard covers that protect against dirt and spillages, although it's rather like working with gloves on. They're most useful in hazardous environments.

Keyboards and mice allow you to interact with your computer and tell it what to do. There are other input devices such as joysticks and trackballs —and to a limited extent it's possible to control a PC using your voice—but you can't yet completely dispense with a keyboard and mouse.

Considering how much time is spent using them, it's surprising how few people change the keyboard and mouse supplied with their computers. Some of this original equipment is best described as cheap and cheerful and may have been selected with an eye to cost rather than quality. Switching to a superior mouse or keyboard, especially one with additional features, can transform the way you use your PC and needn't cost a fortune.

Keyboards

Your first consideration when choosing a keyboard should be the layout and feel of the keys. This means trying it out. When you do, check that the keyboard is a suitable height, that the keys are spaced far enough apart for you to hit them cleanly and that you like the size and arrangement of the non-alphanumeric control keys.

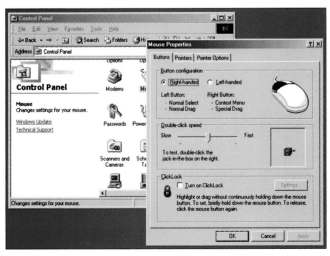

Left-handed users can switch the actions of the left-hand and right-hand mouse buttons by using the Windows Control Panel.

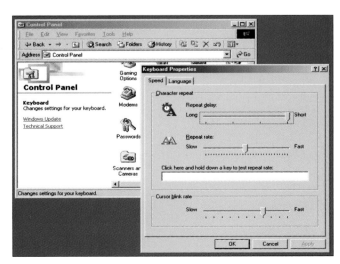

Keyboard settings may be changed by clicking on Keyboard in the Control Panel.

All keyboards send data to a PC in the same way and can be used on any computer with the right type of socket. Keyboards usually have a large DIN or smaller PS/2 plug, but some connect using a USB port. If you opt for a cordless keyboard that uses infrared or radio waves to communicate with your PC, you'll have to make sure the receiver is installed with the right type of plug for your PC.

Mice

Most mice work in a similar way. A ball inside rubs against two rollers in the mouse. At the end of each roller is a disk and a sensor to detect its motion. One roller turns when you move the mouse from side to side and the other when you roll it back and forth. These movements are translated into instructions to move the screen pointer.

Some mice attract more dirt than others and need their rollers cleaned frequently. This might be reason enough to look for a new one, but you're more likely to change because the one you've got isn't comfortable or because you want to upgrade to one of the new breed of mice. These have an extra control wheel or button to scroll through the display without having to use the scroll bars on the screen. The more advanced mice don't have rollers but use optical sensors, scanning the desktop at 1500 times a second to keep the pointer in the right place.

There are three ways a mouse can connect to a PC. Most mice connect to a PS/2 port. Older PCs need a mouse that connects to a serial port. Some mice also connect via USB. If you use a mouse with rollers, it's worth investing in a mouse pad to get the best out of it. These not only provide the right amount of friction for accurate positioning but also keep the ball and rollers clean.

Buying tips

● If you're planning to buy a deluxe mouse with extra features, make sure it will work with your existing software. The early Microsoft Intellimouse, for example, worked fully just with Microsoft Office and it's only recently that the driver was updated for other applications.

● Ergonomic keyboards reduce the risk of repetitive strain injuries, but they're designed for accomplished typists. They won't help you if you're a one-finger typist and might in fact be more awkward to use.

● If you have to put your keyboard close to the edge of your desk, buy a keyboard with a sloping rest for your wrists when you're not typing.

● Adapters are available to convert between PS2, DIN, and serial connectors. These add to the cost of a mouse or keyboard and don't work with every type of PC. It's better to buy equipment with the right type of connector.

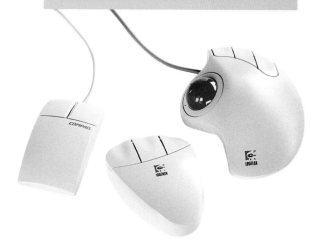

Watch out!

Repetitive strain injury (RSI) takes many forms and affects mouse and keyboard users equally. The most common form is carpal tunnel syndrome, usually caused by resting your wrists on the desktop. To avoid it, try the following:

● Use a mixture of mouse and keyboard operations instead of concentrating on one or the other.

● Use keyboard wrist rests for resting your wrists on when you're not typing.

● When using a mouse don't move just your wrists; move your forearms too.

● Take frequent breaks and stretch regularly.

● Sit with your arms and thighs parallel to the floor and, if your desk is too high, use a footrest.

Top brands

● **Intel** www.intel.com
● **Kensington** www.kensington.com
● **Logitech** www.logitech.com
● **Microsoft** www.microsoft.com
● **PC Concepts** www.pcconcepts.com

Upgrading printers

A mechanical printer switch plugs into the parallel port at the back of a computer. Printers (and other parallel port devices such as scanners) are connected to sockets on the back of the switch unit.

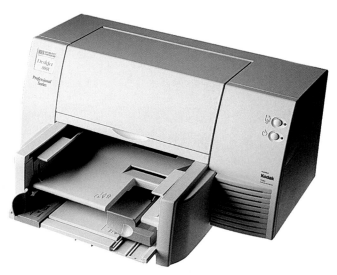

Inkjets are inexpensive, clean, quiet, and versatile. You can buy special papers for overhead transparencies, photos, greeting cards, and T-shirt transfers.

Upgrading a printer means that all your work looks better but you don't have to learn any new skills.

The easiest way to upgrade printers is to buy a new one. This is a blow if you paid a fortune for a laser printer five years ago. For the same money you can now get double-sided printing on 11 x 17in paper at twice the speed and four times the resolution. Old laser printers have virtually no secondhand value.

There have been similar improvements and price cuts in color inkjet printers, to the extent that you'd search hard to find a manufacturer unable to offer color inkjets inexpensively.

Upgrading old printers

A laser printer upgrade worth considering is one with extra memory. Many lasers were sold with only 512KB of memory and can't process a full page of graphics. Adding a few megabytes works wonders, but the extra RAM won't turn a slow printer into a fast one. Neither will it increase the resolution.

Old laser printers might require expensive custom-designed memory modules, but many recent printers will take the same memory modules as used in PCs, making upgrades easy and inexpensive. You might also upgrade a printer by adding extra paper trays to increase the number of sheets it can handle in unattended mode and to make it possible to load envelopes at the same time as ordinary paper.

There is no point in upgrading the internal fonts in a laser printer because fonts and typefaces are provided and manipulated through Windows. The plug-in font cartridge upgrades popularized by Hewlett-Packard were designed to add font capabilities to MS-DOS programs and are largely irrelevant to Windows users.

Jargon buster

Resolution This refers to the number of dots per inch that a printer produces. It is usually expressed as horizontal x vertical dots, for example 600 x 600. As a general rule, the more dots there are, the sharper the print will be.

Adding extra memory to older laser printers makes sense only if the printer is still in good condition and the memory chips are reasonably priced.

The strength of a monochrome laser printer is its ability to produce high-quality output at low cost on ordinary copier paper. It's also a practical way of doing small runs of up to 50 copies.

New for old

If you upgrade your system by buying a new printer you'll benefit from increased speed, increased resolution, and better control and feedback through the printer driver. The most popular budget choice is a color inkjet, but monochrome laser printers are also reasonably priced. Color laser printers are not really an option for the private buyer. They are steadily falling in price, but still cost several times as much as a monochrome model.

Upgraders who need color, but only on special occasions, should consider buying a laser and an inkjet. The laser can be used for everyday work and the inkjet for pictures and presentations, with a simple mechanical switch used to select the appropriate device. The same system could be used to switch between an existing laser that still has some life left in it and a brand new inkjet.

A neat alternative is a multifunction device. These are based on laser or inkjet printers but in the same case as the print mechanism there's a scanner and a fax machine. A multifunction device is suitable for PC users who don't own a scanner and a modem, but there's a drawback inherent in any multipurpose device: if any part of it breaks down, you lose every function while it is being repaired.

The best multifunction devices scan in color at an optical resolution of 300dpi or more and can send and receive faxes when the host PC is not switched on or when it's busy doing something else.

Portable printers like this one run on rechargeable lithium batteries and can print up to 100 pages per charge. An infrared transceiver enables it to receive data from suitably equipped notebooks without a cable.

Watch out!

One of the reasons why inkjets are so cheap is that you pay through the nose for replacement ink cartridges. Printers are often sold at close to cost to ensure a constant revenue from ink sales. Although refills are available from third parties, the use of these invalidates your warranty. So when choosing an inkjet printer consider the cost of running it.

Notebooks

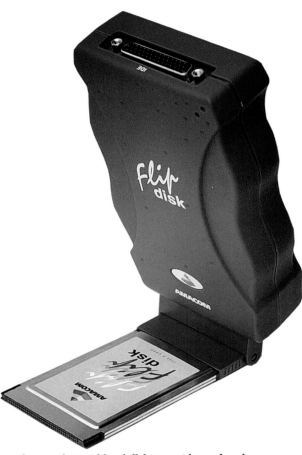

Where an internal hard disk cannot be replaced there's always the option of hooking up an external drive such as the Amacom Flip Disk. This can be cabled into a computer's parallel port or plugged directly into a PC Card slot.

Is it worth it?

Before upgrading a notebook, consider whether the result will be a PC that's exactly what you want or one that will limp along for a few months before its next upgrade. If your computer has a decent sized TFT screen and a newer Pentium processor, it's worth upgrading.

The first thing to tackle is the memory as it yields the biggest performance boost. Then consider the hard disk. If it's a 1GB drive it will be bursting at the seams and should be upgraded. Portable CD-ROM drives can be connected via a PC Card, but be warned that these are far more expensive than their desktop equivalents. You might consider buying a parallel port device that you can also use with your desktop PC.

Notebooks can be upgraded at a reasonable cost and without much technical knowledge.

Today's notebook PCs are very different from those of the recent past. For a start, they're just as powerful as desktop computers and they're equally well endowed with memory and hard disk space. The other big difference is their modularity. It's now the norm to be able to swap a floppy disk drive for, say, a CD-ROM drive or a power pack.

Take it apart

Older notebooks were severely under-specified and many of them have to be partially disassembled to install upgrades. But even if access is tricky, it is in many cases possible to obtain hard disks and memory upgrades from third parties at competitive prices. Where an internal upgrade isn't possible you should be able to plug in an external device.

A decent specification for a notebook PC used to be a Pentium processor, 8MB of RAM and a hard disk of around 800MB. CD-ROM drives and sound facilities were optional. This is still the basis of a decent system, but 64MB of RAM is regarded as the minimum for Windows, a 10GB hard drive is standard, and the lack of a CD-ROM drive is a handicap that restricts the usefulness of a computer. Fortunately, these and other drawbacks can be remedied by easy-to-install upgrades.

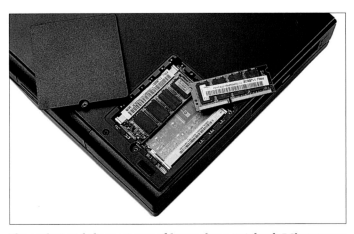

The easiest and cheapest way of increasing a notebook PC's memory is by adding a SO-DIMM module. These have largely superseded expensive proprietary upgrades.

PC Cards often sprout cables to connect the host computer to other pieces of equipment. Appropriate cables are always provided.

Inside and out

Memory can be upgraded using SO-DIMM modules. These are compact versions of the DIMM memory modules used in desktop PCs. Even if a notebook doesn't have a spare DIMM socket, you can remove an original memory module and insert a larger unit. If the original is of a proprietary design, you will need a more expensive replacement module.

Another way of upgrading a notebook is through its PC Card slots (see pages 120–121). Modems, soundcards, network adapters, CD-ROM drives, and hard disks are all available. But if you need this many devices at once, it's probably better to buy a new computer.

PC Card slots almost always come in pairs. Each slot accommodates a type II PC Card or you can use both slots together to house one of the increasingly rare type III PC Cards.

PC cards

Windows makes it easy to expand the capabilities of a notebook computer with PC Cards.

Notebook PCs are so tightly packed with hardware that there's no room for expansion cards. But they need expansion cards as much as desktop PCs, so a set of expansion slots was developed for credit-card sized expansion cards, called PC Cards.

There are three sizes of PC Card. They are all the same length and width (85.6mm long by 54mm wide),

and all use the same 68-pin connector. The only difference between the three card types is thickness: 3.3mm, 5.0mm, and 10.5mm for Type I, Type II, and Type III cards respectively. A thinner card can be used in a thicker slot, so a typical notebook with two vertically stacked Type II sockets can take two Type I cards, or a Type I and a Type II card,

Installing PC Card devices

1 Most notebooks come with Windows, so it is normal to find all the special hardware, such as infrared ports and PC Card slots installed. To check, right-click My Computer and select Properties, Device Manager. Scroll down the list and you'll see a card labeled PCMCIA socket. Next, locate the PC Card slots on your notebook. Most have a pair of Type II PC Card slots, mounted one above the other, but a few may have only one PC Card slot. They should be obvious but sometimes the slots are protected by a flap. Another clue is a pair of buttons, used to eject the cards.

2 The next step is to insert the PC Card. In this example, a Psion WAN Global 56K with Combine IT modem is installed. PC Cards can be inserted one way only, and should be pushed in until they stop. Windows will automatically detect the new hardware and run the Add New Hardware Wizard. It's unlikely that Windows will have the correct PC Card drivers for your card, so will be unable to identify it correctly. As a result, it will probably identify it as a generic device. In the screenshot, the Psion modem is identified as a Standard PCMCIA Card Modem.

or two Type II cards, or a single Type III card. Type II PC Cards are used for modems, network cards and SCSI cards, while Type III PC Cards are for devices with thicker components, such as hard disks. It is possible to fit a PC Card reader which connects the PC Card device to a desktop computer, but there isn't much point.

The three most popular types of PC Card are modems, GSM cell phone cards, and network cards or combo cards that combine some or all of these functions. There are other PC

Cards too: the very latest Iomega Pocket Zip drive (which takes 40MB disks) can fit inside a 5mm Type II card. IBM and Calluna also make tiny hard disk drives that can fit in Type II and III PC Card slots.

And if your digital camera has a removable memory card, such as CompactFlash, it's possible to buy a PC Card adapter for it. To transfer pictures to your notebook you simply unplug the memory card from your camera, plug it into the adapter and plug that in to your notebook.

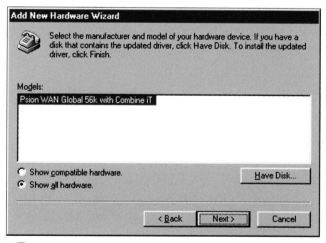

USB tip

You don't have to buy a PC Card modem for your notebook. Most notebook PCs are now equipped with Universal Serial Bus ports as standard. Recently, USB modems have started to appear. These are typically compact devices, smaller than normal desktop modems and are self-powered, that is, they draw power from the notebook batteries. Because USB devices are hot-swappable (you can connect or disconnect them without turning off your PC), it is simple to share a USB modem between several PCs, such as a notebook and a desktop PC, something which is not easy to do with a PC Card modem.

3 Click Next and select Display All Drivers in a Specific Location. Click Next and then Have Disk. Put the modem driver disk in the floppy-disk drive and click OK. Select your modem from the new list and click Next twice.

Note that to overcome the misidentification problem, some vendors recommend you install the driver software first, so that Windows will correctly identify the PC Card first time around.

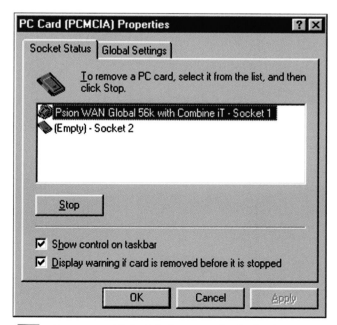

5 To remove a PC Card device, never simply eject it. Right-click on the PC Card icon in the system tray and click Adjust PC Card Properties. Select the PC Card you want to remove and click the Stop button. When Windows tells you it's safe to remove the PC Card, you're free to extract it by pressing the eject button next to the PC Card slot on the notebook. As you remove the card, your PC will emit another two-tone beep to warn you. You can also shut down your PC Card from the PC Card Control Panel applet.

4 Your notebook will now beep twice, signifying that the PC Card is correctly installed, and a PC Card icon will appear in the system tray on the Taskbar. Click Finish to complete the installation. You can now plug the telephone lead in to the PC Card and the phone socket to dial out.

Choosing software

Upgrade tips

● Upgrade only one program at a time. If faults or bugs develop thereafter you'll know where to look.

● So-called service packs are provided free of charge but can be more trouble than they're worth. For example, installing the service pack for Office 2000 means you can no longer add or delete some Office tools without reinstalling the entire package.

The trick with upgrading software is to choose the right upgrade and plan its implementation carefully.

We've looked at upgrading the hardware inside a computer. Here you learn what can be done to upgrade a computer's software, how you can perk up a flagging system using plug-in accessories, and how to keep Windows itself up-to-date.

Soft options, hard choices

Some computer users seem to get a kick out of having the latest, fastest versions of everything and feel compelled to upgrade their computers whenever new products are released. This does not always make sense, especially when the computer is nearing the end of its life and an upgrade won't be used for long enough to justify its cost; nor is it a good idea to buy the latest version of a program when you are using only half the features of the existing one.

When to upgrade

A good indication that it's time to upgrade is when you discover that there's something you want to do with your computer but find your current software can't cope. Alternatively, you might want to take advantage of a software innovation, such as home video editing, that wasn't available when you bought your computer. The best software upgrades are those you can remove at a later date and transfer to another computer if you buy a new one. Software can usually be freely re-installed on a new computer provided you delete the existing copy first.

Keep up-to-date

Make certain you have the latest version of Windows.

There is no such thing as perfect software. All software has faults, known as bugs. Not only that, but software can always be improved so that it runs faster or is easier to use.

During the life of your system, updates will be made to the software on it to fix bugs, make improvements, or add new features. These updates are not usually publicized. You might never realize that a problem you are experiencing has been fixed by an update until you call a vendor's support line. You could spend hours searching the Web for new drivers, but this can be time-consuming.

If you are using Windows 98 or later you can always be sure of using the latest software. The Update Wizard compares the Windows components on your PC with the latest versions on a Microsoft Web site, and enables you to download and install them with a couple of mouse clicks. The Update Device Driver Wizard searches your disk drives, Windows CD-ROM and the Windows Update Web site for the latest drivers for your hardware.

How to update Windows

1 You can access Windows Update from the Start menu. Click on the Update Wizard link to start it. If you have not registered your copy of Windows online you will have to complete a form before being allowed access to the Windows Update site. If this is the first time you have used the Update Wizard you will also have to download the Wizard from the Windows Update site. The Windows Update page has two links: Product Updates and Support Information. Click on Product Updates to begin an update.

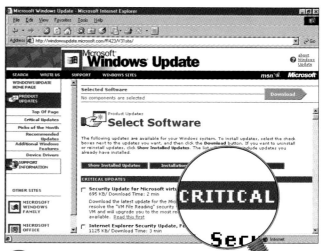

2 After you have clicked Update, the wizard will download a list of the updates which are available from the Windows Update site to your computer. It will then scan your computer to see which, if any, of these updates are appropriate to install on it. When it has completed this task it will display a list of the items that you should update.

There may not be any items at all in the list, depending on how recent your Windows installation is. The updates are graded according to their importance and you should always download Critical Updates. Tick the items you want to download, then click the Download button.

3 When you click Download, you can confirm the updates you've selected before starting the actual download. The updates are installed automatically and you may be instructed to reboot your PC when the process has finished.

5 Next, you will be asked to specify the locations in which the Wizard will search for new drivers. If you have some drivers on floppy disk, select Floppy Disk Drives. Select CD-ROM drive to have the Wizard search your Windows CD. Select Microsoft Windows Update to search the Windows Update site. If you have downloaded drivers to a folder on your hard disk you can also specify that folder's location. Once you have made your choices —you can select more than one location—click Next.

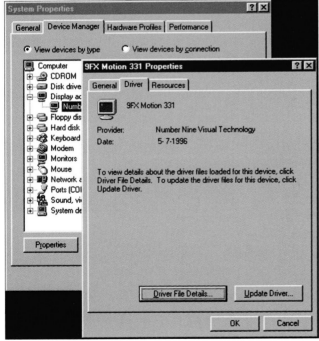

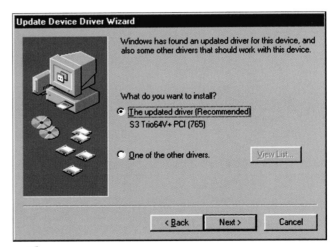

4 You can search for updates for specific device drivers directly from the Device Manager in System Properties. Select the driver you are interested in and click Properties. When the driver property page opens, click on the Driver tab. This page displays information about the driver, including the date it was created. To search for a newer driver, click the button marked Update Driver.

The Update Device Driver Wizard will appear. The first page gives an explanation of what will happen. To start the wizard, click Next. You will be asked if you want to search for a better driver than the one you are using now, or whether you want to see a list of drivers so you can choose one. Choose the first option.

6 If you are using the latest driver the wizard will tell you. Otherwise it will display the name of the newer driver that it thinks you should install. If you select One of the other drivers you can click View List to see and select alternative drivers. You should do this only if you have a good reason for choosing a driver other than the one Windows recommends.

Once you have selected a driver to install, click Next. The wizard is now ready to install it. You can still back out at this point by clicking Cancel. Otherwise click Next again. You will see progress indicators as files are copied to your hard disk. When all the files have been installed the wizard will display its final page, telling you that the update is finished. Click Finish to close the wizard.

Applications

Having the latest versions of the top programs might give you prestige, but is it always worth the money?

Planning a software upgrade begins long before you buy the program itself. First, ask yourself why you want to upgrade. If it's because your skills and requirements have exceeded the capabilities of your present software, then an upgrade is definitely in order. Even so, you have to decide whether to upgrade to a new version of the same product, to a superior product from the same manufacturer, or to a new product from a different vendor.

Buy the right product

A standard upgrade is when a manufacturer sells you an updated version of a product you already own and charges only a third or a half of the full price. A variation is where you switch to a superior product from the same manufacturer, such as from Microsoft Works to Microsoft Office, and pay the same price as for a standard upgrade.

A crossgrade, sometimes called a competitive upgrade, is a marketing ploy to tempt buyers to try a new product. It works like an upgrade, but you don't have to have a version of the software you're buying, just proof that you use a similar product.

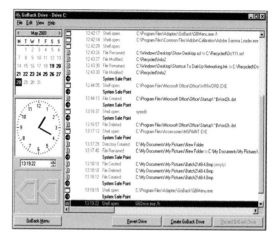

A program like **Rescue Me!** is a boon when you are upgrading. It takes a snapshot of your computer's system files and can return them to their original states if you abandon an upgrade.

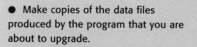

Upgrade tips

● Make copies of the data files produced by the program that you are about to upgrade.

● If you have a backup drive, use it to copy the entire hard disk.

● Read the printed documentation supplied with the upgrade.

● Check the CD-ROM to see if there's a Readme.txt or Setup.txt file on it. If so, read it before installing.

● Follow the manufacturer's recommendations about whether to install the new software on top of the old version or whether you should make a fresh installation.

● Close all other programs, including screensavers and schedulers, before starting installation.

● After installation read the release notes and print them out for future reference.

● Test the upgraded software as often as you can in the days after installation, both by itself and at the same time as other programs.

● Don't delete your backup data files until you are completely confident about the new program, which may be some time after installing it.

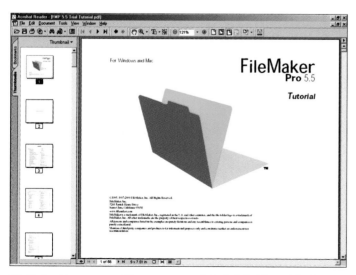

FileMaker Pro comes with an onscreen tutorial that is an ideal introduction to the main features for newcomers, and helps upgraders learn about the new features.

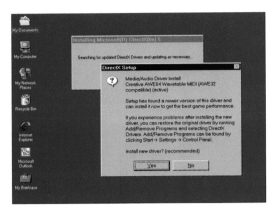

Messages about overwriting existing drivers are common when upgrading. The Setup program will make recommendations which you should follow, but make a note of which drivers have been replaced and which retained in case you need to troubleshoot the installation later.

Checklist

● Make a shortlist of the programs and upgrades with the features you need.

● Find out from stores, magazines, suppliers, or by searching the Internet whether there's a trial or demo version of your chosen upgrade. If so, get hold of it and test it thoroughly.

● Once you've picked a product, check its system requirements to make certain your PC can handle it. Your PC will need to have the correct version of Windows and sufficient memory and disk space.

● If the upgraded program uses a new file format, consider whether this will cause compatibility problems with other programs.

● Vendors may provide copies of reviews, but you'll only be sent the complimentary ones! Browse the shelves of your local news stand for other points of view.

● If you decide to go ahead, find out how the upgrade scheme works and make certain you have the correct proof of purchase.

Upgrades and crossgrades may require a proof of purchase to show you're entitled to the reduced price. This is usually a page torn from a manual or the old product's Setup disk or CD-ROM. When you buy an upgrade you may receive nothing more than an upgrade voucher which you send off together with a proof of purchase. Alternatively, the software may check your PC to see if it can detect an earlier version of the program.

Pitfalls

It makes no sense to upgrade your favorite program just because it has been superseded by a new version. Upgrade only if new features have been added, and they are ones that you really need.

New versions of programs aren't always better than the ones they replace, and the evolutionary nature of software means that the latest programs always require more resources to run well. Another danger is that an upgraded program might introduce a new type of file or document format, which could complicate the process of sharing data between programs and with colleagues.

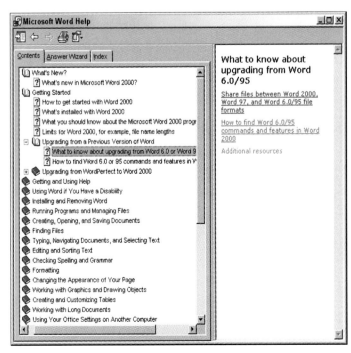

Word 2000, like many other Microsoft programs, includes release information in its Help file. Differences between the last three releases of the program are described.

Speed-up programs

Your PC can use software to speed up its operations without the need for expensive RAM chips.

Most speed-up programs depend on some form of cache, that is an area of memory set aside to act as a super-efficient hard disk. It's an effective ploy because memory, which has no moving parts, is much faster than a mechanical disk.

Happy memories

Disk caches became essential when computer users moved from MS-DOS to Windows and discovered that their hard disks never stopped whirring. This was because Windows and its application programs were too big to load into the 2MB or 4MB memory of the average computer, so constant reference had to be made to data stored on disk. The obvious solution was to add more memory, but 4MB RAM chips were expensive, so people were keen to find less costly alternatives.

Now memory is inexpensive and plentiful, and because memory management and software caching are built in to Windows 98 and later, most users don't need general purpose cache software to overcome slow disks. However, it is needed to overcome slow modems. Every Web browser stores

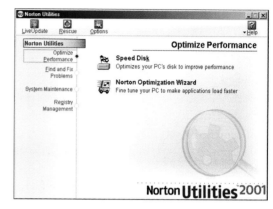

Performance enhancement is not the main aim of Norton Utilities, but two useful tools are supplied.

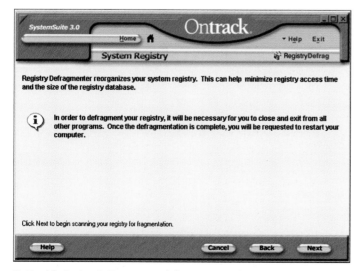

OnTrack's SystemSuite 3.0 can defragment your computer's Registry to improve performance.

Fact file

● **Disk compression** A way of squeezing more data onto a disk by dedicating most of it to a large file that stores data more efficiently. Loading compressed data from disk is quicker than loading uncompressed data, but any speed gains are countered by the time taken to expand the data to its original form.

● **RAM disk** An area of memory designated as a fast disk. Unlike a disk cache, which works invisibly, a RAM disk appears in MS-DOS or Windows with its own drive letter like a real disk. The snag is, when you switch off your computer the RAM disk forgets everything.

● **RAM expander** A utility that claims to make PC memory go further by compressing the data within it, in much the same way that a disk compression utility squeezes more onto a disk. Adding real memory chips to a PC speeds it up, but using a RAM expander might slow it down because of the additional processing involved. However, it should enable your PC to run more programs at the same time.

Top brands

● **Micro Warehouse** www.warehouse.com
● **IMSI** www.imsisoft.com
● **Network Associates** www.nai.com
● **Symantec** www.symantec.com

Buying tips

● Accelerator programs don't have the same dramatic impact as installing extra memory or a faster processor. You should use them as supplementary aids to a hardware upgrade, not as a substitute.

● The disk defragmenter in later versions of Windows (see pages 29–30) differs from the one supplied with Windows 95 in that it not only removes gaps between files but it also rearranges them in the most efficient order. Windows 95 users can achieve the same effect with Speed Disk (from Norton Utilities) and McAfee's Utilities.

● If you can, make a full backup before installing any utility suite because it's easier to reinstate a backup than it is to remove all traces of a program which is firmly embedded in Windows.

Watch out!

The search for extra speed can be self-defeating. Every program, once loaded, draws on some of your computer's processing time. A speed enhancer has to speed up your computer enough to cover its own requirements and then provide some surplus speed for other applications to use. If you load several enhancers at the same time and they all try to take control of disk and memory management, you can end up with a system so busy controlling itself that it slows down. Beware, too, of snazzy-looking control panels and gauges that you do not really need. Switch them off.

Norton Utilities automatically loads resource-grabbing control panels every time you start Windows.

information from recently visited sites, which saves having to download everything from scratch when you return to a site. An extension of this principle is used by NetAccelerator and similar programs that attempt to speed up Web access by caching not just the pages you've already visited, but also those you might visit in the future.

They do this by examining the links on a Web page. While you are reading a page the program logs onto the linked sites and stores them. When you click on one of the links to go to another Web site, it should already be available on disk. It's a great idea, and it works, but only if you are a slow reader. This is because it can take several minutes for NetAccelerator to cache the linked pages, and if you click on a link that hasn't been cached, you end up waiting just as long as you normally would.

Speed systems

Since Windows incorporates some of its own measures to speed up a PC's performance, there's less need for separate Windows tweaking tools. You can still find performance boosting components in certain utility suites, however, and these cover areas still ignored by Windows.

OnTrack's SystemSuite 3.0 can weed out unnecessary entries in the Windows Registry and defragment it, which can shave seconds off a computer's boot time. Norton Utilities has Speed Disk to unclog hard disks and the Norton Optimization Wizard to determine the optimum size and placement of the Windows swap file. McAfee's Utilities is another utility suite that provides similar tune-up tools to make computers work more efficiently and go faster.

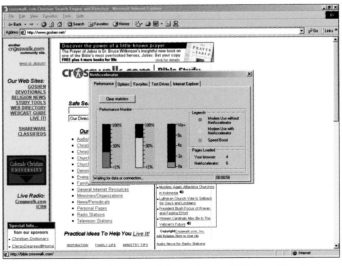

NetAccelerator can take some of the wait out of Web surfing by automatically fetching pages from the backup that are linked to the one you are currently reading.

Web plug-ins

When your browser can't cope with complex Web-page content, you probably need a plug-in.

A Web plug-in is software that adds functionality to a Web browser. Just as your PC opens Word files by associating the Word application with the .doc file extension, so Web browsers associate particular file extensions with a plug-in and open them with that application. Sometimes you may not even realize a plug-in application is being used because it integrates completely with the browser, opening and running the content file on the Web page inside the browser screen. Other plug-ins open a new window and run the file content inside this.

Once a plug-in has been installed you can view any Web pages containing content in that plug-in's format—video, audio, or a magazine layout—on screen, just by connecting to the Web site. Plug-ins are useful because they bring a wider range of complex and exciting content to your PC.

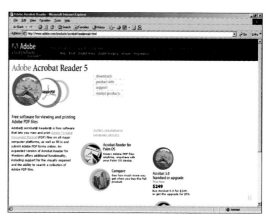

The **Adobe Acrobat Reader is used to bring properly laid out magazines, brochures, and similar publications from the Web to your computer screen.**

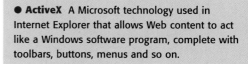

Fact file

● **Plug-in** A program that integrates with your Web browser to allow additional content to be displayed.

● **ActiveX** A Microsoft technology used in Internet Explorer that allows Web content to act like a Windows software program, complete with toolbars, buttons, menus and so on.

RealPlayer has become one of the most popular plug-ins because it delivers both audio and video on the Web page, and by using a special streaming technology allows you to start viewing or listening when just a small part of the file has been downloaded.

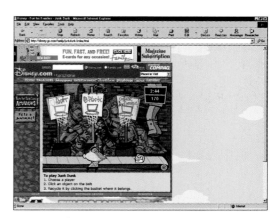
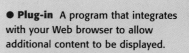

Games such as Junk Dunk from the Disney site at http://disney.go.com/family/junkdunk/index.html are produced using Macromedia Shockwave. If you have got the plug-in, you can play the game.

Buying tips

● Most plug-ins are available to download free from the Net. Software companies make money by selling to Web page designers. The more people who use the plug-in the more Web site designers will want to buy it. This isn't always the case, and some plug-ins are not free. Commercial applications often let you download an evaluation copy that will work for a set number of times or, more commonly, for a limited period. At the end of the evaluation period the plug-in will stop working unless you register.

● Before you decide to pay for a plug-in, you should calculate how much you really need it. If you will use the plug-in for infrequent visits to a Web page there is little point in buying it.

● Ask what value the content delivered by the plug-in has. If it just enlivens otherwise static information with animation, you may be better off saving your money and accessing the information in its old-fashioned format. You may be able to find the same information at another Web site that doesn't require you to use a plug-in.

● Make sure that plug-ins work with your browser. Some will work just with Netscape Navigator and not Internet Explorer and vice versa.

PhoneFree is a great plug-in that enables you to make long-distance PC-to-PC phone calls for free.

Top brands

● **PhoneFree** www.phonefree.com
● **Adobe Acrobat Reader** www.adobe.com/prodindex/acrobat/main.html
● **Inso QuickView** www.inso.com/qvp/index.htm
● **RealNetworks RealPlayer** www.real.com
● **Macromedia Shockwave** www.macromedia.com/shockwave

Careful management

If you change from Internet Explorer to Netscape Navigator or vice versa, chances are that you will have to reinstall the majority of your plug-ins, and download specific versions of some of them. To make managing your plug-ins easier, it's best to install them all in a folder named plugins.

Netscape Navigator and Internet Explorer handle plug-ins in a similar way, but Microsoft has the edge when it comes to ease of installation. Many Explorer plug-ins use ActiveX. When you connect to a page requiring a plug-in that uses ActiveX, a requester box will appear on screen asking if you want to install and run the application. Click yes and the plug-in will be downloaded and installed. Netscape plug-ins usually require you to download the application, run the setup file, install the plug-in, then exit the browser and restart your PC.

Popular plug-ins

There are hundreds of plug-ins available. The most popular include Adobe Acrobat Reader, which lets you view publications in PDF format, complete with magazine indexes and layout. QuickView Plus lets you view the contents of files without having to use the specified application, so you can read, but not edit, Word files without having a copy of Word, for example. RealNetwork's RealPlayer makes it possible to play audio and video files, using a streaming technique that means you don't have to download the whole file before you start viewing. Macromedia Shockwave is the most popular format for bringing animation to the Web. PhoneFree lets you make long-distance PC-to-PC phone calls for free.

QuickView Plus is invaluable if you get a lot of e-mail attachments or want to view files from Web pages in an application you don't own.

DirectX

Make sure your games run as quickly and smoothly as possible with the latest version of Windows DirectX.

DirectX is a set of Windows features that enables games programmers to build direct hardware access into their games without needing to know the specific hardware setup of your PC. Previously they had to assume the lowest common denominator in order to guarantee a game would work. For example, every graphics card supports at least 640 x 480 pixels in 16 colors, but this makes for poor games.

Thanks to DirectX, games can now use the advanced features of any video card, such as 3D or full-motion video, without the need for different versions for every single variety of card. In effect, DirectX acts as a universal translator between the program and the software driver for the hardware device.

With Windows Me and the latest version of Internet Explorer, DirectX is included as standard, but it may not be the most up-to-date version. Windows 98 has DirectX 5.0. If you want the best games performance, you must install the latest version, which you can do by going to the Windows Update Web site.

DirectX consists of a number of components: Direct3D is used for 3D rendering; DirectPlay is used for gaming online; DirectDraw is used for screen graphics; DirectSound3D is used for audio; and DirectInput is used for input devices like gamepads.

How to install DirectX

1 Installing DirectX is simple. The best way to launch the process is to select Windows Update from Settings on your Start menu. A Web site will be displayed that lists all the available downloads for your computer, and if you don't have the latest version of DirectX, it will appear. Just follow the on-screen instructions to download and install it.

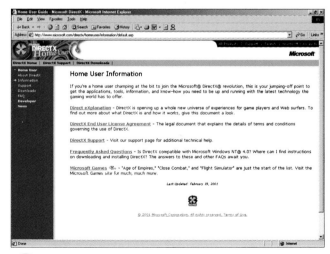

2 It's a small file but DirectX has to be downloaded by itself without any other updates. Check that you have the latest drivers for your graphics and soundcards. If you have any questions about DirectX, visit the DirectX Home User page at: www.microsoft.com/directx/homeuser/information/default.asp.

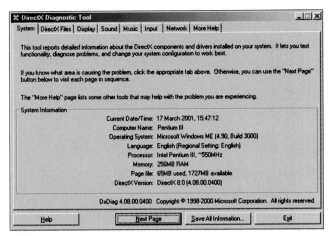

3 Once installed, DirectX is invisible to the user and requires absolutely no tweaking or user intervention at all. However, if you do experience problems with DirectX, a diagnostics program is supplied which will help you test your configuration and pinpoint any problems that you might be having. Click on Start, Run and then type DXDIAG in the Open dialogue box and click OK.

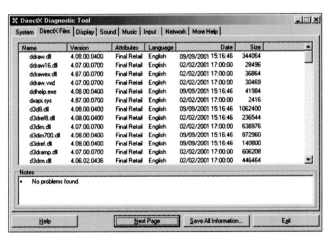

4 The program has a tabbed interface, which lets you test the various multimedia components. The system tab provides system information about your computer and specifies the version of DirectX that is installed on your computer. The DirectX Files tab lists the file name and version number for each DirectX driver installed. If the DirectX Diagnostic Tool detects a problem with a DirectX file, a warning message is displayed in the Notes box.

What's new?

Each new version of DirectX improves upon the performance of the last, adding new features and improving the way in which DirectX software runs.

The latest versions of DirectX make better use of a 3D graphics card's ability to handle how 3D objects are lit and give objects a more realistic appearance. They also make better use of any extra instructions built into the CPU (see Upgrade tip) and provide greater support for multiplayer games.

Upgrade tip

If you want the ultimate games experience, it's important that you install the very latest version of DirectX. This is particularly important if you have a PC powered by the later AMD or Cyrix processors. These processors all support a special set of 3D extensions, called 3DNow!, that has proved very popular with games developers. To make full use of 3DNow! features in games, you need the latest version of DirectX. It also significantly improves the performance of Direct3D games. You probably won't see much improvement in current Direct3D games, but future titles will run faster.

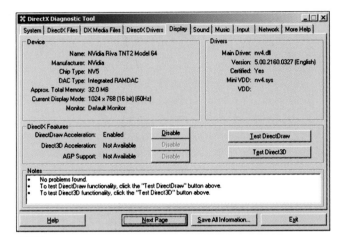

5 The Display tabs list your current display settings, and allow you to disable hardware, while the Sound tab displays your current sound settings, and enables you to test DirectSound.

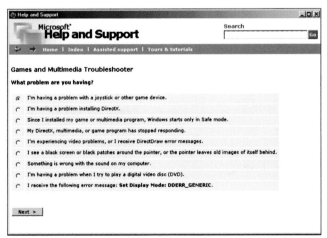

6 For more information about how to solve problems with DirectX, click on the More Help tab and launch the Windows Help DirectX troubleshooter. There's also a useful list of FAQs at www.microsoft.com/directx/homeuser/faq.asp.

4

Making life simpler

Personal information managers

Put your life in order with an integrated address book, phone book, diary and card index.

The term "personal information manager," or PIM, is a misnomer because it gives the impression that a PIM is for storing trivial information such as birthdays and shopping lists. This is not the case—PIMs are powerful data storage tools that are as useful in the office as they are in the home.

PIMs replace the traditional storage system of filing cabinets. Information is kept together in one easily accessible place—your PC's hard disk. The contents of address books, appointment books, diaries, phone lists and notebooks can all be transferred to a PIM. Once they're stored in the computer you can sort them, search through them, print them out and make changes with much greater ease than their physical counterparts allow.

Look before you leap

Having used a PIM, it's difficult to return to traditional ways of storing information. But before you decide to copy all the information from your paper-based systems into your PC, there are two drawbacks to consider. One is that a PIM is only faster than a paper system if you work near your PC and keep it switched on. The other is that you may not be sitting at your PC when you receive data you want to store—people give you business cards at meetings or you may write notes while traveling on the train. Aim to transfer this type of data to your PC at the first opportunity.

Which software?

The different types of PIMs available are similar in function because there are only so many ways of arranging a calendar or address book sensibly. However, they differ in terms of their additional features, and programs written for the latest Windows software are much more capable than older ones.

● **Microsoft Outlook** This is a versatile application that handles your contacts, diary, to-do lists and even e-mail. The latest version is included with Microsoft Office 2000.

● **CorelCENTRAL** This comes with WordPerfect Office 2000. It can handle inward and outbound Internet e-mail messages. It also has built-in support for Palm OS handheld computers.

● **Lotus Organizer** This comes with SmartSuite. It integrates a calendar, contact management and planner, and allows meeting scheduling over the Internet.

● **GoldMine and Act!** Standalone products that offer sophisticated contact management and scheduling facilities, but often at the expense of ease of use.

You will need

ESSENTIAL
Software A PIM such as those supplied with office suites from Microsoft, Lotus and Corel or standalone products from other suppliers.
Hardware A Windows PC. A printer is a useful accessory if you want to produce pages you can slip into a ring-bound organizer.

What's a PIM?

Modem tip

PIMs for Windows 98 and later should automatically detect which modem you're using. PIMs designed for older versions of Windows need to be told about your modem.

Personal information managers are just like a more powerful version of traditional paper-based organizers.

The key elements in a PIM are the address book and diary. The address book stores names and street addresses as well as e-mail, fax, cell phone and pager numbers and Web site addresses. It's difficult to find someone whose name you've forgotten in a paper address book. But a PIM can search for certain details that you can remember about a person, such as their company or the place you last met—if you made a note of these. When you call a number in your address book, you can log the time duration of the call and make notes.

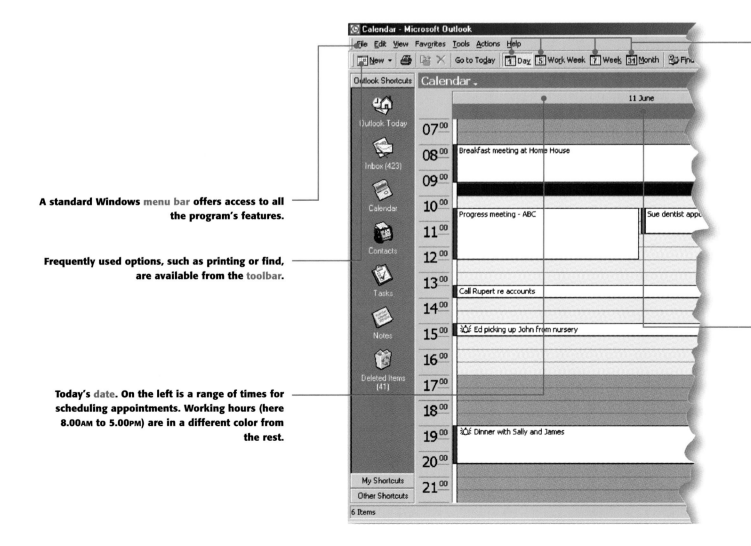

A standard Windows menu bar offers access to all the program's features.

Frequently used options, such as printing or find, are available from the toolbar.

Today's date. On the left is a range of times for scheduling appointments. Working hours (here 8.00AM to 5.00PM) are in a different color from the rest.

More than a list

The diary in a PIM is more than a chronological list of events. It lets you schedule appointments and warns you of conflicting commitments. Tasks can be allocated time slots and the PIM can sound an alarm when one is due. It's easy to juggle appointments by dragging them from one time to another and some PIMs can automatically find free time slots for meetings you're trying to arrange.

Data can be printed out or copied for use in other programs. You never run out of space for entries in your diary or have to hunt around for blank pages in your address book. If you also own a notebook handheld computer, you can download your PIM and carry it around with you. Programs are available to synchronize entries in two computers.

Layout tip

To fit more data on a single screen, alter the size of the fonts used to display information. In Outlook, click on the Organize button and in the pane that appears select Using View. On the bar at the top, select Customize Current View and then click on Other Settings in the box that opens.

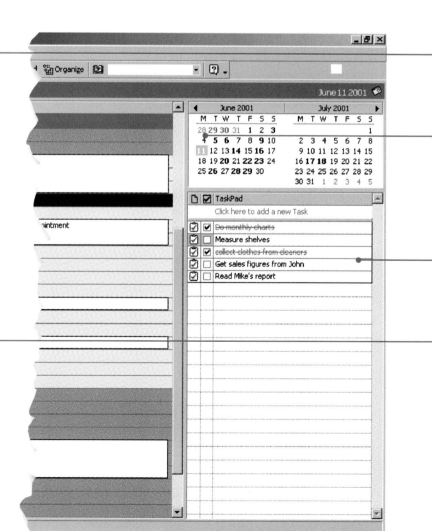

The current view of the calendar is a single day. By selecting the buttons on the toolbar you can change the view to show the working week, a seven-day week or the month.

The calendar for the year. Click on the arrow on the left to move the calendar back a month or on the right arrow to move it forward a month. Days for which appointments have been made are shown in bold.

The taskpad has a list of any tasks for the day. Click in here to list a new entry.

If a reminder has been set for an appointment an alarm bell will be shown here and a window will pop up with details of the event shortly before it is due.

Scheduling

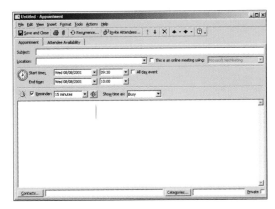

One way to set up an appointment is to go to the calendar's Month view and pick a date. Double-click to open the Appointment dialogue box and you can set various features, including the time, who will attend, and a reminder.

You should never miss an important appointment if you use your PIM to remind you of where you need to be.

Scheduling an appointment or meeting begins with choosing a date for the event. Find a free time slot by setting your PIM to its monthly view, selecting a particular day from the annual calendar or annual view and clicking on it. This will display the daily view for the date you've selected and you can look for a free time slot. Once you've found one, double-click on the nearest appropriate start time to call up an Event box.

In Microsoft Outlook, you can also ask Outlook to find the next free time slot. To do so, go to the Actions menu and select Plan a Meeting. In the box that opens, go to Autopick and select an option. Then click Make a Meeting to get a suggested time and date. CorelCentral and Lotus Organizer also suggest appropriate time slots for appointments.

Find some time

You'll now be able to enter the start and end time for the appointment along with a note reminding you what the appointment is for. This might be all you need if it's a one-off appointment such as "Visit travel agent to arrange holiday" but you also have

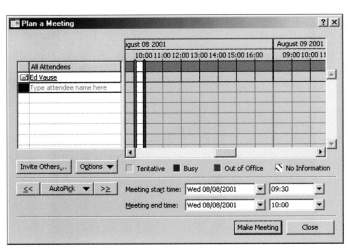

From the Plan a Meeting item on the Actions menu, Outlook can find a free time slot automatically. In addition, Outlook can send e-mail invitations to anyone you want to attend the meeting.

the option of scheduling recurring appointments that take place at regular intervals.

Recurring appointments could be regular events that occur every day or on the same day every week or month, but you can also choose movable days such as the third Thursday in each month and let your PIM work out the dates for you. Alarms can be set to sound at the time of the appointment, or at a designated lead time before the appointment, to give you time to get there.

Lost time

PIMs can tell you how you organize your time. When making appointments, some PIMs let you allocate time to categories of activity. Some of these PIMs are supplied with a pre-defined list which includes meeting clients, administration, planning, expenses, travel and so on. In others you can create your own list of activities.

Good organization

If all your time is allocated to a category you can create a report to tell you exactly how much time you spend working on each type of activity. If you allocate categories to individual clients you can use this information to invoice them for time spent on their behalf. Lotus Organizer takes this one step further by letting you allocate tasks not only to a category but also to customer and cost codes.

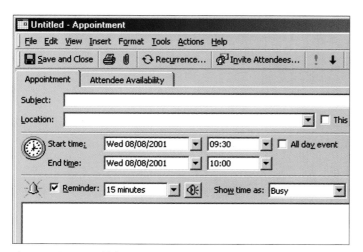

The Appointment dialogue box is setting up an appointment on Wednesay, August 8, 2001 with an alarm reminder to sound 15 minutes before.

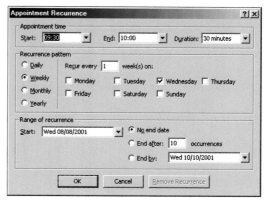

The Appointment Recurrence dialogue box offers flexible choices for scheduling regular appointments. This one will repeat every Wednesday for a period of 10 weeks.

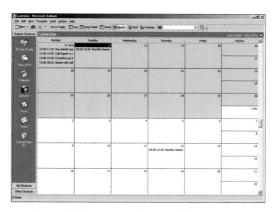

Here is proof that a recurring appointment has been entered for future months. If you are looking at appointments in the future and want to return to the current date, click Go to Today on the toolbar.

Jargon buster

Lead time The lead time is the number of minutes, hours or days prior to an appointment that its alarm will go off. A 10AM appointment with a lead time of 30 minutes will sound an alarm at 9.30AM.

Address books

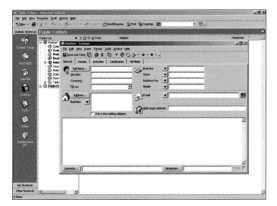

To make the first entry in a new card file: click the arrow next to an entry and it enables you to enter a second option. For example, in Address you can enter your contact's business and home address.

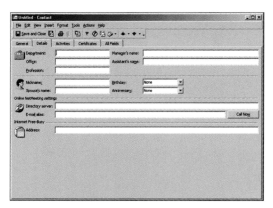

Selecting the Details tab enables you to put some additional information, such as a nickname, a spouse's name or a birthday.

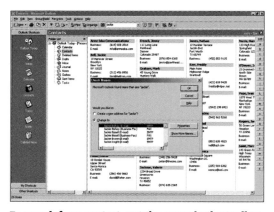

To search for a contact, put the name in the toolbar address box. The contact card opens. If there are other people with that name, they are all listed. Highlight and click Properties for more details.

It always pays to put some thought into setting up your PIM address book for the first time.

Setting up a new address book is a major task, but try to get it correct on your first attempt. When entering a contact in an address book it's easy to add just a name and phone number and ignore other information that may be on hand. This can cause problems later when you realize you need to send an e-mail or fax to a contact and you haven't got the details.

Address books

Some PIMs have templates for creating cardfiles that you can customize. In Outlook, press Ctrl+N to get a new contact file. Fill in the details and then save your file.

Once you've entered the names and addresses, you can choose how you want your contacts displayed, by selecting an option from the dropdown list beside the File As: box. You can view the contacts with their full details, by phone-list or grouped by business name and so on.

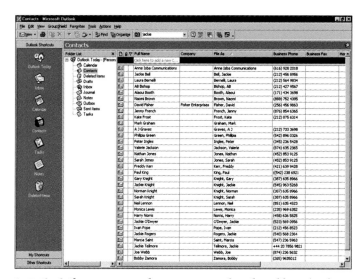

In Outlook there are several ways you can view the address book. This is the phone book-style listing but you can also arrange your contacts by location, by any categories you have assigned them or by any follow-up action that is needed.

To-Do lists

Organize your time and make sure you are up-to-date with all your plans with a To-Do list.

To-Do lists in a PIM offer numerous advantages over something hastily written on a scrap of paper. For example, they're flexible, so you can move an item up or down the list if circumstances change. Items in the list appear alongside other tasks and appointments for each day, so you can't ignore them.

To-Do tasks can be prioritized and given dates for completion. Those you don't finish or ignore will pop up in red until you deal with them. They will also appear alongside appointments in the weekly view of a diary. Tasks may be scheduled to repeat at regular intervals.

Tasking times

Unlike appointments, To-Do tasks carry forward from day to day. There's no set time slot for them, just a start time and date. Once they're completed, they are no longer displayed. You can categorize tasks into related groups or assign them to individuals—the person who instigated it or the person who's going to carry it out.

Sorting tip

When you set up a task, you can assign a priority. The priorities are low (shown by downward pointing blue arrow), normal (shown by nothing) and High (shown by a red exclamation mark). To sort by priorities, click on the black exclamation mark at the top of the column.

A **red** entry in the To-Do list shows an uncompleted task. When a task has been marked as completed, it becomes gray and is crossed out. To delete it, highlight it and select X on the toolbar.

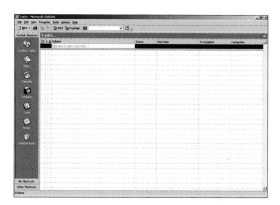

To enter a **new task**, click on the New Task button at the top and enter the details. Alternatively, double-click here and a separate dialogue box opens for you to fill in.

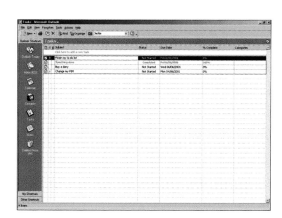

Sorting tasks makes it easier to see at a glance what needs to be done. Here the list is being sorted using the priorities assigned to each task, so what needs doing most urgently is at the top.

Printing

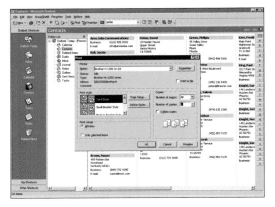

In the Print dialogue box for the address book, the print range has been set to print all items but you can just highlight a selected range and print that. To further customize your printout, click on the Page Setup button.

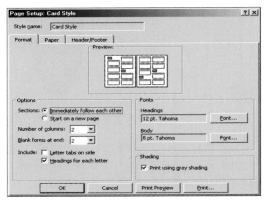

In Page setup you can change the font style and size and alter the layout to increase the number of columns on the page, or change how the different sections follow on from each other. You can also include a letter tab at the side of the page for easier indexing.

Printing tip

When setting up a print session using special papers, always use the Print Preview button to check the layout on screen before you print it out. Then try a test print on plain paper before using expensive organizer refills or labels.

You can print out any kind of data from your PIM to use as a physical reminder or to file in an organizer.

Data from a PIM can be printed on address labels, envelopes, phone lists and in many pocket and desktop organizer formats.

Outlook's print features depend on the view you're using. In Calendar, daily, weekly and monthly views offer different print facilities. To print from Calendar on plain paper, switch to a view that's closest to the output you want by going to File on the Menu bar and choosing Page Setup.

Contacts printing

Contacts offers more versatile options with a wide choice of paper. From the File menu choose Print and select the style you want. In the Print dialogue box you can also choose whether you want to print all of the cards or only a selected range. Choose a paper type and edit the layout if you need to.

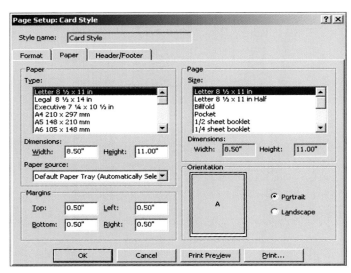

On the paper tab you can modify the layout to fit different paper types, such as labels and filofax sheets, and sizes, such as a day planner. On the Header/Footer tab you can alter some of the elements automatically printed at the top or bottom of the page, such as the page number and date printed.

Contact managers

Contact management software helps you to keep an eye on all your business and social contacts.

Broadly speaking, contact management software first arrived on the computer scene courtesy of some business people who believed that the only successful salesperson was a well-informed salesperson. They decided that it wasn't enough just to have a record of a potential customer's name, address and telephone number, but that it was also important to track the conversations you had with them and to keep a note of what their interests were outside work, whether they had a family, what kind of food they liked to eat and so on. Thus the contact manager was born.

All aboard

Professional people such as lawyers and consultants liked the fact that some contact managers allowed them to assign their time so that they could bill clients more easily and accurately. By the early 1990s there were a number of powerful programs such as ACT!, Maximizer and Goldmine which promoted the notion that the contact manager was the main program professionals, typically salespeople, should use, and that other related

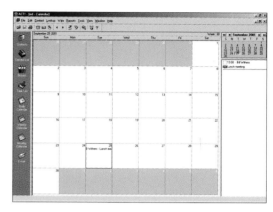

Primarily designed for corporate use, ACT! is a highly sophisticated contact manager.

Reporting

Heavy-duty contact managers such as ACT! and Goldmine have many reporting features so you can have a print-out describing exactly what the situation is with a set of clients or a project. For home use, such facilities are not necessary, but the organization that contact managers inject into a business can be invaluable.

Fact file

● **PIM** A personal information manager. The emphasis is more on diary management than complex lists of contacts. Examples include Lotus Organizer.

● **Contact manager** Although this will have elements of a PIM (particularly for appointments and to-do lists) the emphasis here is on keeping up-to-date with your contacts (typically a client list) so that you can quickly extract relevant information before or during a sales call and generate a report on it afterward.

● **Data protection** If you keep records of contacts on your PC, you may be required to register that fact under law.

● **Windows CE / Pocket PC** The version of Windows that runs on palmtop PCs. Some contact managers such as ACT! and Maximizer are either able to exchange data with handheld PCs, or have pocket versions that work on these tiny computers.

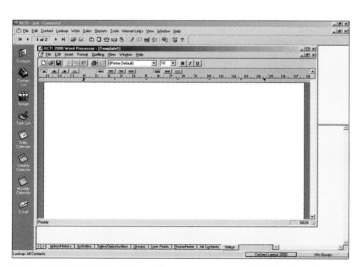

Using Act! 2000's built-in word processor you can instantly write letters and mail merge them with your address book to send to hundreds of people.

Buying tips

● If your requirements are simple, you can produce your own contact manager in a program like Microsoft Works.

● Investigate shareware sites on the Net. They are a good source of contact managers and there's the advantage that you can try them out before deciding whether or not to buy. Start at www.hotfiles.com or www.shareware.com.

● For a sole trader or small business, a program such as Outlook, which combines appointments, contacts and To-Do lists, will do the job. There are more specialized programs, but you may find them too top-heavy and complicated to use, and they'll contain features that are useful if you're working as part of a group such as a sales team, but not so much if you work on your own.

● Links to other programs are important. A good contact manager will either include a simple word processor for writing letters or allow you to use your existing one. In this way, you can click on an address entry, tell the program you want to write a letter and your word processor will automatically load, with the name, address, the date, a salutation and sign off already in place.

● A contact manager is only as good as the data you type into it. Get someone's details wrong, and all the technology in the world won't help you.

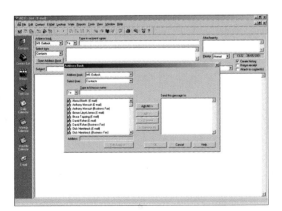

GSP's **Instant Addressbook** allows you to e-mail anyone in the list easily.

Top brands

● **ACT!** ICC www.act.com
● **FastTrack** AEC Software www.aecsoft.com
● **Lotus Organizer** Lotus Development www.lotus.com
● **Maximizer** Multiactive www.multiactive.com
● **Outlook** Microsoft www.microsoft.com

activities such as letter and e-mail writing, faxing and Web browsing, should be accessible from inside the contact manager.

At home of course, it's unlikely that you will ever need such sophistication. But if you have any kind of irregular contact with a group of individuals such as a sports club or society you belong to, and especially if you are running a business from home, where every advantage counts, you will find them worth investigating.

A collection of names

At its simplest, a contact manager is an up-to-date collection of names, addresses and phone numbers. You'll probably find that you can use one of the programs that came with your PC to do this, such as Word, Works, or even Excel. Alternatively, you may have bought a diary program—often called a PIM or personal information manager—such as Lotus Organizer, which has an excellent address book and other features that allow you to keep notes on telephone conversations or assign a particular task to a client or category. (For more details on PIMs, see pages 135–142.)

E-mail

You'll also some find some good, inexpensive programs, which as well as handling conventional contact details are clever enough to link to your existing e-mail program so you can compose and send e-mails to your contacts, and to your Web browser so you can visit their Web sites. Other features to consider are good links to your word processor for writing standard letters, the ability to fax from within the program, and the ability to communicate to an accounts program or spreadsheet for easy billing.

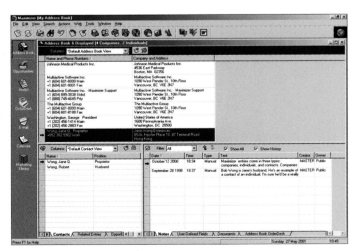

A trialware version of the **Maximizer** contact manager can be downloaded from the Internet at www.maximizer.com.

Collect your e-mail while you're away

Wherever you are in the world you'll never have to miss that vital message.

While you're sunning yourself on the beach in California, or enjoying a weekend break in New York, it's possible to keep in touch with your e-mail. Even if your location is more exotic, you can still pick up vital e-mail messages.

All you need to do is locate a PC that has an Internet connection, perhaps at an Internet café. It's all thanks to a little piece of technology called POP3, which is used by most Internet service providers (ISPs) to deliver e-mail.

One of the benefits POP3 bestows is that it lets you read your e-mail from anywhere on the Internet. To send messages, see the Sending E-mail box on page 146. Messenger, as found in Netscape Communicator, Microsoft's Outlook Express or any other e-mail software program that supports POP3, including Eudora, will let you do this. In the examples on the following pages you will learn how to access e-mail using Outlook Express 5.5 and Messenger Netscape Mail.

Before you start, see the Redirection Tip on page 148.

You will learn

● How to send and receive e-mail messages from anywhere in the world using Microsoft's Outlook Express and Netscape Communicator's Messenger.

You will need

Software Microsoft Outlook Express or Netscape's Messenger.
Hardware A Pentium PC or better, running Windows Me or 98, with at least 32MB RAM.

Collecting e-mail with Outlook Express

1 Start Outlook Express. Click on Outlook Express in the left-hand pane to bring up the main Outlook Express toolbar. Click on the Tools menu and select Accounts. In the Internet Accounts dialogue box click on the Add button and select Mail. The Internet Connection Wizard will pop up. Type in your Display Name—it will now appear in the From field in all your outgoing messages. Click on Next.

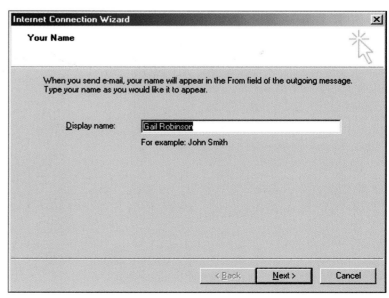

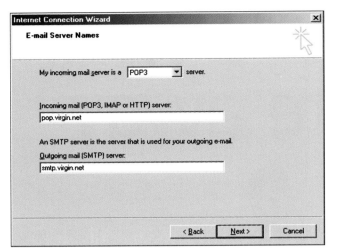

2 Type in your e-mail address and click Next. You need to change the incoming mail server details to tell Outlook to pick up e-mail from your Internet service provider's mail server. Most ISPs use POP3 mail servers for incoming mail, so make sure that option is selected. Then type in the Incoming mail server name (see the Get This Info First box on page 148 for details.) You are also asked for your SMTP server details. SMTP handles your outgoing e-mail. Type them in and click on Next.

3 In the next dialogue box, type in your POP name—this is your e-mail name. Then type in your e-mail password. You can check the box for Outlook Express to remember your password automatically. You'll also be asked to check a box if your ISP uses Secure Password Authentication. Most don't, apart from MSN. Click on the Next button. You're then asked what Friendly Name you want to give to this e-mail account—give it a name such as the name of your ISP and click on Next. Select how you're going to connect to the Internet. Click on Next. Finally, Express needs to know which dial-up connection you're going to use to connect to your mail server. Select Use An Existing Dial-up Connection. Now click on the dial-up connection being used by this computer. Click on Next and then on Finish.

Address tip

AOL and CompuServe have member directories. If you don't have an account with them but know someone who does, you can ask them to look up the address of someone you are looking for.

Etiquette tips

If you are e-mailing from a cybercafé, there are a few tips on good etiquette.

● While you are waiting to use a machine don't stand reading over people's shoulders however tempting it is. It's rude.

● Clean up the trash you left on the computer. Most mailer programs keep copies of the messages you send. If you don't want someone to read your e-mail, make sure you find the sent message folder and delete your mail. Then empty the trash. You may not want to share that love letter signed Bunnikins with everyone who uses the machine after you.

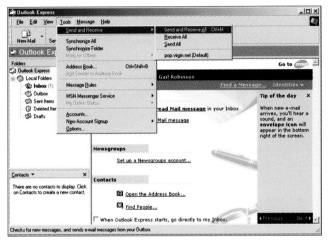

4 Your new mail server details should now be listed in the Internet Accounts box. Click on Close. To pick up your e-mail, go the main Outlook toolbar and choose Send and Receive from the Tools menu. Double-click on the e-mail account you've just set up. Express will now download your e-mail. Using this method, no matter where the computer you are using is located, you should be able to read your messages.

Sending e-mail

The quickest way to send an e-mail when you are away from your computer is to use someone else's e-mail account. An e-mail message sent this way will carry the address of the account you've used. Include your real e-mail address in the body of the message for any replies. Alternatively, sign up with one of the numerous free Web-based e-mail services. These let you send and receive e-mail from any PC with Internet access. There's Hotmail at www.hotmail.com, Yahoo! mail at www.yahoo.com, and Excite Mail at www.excite.com. These free e-mail services can also handle POP3 mail so you can set them up to pick up e-mail direct from your Internet service provider.

Address tips

● If you cannot remember some friends' address and you want to e-mail them, you can always check out an online newsgroup they use. Use a search engine such as AltaVista to search through Usenet or check out http://groups.google.com. Do remember, however, that your friends may not use their full name or anything like their real name, but it is always worth a try.

● There is no online directory that lists everyone's e-mail address. But some people do choose to list themselves in a directory. You can try out the Yahoo People Search at http://people.yahoo.com and do an e-mail search. If you want others to find you, you can list yourself. (See pages 153–156 for more information on finding people online.)

Collecting e-mail with Messenger

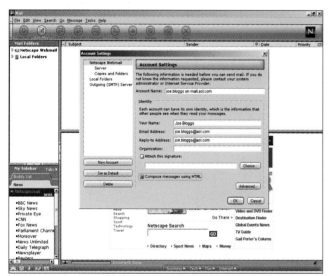

1 Start Mail. From the Edit menu select Mail/New Account Settings and click the button on the left marked New Account. This launches the Account Wizard. If you are using a friend's computer, you can set up this new account and then delete it when you have finished without affecting his/her settings.

Address tip

You may find that you want a reply from someone when you are away from home, only to find that you don't know the e-mail address of the computer you are working on—if you are in a cybercafé, for example. E-mail a friend and ask them to e-mail you back. All messages have return addresses and you will be able to work out your e-mail address from there. Don't be surprised if the address has a lot of strange punctuation. After going through a few gateways it may look odd, but if you type it back in it usually works.

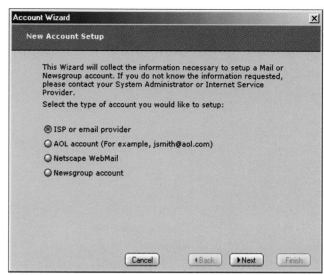

2 You are asked which type of account you wish to set up. Select the top option—ISP or e-mail provider—and then click on Next.

3 At this Identity screen, enter your name and any existing e-mail addresses that you have. Then click on Next.

Jargon buster

● **Mail servers** The computers at your ISP that handle the e-mail coming into your account and all the e-mail you send out.

● **SMTP** Simple mail transfer protocol is the standard method for moving e-mail around the Internet.

Get this information first

There are four important pieces of data you need from your ISP: your e-mail account name, your password and the names of your ISP's incoming and outgoing mail servers. Your e-mail account name will be something like my.name@isp.com. Your initial password is allocated by your ISP although you can usually change it to one of your choice afterwards. The name of your ISP's incoming mail server will be something like mail.ispname.com. And the ISP's outgoing mail server will be something like smtp.ispname.com. This data should be in the documentation that came with your ISP account. Below you'll find mail server details for some of the major ISPs. If they don't work, contact your ISP.

AOL AND ATT
Both AOL and ATT have features which let you pick up your e-mail over the Web from any computer. Contact www.aol.com or www.att.com.

COMPUSERVE
Incoming pop.site.csi.com
Outgoing smtp.site1.csi.com
www.compuserve.com

EARTHLINK
Incoming pop.earthlink.net
Outgoing smtp.earthlink.net

NETZERO
Incoming pop.netzero.net
Outgoing smtp.netzero.net

VERIZON
Incoming mail.verizon.net
Outgoing smtp.verizon.net

MSN
Incoming pop.email.msn.com
Outgoing smtp.email.msn.com

Redirection tip

Before you start trying to redirect your POP3 mail, check to see if your ISP provides web-based mail. You can access webmail from any computer with an Internet connection by simply going to the ISP's website. And some ISPs encourage subscribers to use webmail rather than POP3. When you're traveling or need to access your personal e-mail at the office, webmail is more convenient than POP3 mail and it's great for messages that you only need to read once; however, you can't automatically save a webmail message to your computer as you can with POP3 mail.

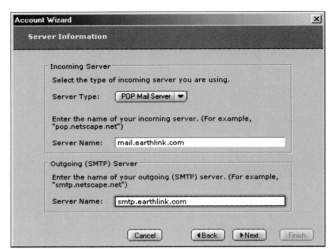

4 Add in the name of your POP mail server for incoming mail. Even if you have several e-mail accounts, you use only one outgoing (SMTP) server which will normally be that of the ISP you connect to the Internet with. At the next screen enter your user name given by the ISP and then a friendly name for the account to make it more recognizable such as home or work mail.

5 With your new account set up you will be prompted for your password when you first connect to the email server. If you check the Use Password Manager box this will be entered automatically on subsequent visits.

Filtering e-mail

Set up a virtual secretary to open e-mail and sort it into relevant folders.

E-mail is quick, efficient, and inexpensive, but this is starting to cause problems. Information overload is a reality. If you receive 25 e-mails per day, that's 175 each week, or a staggering 9,125 a year. Often the figures are higher, thanks to the amount of junk e-mail, or "spam" as it's called, that's sent.

Junk e-mail distribution has become big business, attracting unscrupulous people who don't care who receives it. Even managing everyday e-mail can be a task. With 175 e-mails coming in each week, it's all too easy to skip or delete an important message that has been lost among the rest.

The solution is filtering. You could set up a filter with a rule that looks for e-mail from Aunt Bessie and an action to move such messages to a folder called Auntie; or you could have a filter that looks for a phrase such as Get Rich Quick in the subject of an e-mail and moves it to a junk folder because it will almost certainly be spam. Set up the right filters and your e-mail will manage itself.

You will need

Software Just about any dedicated e-mail program, such as Outlook, Netscape Messenger or Eudora, will let you filter mail.
Hardware A modem or other means of connecting to the Internet.
Other An account with an Internet service provider that gives you with an e-mail address.

Organizing incoming e-mail messages

1 Here you can learn how to organize your e-mail using Microsoft Outlook, but the same principles apply to all e-mail filtering. Only the procedure will change, so check your manual for details of how to apply these steps in your software. Your first step to a more organized life is taken by selecting Organize from the Tools menu or clicking on the Organize button on the toolbar.

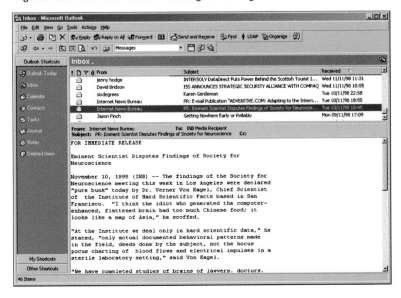

You will learn

- How to use the built-in filtering features of your e-mail software.
- How to set up filtering rules that sort your incoming e-mail into separate named folders.
- How to consign junk e-mail straight to the bin.
- How to send automatic replies to let friends and family know you've received their e-mail.

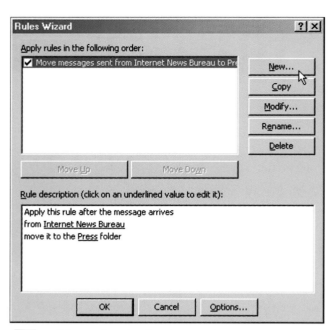

2 A new pane opens at the top of your e-mail window, and offers four options: Using Folders, Using Colors, Using Views and Junk E-mail. Using Colors option lets you display messages from different people in different colors, so you can spot an e-mail from a member of your family, for example. Using Views will change the way your e-mail is displayed and sorted, enabling you to sort alphabetically by sender, or in date order.

3 The Junk E-mail option lets you color or move messages which Outlook recognizes as spam or adult. This is a useful way to filter out unwanted or inappropriate messages, especially if the whole family uses the e-mail account. You can even get updates of suspect e-mail addresses to be added to the filter list automatically by selecting Click Here and downloading the updated data from the Microsoft Outlook Web site as directed.

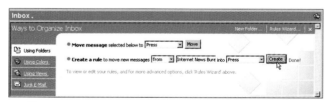

4 Now look at the Using Folders options, the simplest of which is highlighting a message and using Move to copy it to another folder. Use the New Folder button to create an appropriate folder. Alternatively, you can create a simple rule that does this automatically every time a message is received from that sender. Choose the folder you want the messages to be moved to, and click Create. You can do cleverer things than just moving a message to a folder, and the key lies with the Rules Wizard.

5 Click on Rules Wizard at the top right of the organize pane, and a new window will appear. If you have just created a rule, as in the previous step, details of this will be shown. The top pane of the window shows rules that exist, with a checkbox to the left of each that determines if they are activated. The bottom pane describes the action performed by that filtering rule. To create a new filter, click the New button.

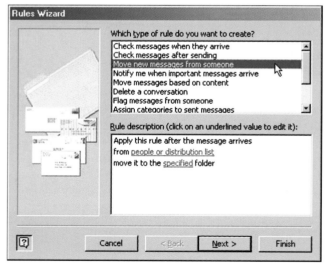

6 A new window appears with lots of options. The top box contains the most common types of filter, while the bottom box explains the action that will be taken. Start with the most useful filter of them all, one that moves messages from specified senders into specified folders. To set up this filter select Move New Messages From Someone and click on Next.

Address book tip

Make full use of the address book that comes with every e-mail program. When you get e-mail from someone you may want to contact again, add their details to your address book straightaway. Most e-mail software makes this easy—often a right-click over the message opens up a menu that includes Add to Address Book as an option. Failing that, the same option can be found in the main program menus. Familiarize yourself with the process and it will soon become second nature.

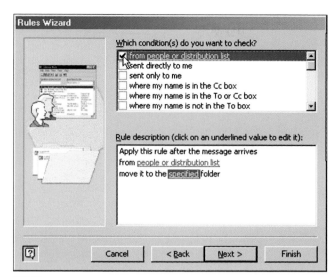

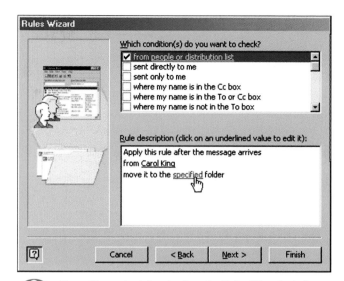

7 You are now faced with a long list of conditions. These are the rules governing which messages the filter will apply to, and there are plenty of them to cover all possible requirements. You can choose to move e-mail that has a specific word in the sender's address, so that all e-mail from one domain or mailing list is moved, or with specific words in the subject line or message text so that all messages that contain that word (maybe the name of your business or of a hobby) are moved to a folder. You can choose to move messages which are marked as important, or which have an attachment, or are over a certain size. The possibilities are enormous, but for this example check the option at the top of the list From People or Distribution List.

9 You will now be taken back to the Rules Wizard window, but if you look in the action pane you will notice that the sender's name now appears there. Next you need to select a folder in which to move e-mail from this person—in this example, a tutor called Carol King. To do this, click on the word Specified which is highlighted in the same pane.

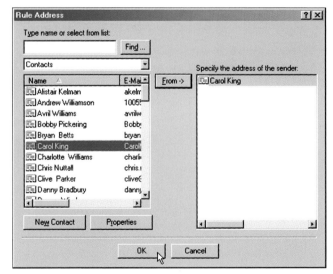

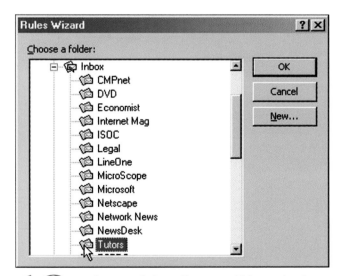

10 A directory window will appear which contains the folders in your e-mail inbox. Either select a folder from here by clicking on it, or create a new folder using the New button. When you have finished, press OK.

8 Move to the lower action pane and click on People or Distribution List. Select the name from the address list that appears, which is a copy of your e-mail address book. If the name isn't shown, you can create a new entry for your address book. To do this, click New Contact and fill in the details. This can then be chosen from the list. Once you have made your selection, click OK.

Watch out!

Internet e-mail services provide you with an e-mail address and mailbox free of charge. The only trouble is that they are Web-based: you collect, view and reply to e-mail using your Web browser. You can't use e-mail software to collect Web-based free e-mail from all online services, which means that you cannot filter it using your existing filters either.

Some, such as Hotmail, do allow you to set up Web-based filters. You would be well advised to check if filtering options are available before you sign up with a free e-mail service.

Jargon buster

Spam This is junk e-mail, which can be sent to millions of people for little cost. Targeting methods are rarely used, resulting in all kinds of rubbish being sent.

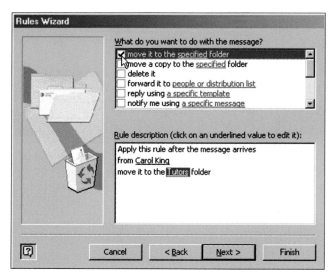

11 You will find yourself back at the Rules Wizard window, with the folder name now shown in the action pane as well as the sender's name. Click Next and the upper rules pane changes to show further options that specify what you want the new filter to do. You can move the message to the folder, or move a copy, reply to the sender using a template, be notified of the arrival of the e-mail by way of a sound or a written message, and much more. Explore all the options and have fun at the same time as making your e-mail work for you. Because you want to Move It To The Specified Folder, check this option. Press Next.

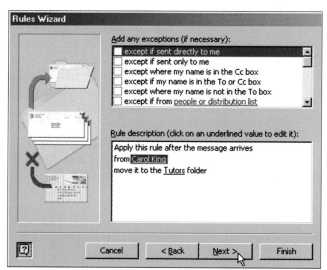

12 You now have the option of including as many exceptions to the rule as you want. This enables you to override the action of the filter in specified circumstances—if the e-mail address contains a specific word (useful to separate business and personal e-mail from the same person sent using different accounts), or if your name is in the CC box instead of the main recipient, and many other exceptions. For this example there are no exceptions, so click on Next.

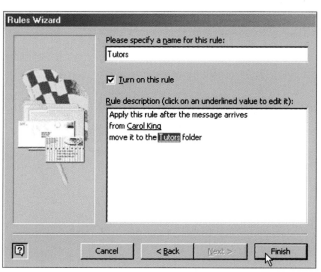

13 The final step involves giving your filter a name by which you can easily identify it. Since you can apply as many filters as you like, this is important. Then check the box to turn the filter on, and press Finish.

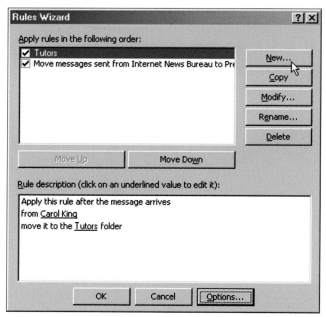

14 You will now see two rules present in the top pane. You can turn these rules on or off at the click of your mouse and edit them simply by using the highlighted sections in the lower action pane. To create the next filter, press New.

Watch out!

You may want to filter out all junk e-mail, which can be easily done by using certain keywords such as Get Rich Quick. However, if you do this you should always make sure something important hasn't slipped through as well. The solution is simple: set up your filter so that it moves all junk e-mail to a folder called junk rather than deleting it instantly. This way you can quickly scan the contents of the folder before you trash them.

Finding people online

Finding someone online may seem a difficult task, but it needn't be.

The bigger the Net gets, the harder it becomes to track people down. With more than 100 million people around the world already online, and more than a million newcomers joining every month, locating the Dave Smith you used to know is like looking for a needle in a whole field of haystacks.

There is no such thing as a printed e-mail directory, like a telephone directory. So if you've got a name, and you think they have an e-mail account, how do you go about tracing them? Fortunately, this is something that is becoming easier all the time.

Most Web search engines let you look for people as well as topics, and they make the searches as speedy and accurate as possible. If you are using one of the latest e-mail programs, you will find it has a people search facility built in. Windows 98 and later let you search for people straight from the Start menu.

You will learn

- How to use the search features in your electronic address book.
- How to use the online directory services to locate e-mail addresses of people for whom you have no mailbox details.
- How to make the most of the search options available from these directory services to ensure an efficient and accurate search.

You will need

Software A Web browser and e-mail program, such as Microsoft Internet Explorer and Microsoft Outlook, for example.
Hardware A modem or other means of connecting to the Internet.
Other An account with an Internet Service Provider.

How to find someone online

1 Start at the beginning, with the easiest option, the Windows Start menu. Simply left-click the start button to open the menu, move up to Search and then select People from the sub-menu that appears. Click on this and a new window will appear, with various options for finding people.

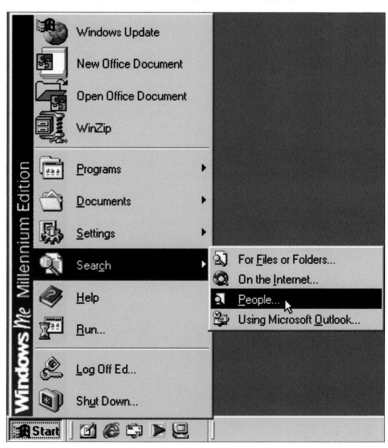

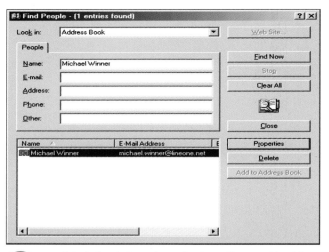

2 By default the Find People application will open with Address Book selected in the Look in panel. Entering a name in the relevant box and clicking the Find Now button will perform a search of your e-mail address book. A right mouse click over the resulting entry in the lower window will bring up a menu that lets you compose an e-mail to that person. However, this is only useful if you already know the e-mail address of the person in question. If you don't, you will need to use one of the online directory options.

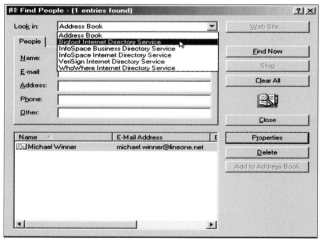

3 To do this, click on the arrow at the end of the Look In selection box, and a dropdown list of more choices will appear. Selecting one of these, Bigfoot, for example, will change the database of information that is searched when you ask the program to find someone. Bigfoot and the other services listed are online resources and so a connection to the Internet has to be made. Enter a name as before, make sure that your modem is switched on, then click on the Find Now button.

Jargon buster

White Pages Any online directory that contains real world information such as street addresses and telephone numbers, rather than just e-mail details, is referred to by this generic term.

LDAP Stands for Lightweight Directory Access Protocol, and refers to the method used to search the databases of Internet people-finding services.

4 Your computer will now dial up your Internet service provider and connect to whichever directory service you have chosen to use. It only takes a few seconds for the results to appear on your screen. If the search is successful, the relevant e-mail details will appear in the lower window as before. If not, you will see this warning box. If this happens, just click on the OK button to clear the warning, then either revise your search criteria (perhaps only use the surname or a first initial and surname to widen the search) or choose another directory service and continue until you are successful.

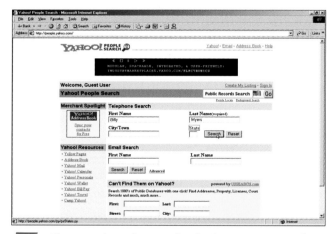

5 There are alternatives to using the Start menu approach. The most popular and efficient alternative is to use one of the many Web-based search sites. The biggest and best known for finding Web sites and services is Yahoo!, which can also help you find e-mail addresses. Yahoo! bought the most popular address directory, Four11, and merged it with its own site to create the Yahoo! People Finder. To get here you must use your Web browser and type http://people.yahoo.com into the address box. Enter a name (first and last names have separate entry boxes) and click on the Search button.

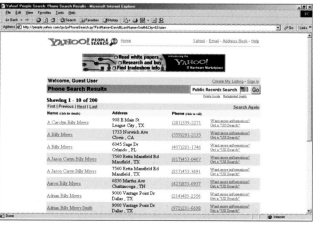

6 This search was successful—too successful, in fact, as it turned up 200 people called Billy Myers living all over the world. However, you can reduce the number by narrowing the search criteria.

Welcome, Guest User
Advanced Email Search   Create My Listing - Sign In

Public Records Search   Go

People Locate Background Search

Fill out as much or as little information as you want. All fields are optional. Enhance your search by choosing an organization name and type.

First Name Billy
Last Name Myers
City/Town New York
State/Province
Country US
Domain
Old Email Address

Organization Name

Organization Type
○ Company
○ University/College
○ High School
○ Military
○ Other
● All Organizations

☑ SmartNames™ (Bob = Robert)

Search   Reset

7 The Advanced Email Search lets you enter more details so that you are more likely to find the right person. Let's assume you are fairly certain that Billy Myers lives in New York. You can enter this and press search. If you know any other details about him, you can enter things such as the type of organization (university, company, or military) to narrow the search further, or the domain (if Billy Myers worked at Microsoft you might enter microsoft.com as a domain) to narrow it down even further. In this example, New York and USA were entered because that's all that was known. Check the SmartNames box, which will search for William and Bill as well as Billy.

Welcome, Guest User
Email Advanced Search Results   Create My Listing - Sign In

Free Online Credit Report Click Here
Offer Ends June 30th
Secure, Online Results. Offer Ends June 30th

Showing 1 - 3 of 3
First | Previous | Next | Last   Search Again - Basic Search

Name (click for details)	Location	Email	
J Billy Myers	New York	j_billy_myers@msn.com	Want more information? Get a "US Search"
Billy Myers	New York	bmyers093@yahoo.com	Want more information? Get a "US Search"
Billy Roy Myers	New York	bandbm96@aol.com	Want more information? Get a "US Search"

First | Previous | Next | Last   Search Again - Basic Search

8 The difference is amazing. It took less than 20 seconds for the Yahoo! People Search to get it down to just three people called Billy Myers based in New York. Now it's just a case of e-mailing three people a polite and brief letter to see which is the Billy Myers you are trying to contact.

9 With a database containing the e-mail addresses of more than 13 million Internet users, the Yahoo! People Search still only has a fraction of the people who are using the Net. The chances are therefore high that you will have to try more than one service before hitting the jackpot. Some services offer country-specific searches, such as the Excite People Finder, for example. Connect your Web browser to www.excite.com and select the People Finder option.

Troubleshooting

While online directory services are improving all the time, they are still not perfect. Printed telephone directories are only updated every few years, and numbers can be out-of-date if people move or are unlisted.

Online directories can also contain out-of-date information. E-mail addresses are easy to change; if you change your Internet service provider, you get a new e-mail address; if you decide to use one of the many free e-mail services, you get a new e-mail address; if you change jobs, you get a new e-mail address. It may not be unusual for a search to return a handful of addresses that are accurate as far as the person is concerned, but dated from the point of view of the mailbox. The date of creation of the address cannot be given, nor can you find out when it was last used; most people consider this information to be private.

Perhaps more of a problem is the fact that it can be very difficult to ensure you have the right person, especially if the name is a common one. Take US president George Bush. A search for this name will produce dozens of addresses, all for George Bush. Unless you know that an official government address ends in .gov you wouldn't be able to filter out the fakes and namesakes. It is vital, therefore, that you verify an identity by sending off a polite Is this you? message before getting down to the confidential nitty-gritty.

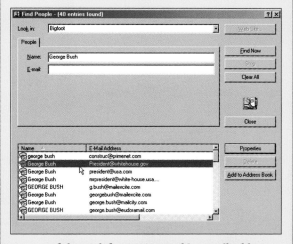

A successful search for George Bush's e-mail address turns up 40 different mailboxes. The real one is at whitehouse.gov but if you already knew that you probably wouldn't be using a directory service.

Jargon buster

Domain A domain is an Internet street address— that part of the e-mail address that comes after the @ symbol. If you know this much of someone's address you are 90 percent of the way to finding the whole thing.

Lookup The act of one computer requesting information from a directory held on another computer.

10 Excite offers a number of choices. Your first move should be to enter the name in the search box and press the Look It Up button. Billy Myers is used once more for this example.

11 Although the search this time returned a staggering 500 people called Billy Myers, each entry has the full e-mail address, details of the geographical location and the mailbox service provider to help narrow the options down. Even better is the addition of a More Details About Billy Myers link under each entry. Click on this and you get much more information, including an exact location (with zip code where known) and the date the entry was last updated, giving you a much better chance of not only finding the right person but finding an up-to-date e-mail address.

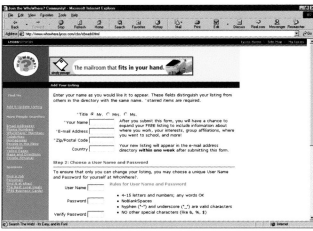

12 And finally, back at the Excite People Finder home page there is the option to add your e-mail listing to the database, free of charge. Selecting this takes you to this data entry screen and allows you to add your details to the WhoWhere directory service used by Excite and many other services online. It's just a matter of entering your details, choosing a user name and password combination so only you can change those details, and clicking Submit. Note that you can update your details whenever necessary. Then your friends should always be able to find you electronically.

Address book tip

The simplest way to keep track of the people closest to you is to ensure that you keep your e-mail address book as up-to-date as the one next to the telephone. If someone gives you their e-mail address, you find it online, or you receive e-mail from a person you want to keep in touch with, enter the details into your e-mail software's address book straightaway so that you don't forget it. It's a lot less hassle searching for a name in your private e-mail address book, no matter how big it gets, than going online to search through a database of millions.

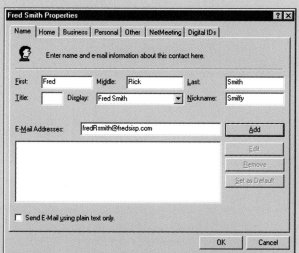

Microsoft Outlook lets you store a great deal of information in its Address Book, which is perfect for keeping track of those people important to you.

Project management

Keep long and complicated tasks on track and on schedule with a project management package.

Project management (PM) is a PC application that is becoming more important. Although PM software is not as straightforward as word processing or spreadsheet software, it's worth examining in some detail as it's likely that you'll encounter it sooner or later. This section shows you how to get the most out of PM software, so that you can plan and schedule projects of all types and sizes.

What does it do?
Project management software does as the name suggests—it helps you to manage a project. Whatever it consists of, any project will always have a series of tasks and an objective. PM software helps you to arrive at this objective within an agreed time, using available resources and equipment, and at minimum cost.

You will need

ESSENTIAL
Software Microsoft Windows and a PM package. Microsoft Project 2000 is used here, but there are several other similar packages.
Hardware A PC capable of running Windows Me or 98, ideally a Pentium with at least 32MB of RAM.

Jargon buster

Collapse To hide subordinate tasks under their summary task, leaving only the summary task visible. In some programs this can be applied to the entire project with one click.

Expand To show all sub-tasks below a summary task, so as to see a detailed view.

The most popular project view is a Gantt chart, and Microsoft Project's format is typical, with task information listed on the left and bars representing each task alongside.

Buying tips

● If your projects are small then any package will suffice, but if they are likely to have thousands of complex tasks, check the program's detailed specification carefully to make sure it won't run out of steam.

● Do you have specific requirements that the program must handle? All programs allow you to specify that one task can't start until another has finished. But there are situations where you might need more complex relationships, even multiple relationships, and not all programs can do this.

● Is the program easy to learn and use? Each of these products strikes a different balance between the power of its features and its ease of use. You'll need to consider your technical requirements and your personal preferences for the user interfaces they offer. For example, how quickly can you enter data and navigate between its areas, and how easy is it to view your project in different ways?

● In practice, it can be difficult to find out about the quality of after-sales support until you need it, but one useful source is the Internet. Look for newsgroups discussing the product, search for messages about it, and use online services such as the CompuServe forums for user feedback.

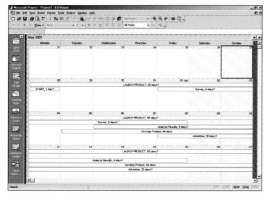

Every project needs to be associated with a calendar. PowerProject's calendar distinguishes clearly between working and non-working days.

Top brands

● **Asta PowerProject**
Asta Development
● **CS Project Professional**
Leach Management
● **Microsoft Project** Microsoft
● **Project Scheduler** Tekware
● **SureTrak** Primavera

Who needs it?

Virtually anyone can use PM. An appropriate project could be any set of planned activities. At home you could use a PM package to help with fairly complex jobs such as redecorating your home or organizing a wedding.

However, you're far more likely to need PM at work. Its use could range from relocating an office, planning a large conference or designing a new product—right up to building a high-speed train link or launching a manned space station. The same principles apply to all of them; only the scale varies. So, whether you're a professional, a manager or a senior executive, and whether you work alone or in a multinational corporation, there are many opportunities for using PM software.

Key areas

It's important to have a clear perspective about the various parts of PM and how they fit together.

A good PM package helps in at least six ways. Entering a plan lets you record details of each task and the relationships between tasks, which is crucial to the accuracy of all later work. Scheduling estimates the duration of the task, allowing the program to calculate the project's finish date and other key dates. Resource assignment allocates people and equipment to each task, with allowance for all the complicated variables, such as vacations, part-time work and so on. Progress tracking updates the plan to reflect any changes that arise during the project's implementation. Resource Management resolves shortages or over-allocations and levels out peaks and troughs to get an optimum balance.

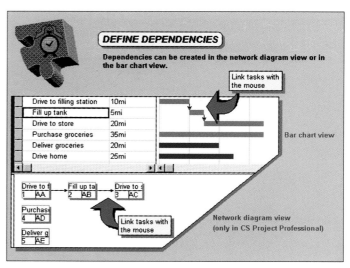

If you're a newcomer to project management, it's an advantage if your package has a good on-screen tutorial **explaining the basics, such as this one in CS Project Professional.**

Communication deals with aspects before, during and after the project, both within and outside the project team, and often includes selling the project in the first place, to secure approval and funding.

What kinds of packages are there?

At the top end there are still a few specialists using highly advanced and expensive products such as Artemis. But the most thriving market is for the mid-range project management products, such as those listed here. These products all have their own distinct characteristics, but one thing they have in common is a balance of power with ease of use.

How does it work?

In essence there are three stages for any project—developing a plan; tracking and managing the plan; and finishing the project and seeing what lessons can be learned for the next time.

PM software is in effect a giant database waiting to be filled with information about your project. From the information you supply it can create and maintain the project's schedule, costs and other items. The more information you supply, the more accurate the plan will be.

Information is entered in fields. Each field is filled with its own specific type of data, such as the name of a task or how long it will take. These fields usually appear in columns.

As with any database, Project can hold a massive amount of information which is impossible to see all at once. In fact, at any one time you would normally just want to see a part of the information, such as the deadlines or the costs. To make it more manageable, Project shows subsets of the information in different views.

Information can also be sorted in various ways, such as using Tables which alter the columns shown, or Filters which sift information according to set criteria. While these views alter the data that's shown, they don't delete it. The information remains in the database and is still updated.

Fact file

● **Task** A single work activity making up a project.

● **Duration** The estimated time to complete a task, usually assuming normal working hours.

● **Link** A dependency or relationship between two tasks, specifying when one begins or ends relative to another.

● **Resource allocation** Assigning resources to the tasks in a project.

● **Baseline** The original schedule and resource allocations, against which you can then compare actual progress to track a project.

● **Gantt chart** A view showing a list of tasks and a graphical representation of them in horizontal bar format. This is the most popular view of a project, and can be found in all programs.

● **Critical path** The series of tasks that must be completed in time if the overall project is to be finished on schedule. Each task on the critical path is called a critical task; delaying any one of them would delay the project.

● **Slack** The amount of time a task can be delayed before it affects other tasks or the project completion date.

● **Milestone** A significant event during a project, such as completion of a major section.

The working screen

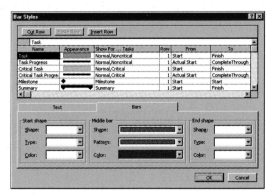

The appearance of bars can be customized in several ways, such as by using this dialogue box. You can highlight all critical tasks with a distinctive color or give milestones a special shape. Using the Text tab, you can also add additional information to Gantt bars instead of, or in addition to, viewing it in the data columns. Names, resources, completion percentages, and start dates can be shown at the top, bottom, left, right, or inside the bars.

Jargon buster

● **Constraint** A logical or chronological relationship imposing some limits on when a task can be performed. The most common type is Finish No Earlier Than, but others are: Finish No Later Than, Must Finish On, Must Start On, Start No Earlier Than, and Start No Later Than.

The title bar contains the name of the active file representing the project on which you're currently working, in this case New Wheel.

The basic entity on which all projects are built is a task. Six have been entered here.

Task duration is one of the many fields associated with a task and displayed optionally in a column. Its width has been minimized here by dragging the divider line, to maximize space for other bars.

This is an example of a special sort of task, called a milestone. They are used to represent a significant point in time, rather than action that must be taken. You create one by entering a duration of zero.

The tools and techniques of PM are easy to master once you've grasped the basic elements.

The Gantt Chart view is the default that appears when you start a new session in most PM programs. It's the screen you'll work with most often because of its helpful combination of two panes. On the left there are columns of text data organized like a spreadsheet, and on the right there's a graphical representation, usually with one bar for every task. This proves a convenient arrangement for many aspects of PM. In particular, it's the best working screen for the most important stage: entering the project's tasks into a detailed plan.

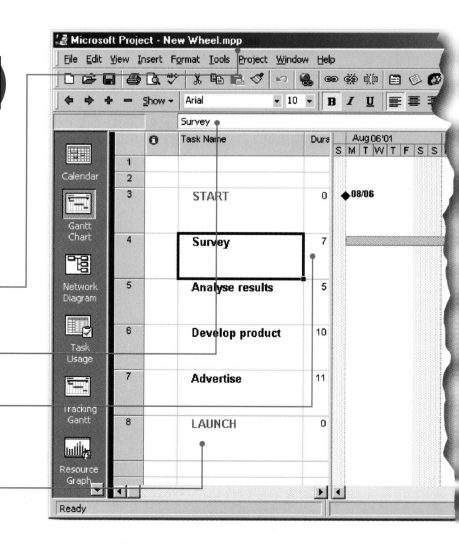

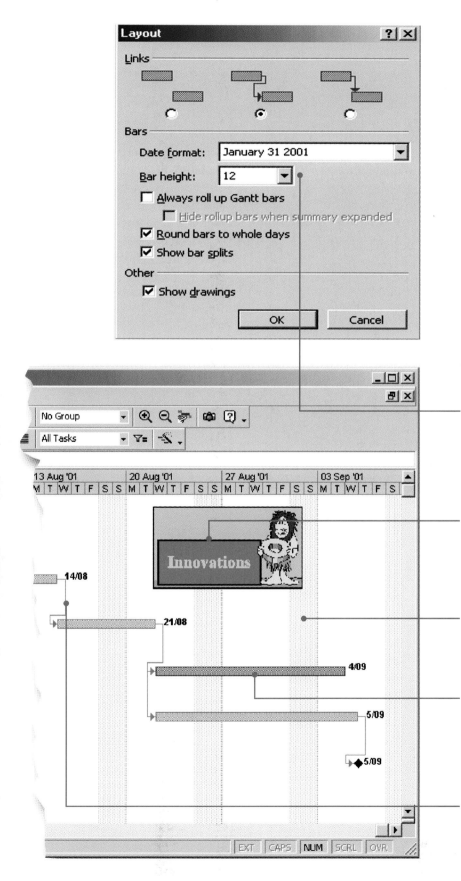

Gantt bars are initially displayed with a default height, but, like most aspects of a good project management program, it's easily customized. If the screen is cluttered with information, you could reduce the height, or, to make bars prominent for a printout, you could increase it.

Using the **Insert/Object** menu, or by pasting from the Windows clipboard, you can add logos and other pictures or symbols to the Gantt Chart. You can also insert sounds or videos to help you sell the project or to celebrate a milestone event.

It's usual to distinguish **non-working time** such as weekends by shading it with a different color. Note that the seven days work duration for Survey actually covers an elapsed period of nine days.

This is one of the **critical tasks**. It lies on the critical path and has been given a distinctive color. The critical path is defined as the series of tasks that must be completed by a certain time if the project is to be finished on schedule. Delaying any critical task will delay the project's completion.

The **relationships** between tasks are represented by various types of link, of which this Finish to Start (FS) link is by far the most common. Other types of relationship available are Finish to Finish, Start to Finish and Start to Start.

Getting organized

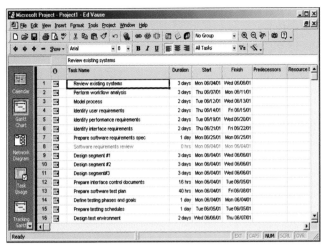

1 Consider this software development project. At the stage shown here the initial list of sequenced tasks has been entered. Line 8 could also have been entered as a brief task, but such activities are often better shown as milestones, with zero duration. The tasks have not only been placed in order of work completion but have also been grouped into appropriate phases.

Outlining tip

To get the best order for your tasks and groups, you'll often need to move tasks around. Details vary, but Microsoft Project's approach is typical. You select the task you want to move, copy it to the Windows clipboard, select the row above which you want to place it, and just paste it in.

PM programs provide tools to help you keep projects organized and logically structured.

Even with relatively simple projects things can soon seem overwhelming. To overcome this, you need to organize tasks logically. This helps you to spot missing tasks and mistakes in the logical flow, and lets you plan to complete each phase at the right time.

PM programs vary in the degree of assistance they provide to help you achieve this. A PM program should be able to help with the three steps involved: sequencing tasks in a logical order; grouping related tasks; and outlining. Sequencing means that you enter or move tasks so that they are in the most efficient order.

Usually it's just a matter of placing them in chronological order. For example, in a building project, Dig Foundation would come before Pour Concrete. But judgment might enter into the sequencing as well. For instance, you would sensibly plan to put up a building's roof before constructing the internal walls, in order to minimize the impact of bad weather.

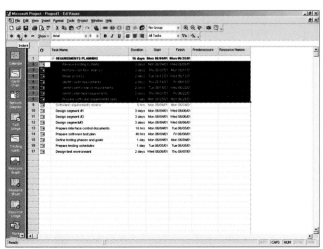

2 The first seven tasks fall into the same logical group, so you should use outlining to show this. First make sure that the Formatting toolbar is displayed. Now insert a new blank task at the top, by selecting Review Existing Systems and pressing the Insert key, or using the Insert menu. This new entry will become the summary task, so give it an appropriate name. Select the seven tasks, now in lines 2 to 8, and click the Indent tool.

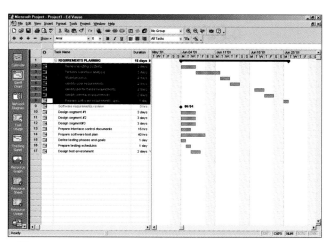

3 The result is that the seven subordinate tasks, or subtasks, are shifted to the right, and the summary task is made bold and given a distinctive bar spanning the period involved.

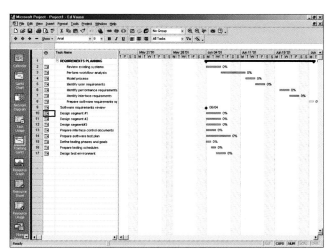

4 It is much easier to understand the structure with the outlined version of the project. With a complex project, outlining can be an invaluable tool.

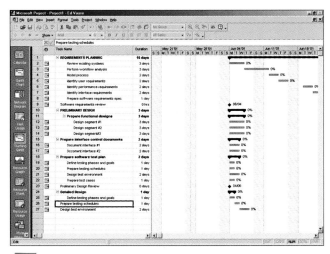

5 Outlined tasks resemble the chapters and topics in a book's table of contents. You can see that clearly here, after repeating the same procedure with other groups of tasks. Some tasks, such as Design Segment #1, have been indented a further level, just as you might find in a hierarchical index.

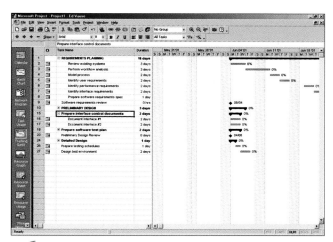

6 Outlining allows you to focus on the details of one group at a time. It's also a dynamic facility because you can expand or collapse summary tasks by clicking the plus and minus symbols alongside the summary task.

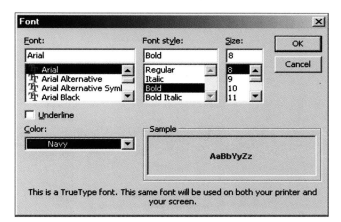

7 It's easy to change the format of the text for summary tasks to make them stand out. Simply highlight the task and select Font on the Format menu. With several levels of summary, for some of them you may want to override the Text Styles dialogue with individual font settings.

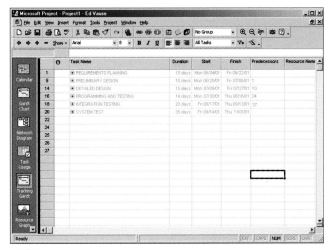

8 Here on the left is the same project with all of its summary tasks collapsed, which can be accomplished with a couple of clicks. Using the multiple windows facility, you can set up a follow-on project applying the same sort of outlining.

Task relationships

Dependencies between tasks can make projects complex, but a PM program handles them easily.

When you enter a list of tasks, PM programs assume by default that all tasks begin on the project's start date. So, in order to ensure the program starts each task at the correct time, you need to link the tasks to each other, based on their start and finish dependencies.

These relationships, plus other constraints imposed on individual tasks, would soon give you a headache if you tried to calculate the project schedule manually. That's where PM programs come into their own.

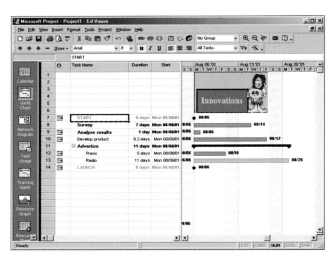

1 This is how the New Wheel illustration might look after the tasks have been entered and Advertise has been split into subtasks. All tasks are assumed to start on August 6. The project finishes on August 20 after 11 days' work (that's 15 elapsed days inclusive, less four for the two weekends). You won't be surprised to note that the critical path, shown in red, is also 11 days in duration, as that's how it is defined.

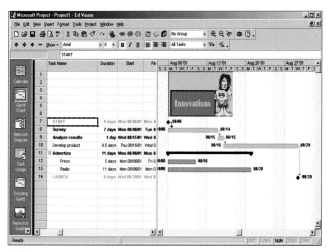

2 Now some appropriate relationships, or links, need to be entered. You don't want to start development until you've analyzed customer opinion, and equally obviously you can't start the analysis until you've finished the survey. It's also logical to make the final launch dependent on finishing development. Those three relationships are all of the Finish-to-Start type (usually abbreviated to FS), which is by far the most common dependency. Note how the critical path (shown in red) has now changed, and that the project completion date is now August 29.

Link tips

● To unlink a task from all its predecessors, on the chart portion of the Gantt Chart view, select the task and click Unlink Tasks on the Standard toolbar.

● You can link a series of tasks sequentially by selecting the tasks and then clicking Link Tasks on the Standard toolbar.

● You can change the task dependency between two linked tasks on the Gantt Chart or the Pert Chart by double-clicking the link line to display the Task Dependency dialogue box.

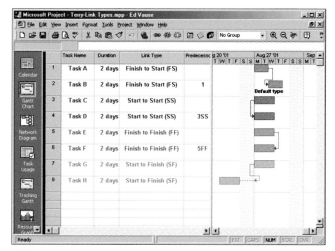

3 The other types of link available in most PM programs are shown here. For example, in a Start-to-Start relationship, task D cannot start until task C also starts. This might be useful in situations involving contractual arrangements; if the start of one task is delayed, then the other must be held up too.

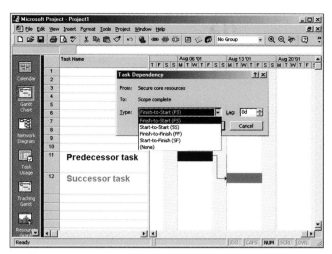

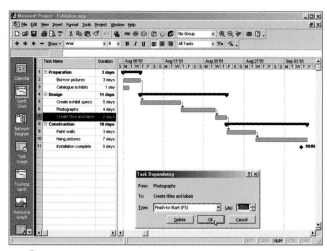

4 To make the links in Microsoft Project, you simply drag a line with the mouse from the predecessor task's bar to the successor task's bar. You can also select multiple tasks first and then click the Link tool, or use the Edit/Link tasks menu, or apply the keyboard shortcut Ctrl+F2. If you then want to change the type of link, you double-click on it and use this dialogue box.

6 Links alone might be inadequate to show accurately when tasks will really start. For example, this plan shows that pictures can be hung after the painter finishes painting with no allowance for the paint to dry. So you insert lag time—a waiting period between the finish of a predecessor task and the start of a successor task. With lead time, you overlap two tasks so that a successor task starts before the predecessor task finishes. For example, you could start creating titles and labels soon after the first photograph is taken. This is entered as a negative lag time, measured in time or percentage complete, as here.

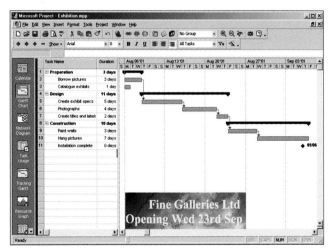

5 The advantages of linking are powerful. First, you can let the program calculate all dates, task start and finish dates, as well as the overall project finish date. You don't need to worry, for example, about pictures being hung before walls are painted because their links maintain the proper sequence of tasks as scheduling changes occur. And if you change the duration, start or finish date of any task, such as the photography, you can see how it affects related tasks and the schedule as a whole. Finalizing announcement posters should be one of the last tasks here.

7 There will often be times, especially with a large project, when you'll get lost and be unable to find the task bars you want to work with. Most PM programs offer navigational and zooming tools to assist. In Microsoft Project, as well as setting the timescale to cover a particular period, you can quickly see the entire project at a glance.

Watch out!

Just as you can type nonsensical rubbish into a word processor it's not difficult to enter tasks into a PM program that defy the laws of logic. One of the most common is a task with inflexible constraints, meaning they must start or finish in relation to a specific date. Better PM programs have tools to help identify the problem. Microsoft Project has a PlanningWizard, which warns you if you try to set a constraint which might cause a scheduling conflict.

View options

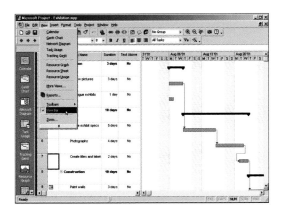

As well as the popular Gantt chart, most programs include many other **predefined views**, and in some programs you can also create your own special purpose views. By using the most appropriate one, you can get your work done more efficiently. Microsoft Project offers a View bar on the left, or you can select one of the five main types directly from the View menu, or click More Views...for a choice of nearly 30.

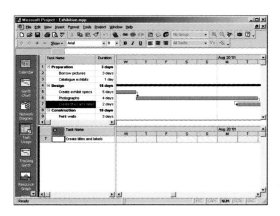

Usually the lower pane of a **combination view** provides further details about whatever is selected in the upper pane—usually a task. In this example, the original view was the Gantt. This was then split into two panes, using Split in the Window menu, or by dragging the pane separator at the bottom right. Finally, with the bottom pane active, Network Diagram view was chosen.

Jargon buster

Filter A set of criteria for displaying a particular group of tasks or resources. You could use a filter to display completed tasks only, and another to display over-allocated resources.

You can focus in on particular aspects of a project and view them in a variety of ways.

Project planning requires a lot of data about every task, all of which is recorded in its database. You usually want to work with just one subset of this data at any one time. A PM program's views, filters and tables can make this easy to achieve.

In Microsoft Project, views can be grouped into two categories—task views and resource views—reflecting the type of information you work with in them. These are further divided into sheets, charts and forms. Sheets are best for viewing text-based information, in a spreadsheet representation, in row and column format. Charts are for graphical data such as horizontal time bars and vertical resource or cost graphs. Forms can be the best way to enter detailed information.

Jargon buster

Table A set of fields displayed in a sheet view of columns and rows, with each column displaying particular information, such as the start date or duration.

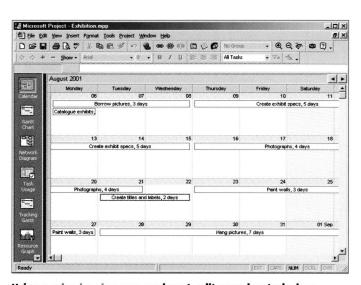

Using a **calendar view** you can insert, edit or review tasks in a familiar calendar format. Task bars span the relevant period, so you can quickly see which tasks are scheduled on particular days, weeks or months. While still in this view you can even establish links between tasks, or assign resources to them.

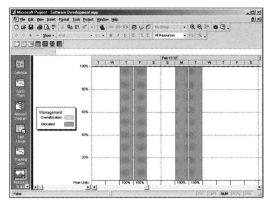

Similar information about Researcher resource can be displayed in the Resource Graph view, a graphic view. It's especially useful for seeing at a glance whether a scarce resource is over-allocated. There are no red warning bars here, however.

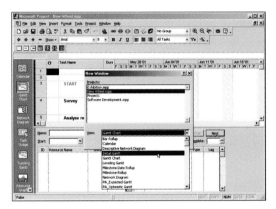

A powerful advantage of some PM programs is the facility to display multiple windows. Here, the existing window is being supplemented, which itself contains two views. A new window will be opened for the same project, and we are choosing to display it initially with a Detail Gantt view.

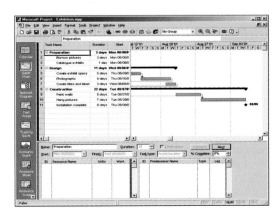

A useful way to enter detailed data about tasks and resources is to use form views. An example is the Task Form, which has fields for entering data such as the task's name, duration, start and finish dates, and the resource assigned to it. Use a form in conjunction with another view. The pair is called a combination view.

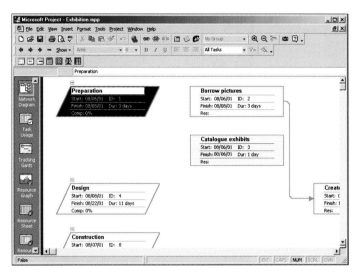

Pert is sometimes used as another name for the classic network diagram shown here. This view helps you to see relationships between tasks more clearly. Pert stands for Program Evaluation Review Technique, an analysis method developed in the 1950s by Lockheed for the Polaris space project.

This original meaning persists to some extent in modern computer project management software. For example, in Microsoft Project you can perform a what-if analysis, which is sometimes called a Pert analysis, based on three estimates of task durations: optimistic, pessimistic and expected.

For planning and adjusting resources, the combination of the Work Usage and Gantt views can also be very useful. It shows a list of resources, with assignments for each resource. This view is best used to show work allocation or cost allocation information. Here the work is unassigned and some has no time allocation. Painting the walls, however, is reckoned to take 42 hours, starting on August 7.

Printing

After selecting the required view, go to Page Setup **on the File menu. Here you can change various settings, including the number of pages to print it across and how many columns to include. When you're ready, click on Page Preview to see how the printout will look.**

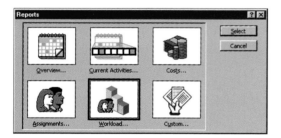

This window appears when you click Reports **from the View menu. Choose the report type you want, and then click Select. A similar window showing further choices of specific reports then appears for your final selection.**

Instead of a general type of report such as Overview or Workload, you can choose a Custom **report. This allows you to select from a long list of many reports, which can be edited and re-sorted before printing.**

From eye-catching summaries to detailed reports, project information of all types is easily printed.

With the trend toward portable multimedia presentations, supported if necessary by the Internet and company intranet, it's possible that much of your communication about a project can be done without touching a printer. Curling up in bed with your project schedule might not be one of them, but there are still occasions when paper output is the best medium. You might want to impress the board or your boss with an overview of your plan, present a detailed task schedule to each team member or pin up a detailed project calendar in the office. Whatever the aim, most modern PM software packages have the tools for it.

Views or reports?

In Microsoft Project, you can choose to print either a view or a report. A printed view includes only the information that's displayed on your screen when scrolling, and you can preview how the printed version will look. If you have a color printer, output should be very similar to the screen display, but size and scaling will obviously determine how many pages it will need.

A printed report uses one of a large set of predefined layouts. For example, the Who Does What report automatically includes each resource's task assignments, as well as the work, delay, and start and finish dates for each assignment. Views and reports each have their advantages and disadvantages. For example, reports can offer output in a format that's not available as a view, but editing a report is less flexible.

Printing tip

Gantt charts often run across several pages. If they're intended to be placed along a bulletin board or wall, reading can be helped by repeating some common data columns on each one. To do that, from the File menu click Page Setup, then the View tab, select the Print First check box, choose the number of columns you want repeated, and finally click Print.

Watch what you spend

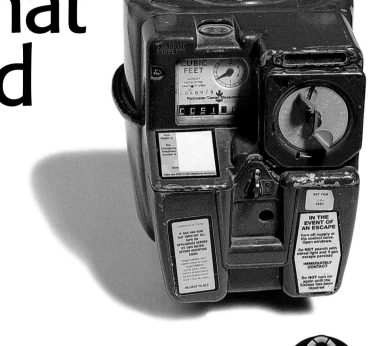

You can keep track of all your household bills using Microsoft Excel.

Keeping track of bills isn't easy, especially when you receive a bill that's larger than you expected. Even if you have a choice of suppliers for gas or electricity—as is increasingly the case—how do you work out which is the best value or estimate the cost of your bills for the winter?

You could work everything out on paper, but that could take a long time. And how can you work out whether it's better to pay one company when they send you the bills, or another company by direct payments from your checking account? You can use your PC to help you calculate this.

With a spreadsheet you can see quickly if it's better to use a company that has a higher basic service charge, but a lower usage cost for the gas or electricity you use. Most spreadsheets can do the basic calculations. This project is a simple theoretical comparison to explain the idea. You can use a similar system to compare, for example, the cost of cell phones and many other things.

You will learn

- How to create spreadsheets with IF statements.
- How to use validation in a spreadsheet.
- How to use conditional formatting.
- How to use the database functions of your spreadsheet.
- How to use a fixed cell reference.

You will need

Software Windows and a spreadsheet package. Excel 2000 is used here, which is part of the Office 2000 suite.
Hardware A Pentium PC, with as much RAM as you can afford or will fit into your computer.

Keeping track of your bills

1 When you first start Excel, you'll see a blank screen. Since you want to make sure you can enter information without any problems, the first thing you have to do, apart from entering a title, is to make a space where you can list the type of payments that you will make. You can put this anywhere; it doesn't have to be with the rest of the information. When you have finished, add the other headings you'll need.

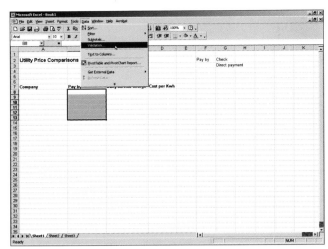

2 Now you need to make sure that you can't make mistakes entering the type of payments that can be made for each company, so you use Validation, which means the spreadsheet checks the information you enter. Assume that you want information on up to six different choices on your spreadsheet, so highlight the six cells beneath the Pay By column with the mouse, and then choose Validation from the Data menu.

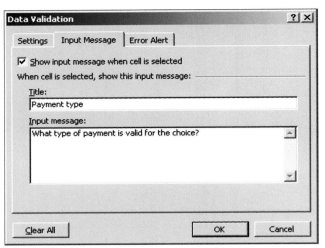

4 Next click on the tab marked Input Message and you'll see a screen like this one. Click the box marked Show Input Message When Cell Is Selected and then type a title and a message in the boxes below. These will appear each time you try to enter information in the spreadsheet cells.

When you've typed in that information, click on the OK button. You'll be returned to the main spreadsheet, and the cells are now set up to allow the information you specified only.

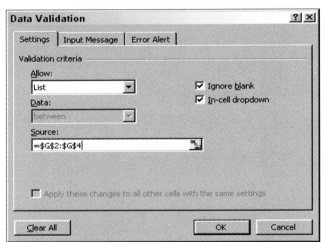

3 This is the Settings tab for the Validation you should perform. You need to show a list of valid choices for the payment method, so from the dropdown list under Allow, choose the item that says List. Click the checks for Ignore Blank and In-cell Dropdown and then click the tiny spreadsheet icon to the right of the blank space labeled Source. Now, you'll see the Data Validation window turn into a small bar, and you can highlight the area on the main spreadsheet where you entered the different options for payments. When you've done that, click on the right of the Data Validation window, to make it reappear.

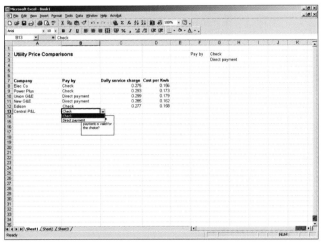

5 Now start filling in the information that you want to compare. Since you need a final figure in dollars and cents, remember to be consistent. For example, if cost per kilowatt hour is quoted as 15.668 cents, you should enter it as =0.15668, otherwise the calculations won't work.

When you go to fill in a cell with validations, you'll see the message you entered appear, and a small arrow to the right of the cell. Click on it, and you can choose one of the items from the list that you made earlier.

Troubleshooting

If the message You Must Enter a Source appears when you try to set up options for Data Validation then you've forgotten to select cells that include the choices you want to appear in a dropdown list. You must enter the data first, and then select the cells when the Settings tab of the Data Validation screen is displayed.

You can't select the options until you've done this. Click OK to make the error message go away, then highlight a range of cells in the spreadsheet, before continuing. You can switch between the spreadsheet and the Data Validation box by clicking the small icon at the right of the blank Source space.

Microsoft Excel - Book1 — B20

	A	B	C	D	E	F	G	H	I
1									
2	Utility Price Comparisons					Pay by	Check		
3							Direct payment		
4									
5									
6									
7	Company	Pay by		Daily service charge	Cost per Kwh				
8	Elec Co	Check		0.275	0.156				
9	Power Plus	Check		0.293	0.173				
10	Union G&E	Direct payment		0.299	0.179				
11	New G&E	Direct payment		0.285	0.162				
12	Edison	Check		0.277	0.158				
13	Central P&L	Check							
14									
15									
16	Start of period	01-Jan-02							
17	End of period	01-Apr-02							
18	Total days	90							
19	Kwh used	327							
20									

6 You've entered the basic figures, so set up the information you need for calculating your power bills. You need to know the period covered by a bill, and the estimated amount of power that will be used, so create headings for those.

Rather than add up the number of days covered, you should enter the days and format the cells as dates. Below those, use a cell with the formula =days360(B16,B17), which works out the number of days between two dates. Not all spreadsheets do this accurately, so you might want to enter the number of days yourself.

Microsoft Excel - Book1 — E12 = No

	B	C	D	E	F	G	H	I	J	K
1										
2	sons				Pay by	Check				
3						Direct payment				
4										
5										
6										
7	Pay by		Daily service charge	Cost per Kwh	Discount?	Days free				
8	Check		0.275	0.156	No					
9	Check		0.293	0.173	No					
10	Direct payment		0.299	0.179	Yes	21				
11	Direct payment		0.285	0.162	Yes	21				
12	Check		0.277	0.158	No					
13	Check				Yes					
14					No					
15						Does the				
16		01-Jan-02				service charge				
17		01-Apr-02				discount apply?				
18		90								
19		327								

7 Suppose that one of the companies doesn't charge its daily service charge in the winter for a number of days. You need to include that in your calculations, so add some extra columns in the spreadsheet, to the right of your figures for the charges. You should have added one column called Discount, which you use to determine whether a discount applies, and another for the number of free days you'll receive if it does. To make it simple to enter information, enter the words Yes and No in two spare cells on your spreadsheet, and use the Validation option on the Data menu to make these cells give you the option of choosing Yes and No from a list, as you did for the payment types earlier.

Microsoft Excel - Book1 — H8 = =D8*B19

	B	C	D	E	F	G	H	I	J
1									
2	sons					Pay by	Check		
3							Direct payment		
4									
5									
6									
7	Pay by		Daily service charge	Cost per Kwh	Discount?	Days free	Total service charge	Usage	Total
8	Check		0.275	0.156	No			51.012	
9	Check		0.293	0.173	No			56.571	
10	Direct payment		0.299	0.179	Yes	21		58.533	
11	Direct payment		0.285	0.162	Yes	21		52.974	
12	Check		0.277	0.158	No			51.666	
13	Check								
14									
15									
16		01-Jan-02							
17		01-Apr-02							
18		90							
19		327							

Sum=270.756

8 Now you have all the information that you need and you can start to calculate the charges. The usage charge is simple: you need to multiply the cost per unit by the number of units. For the first company in this example, the cost is in cell D8 and the number of units is in B19, so the amount is given by the formula =D8*B19. Highlight the first cell in the usage column and type that formula in the formula bar. Then copy it into the other cells in the usage column to calculate the figure for the other options. D8 is automatically changed to D9, D10 etc. This is called a relative reference. The use of the dollar sign in the B19 part of the formula makes this a constant, that is it stays the same when the formula is copied into subsequent cells. This is called an absolute reference. Look at the formulas—each time you highlight a cell, the formula appears in the formula bar—and you will see they're using the correct cost per unit.

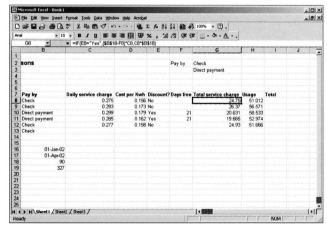

Microsoft Excel - Book1 — G8 = =IF(E8="Yes",(B18-F8)*C8,C8*B18)

	B	C	D	E	F	G	H	I	J
1									
2	sons					Pay by	Check		
3							Direct payment		
4									
5									
6									
7	Pay by		Daily service charge	Cost per Kwh	Discount?	Days free	Total service charge	Usage	Total
8	Check		0.275	0.156	No		24.75	51.012	
9	Check		0.293	0.173	No		26.37	56.571	
10	Direct payment		0.299	0.179	Yes	21	20.631	58.533	
11	Direct payment		0.285	0.162	Yes	21	19.665	52.974	
12	Check		0.277	0.158	No		24.93	51.666	
13	Check								
14									
15									
16		01-Jan-02							
17		01-Apr-02							
18		90							
19		327							

9 To calculate the service charge, you need to multiply the charge per day by the number of days, which would normally be given using the formula =3DC8*B18, since cell B18 contains the number of days, and C8 the cost per day for the first company. But what about those discounts? If the discount applies, there are fewer days to include.

You need to use an If command in the spreadsheet. This has three parts: the first is the If, the second is what to do if it's true, and the third is what to do if it's false. If the Discount column (column E in this example) has the word Yes then you need to subtract the number of free days, in column F, from the total, before multiplying by the daily charge. The formula you need is =IF(E8="Yes",(B18-F8)*C8,C8*B18). Type this into the cell where you want to calculate the standing charge for the first company and then copy it to the others below.

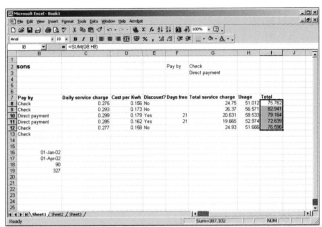

10 Now that you have all the figures you can add them up for each company. You'll see that if you change one of the discount figures, the total service charge changes. Switch an option to No instead of Yes and you can see the difference. Here the total service charge and usage were added to give a total, and then the totals cells were formatted using the Cells option on the Format menu.

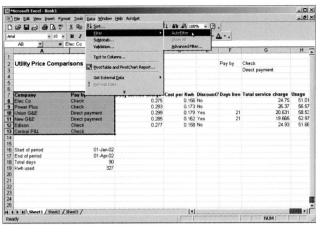

13 If you want options for paying by check only, use Data functions. Highlight the headings for payment method, and the cells beneath, then choose Filter, Auto Filter from the Data menu.

Conditional Formatting ? X

Condition 1

| Cell Value Is | equal to | =min(I8:I13) |

Preview of format to use when condition is true: AaBbCcYyZz   Format...

Add >>   Delete...   OK   Cancel

11 To make it easy to see which is the best deal, ask the spreadsheet to highlight it. Select the cells in the Total column and choose Conditional Formatting from the Format menu. Select Cell Value, Equal To and in the box on the right type = min (I8:I13), then select the cells again. Click Format and from the screen that appears, select a color to highlight the best deal. Click OK after choosing the color, and again to confirm the Condition you just set. Make sure there's a closing bracket on the end of the= min (I8:I13), otherwise you'll see an error message.

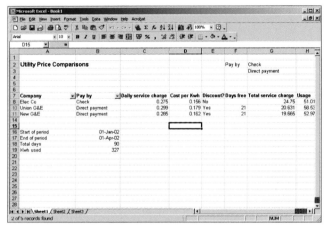

14 Click on the payment type and you'll see only the options you want. Click the arrow to the right of the column heading and you'll see the choices available. You'll also notice the conditional formatting you applied changes. It's applied to all the data, not just the parts you selected. By combining the two with the If statement you can create a spreadsheet that makes it easier to work through complicated sets of numbers and make sure you can see the bottom line.

12 Here's the result with the best deal highlighted in green. If you change any of the figures so that another option is less expensive, you'll see that it changes to green instead, and the current one turns back to black.

Spreadsheet tip

If you don't have a spreadsheet with Validation features, avoid using words such as check and direct payment as they can be mistyped. Use a single letter, C or D. That way you'll fill in the data without making any mistakes. You can still get the spreadsheet to fill in the full text by adding a column which refers to the letter you typed in an IF command, like this: = IF (B2="c", "Check", IF (B2="d", "Direct payment", "Invalid"))).

Now, if you type a letter C or D in cell B2, the type of payment will be displayed in the cell that contains the formula. If you type anything else, the word Invalid will appear.

Financial advisers

Personal finance software helps you to analyze your financial past, manage the present and plan your future.

This section looks at some of the common functions in personal finance software and how to get the best from it. Here we are using Intuit's Quicken, but Microsoft's Money has similar capabilities and is used in much the same way. Of course, there are other products on the market but they offer fewer features and less versatility than Quicken and Money.

Top of the range
The two leading products are available in standard or advanced versions, the advanced being Quicken Deluxe and Microsoft Money Financial Suite. The interfaces are the same, but the top versions have additional features. Broadly, these fall into four areas: planning, online, investments and business.

Online features include Web access from within the main programs to sites offering financial data and advice, real-time share price quotations and currency rate updates. Both programs also offer online banking in various forms, in conjunction with some of the major banks and other financial institutions, but this market is at an immature stage. Consistent standards have to emerge and public acceptance is still some way off.

Invest wisely
Investment features in Quicken and Money are extensive. For example, you can set up a portfolio of stock market shares, mutual funds, bonds, and so on, and track their performance.

Those buying a package for business should look at products designed expressly for that application. Examples include Sage Instant Accounting, Intuit's QuickBooks and MegaTech's MYOB and TAS Books.

You will need

ESSENTIAL
Software Some personal finance software such as Intuit's Quicken or Microsoft Money.
Hardware A Windows PC (Pentium or faster) with 32MB of RAM recommended.

ALSO RECOMMENDED
Hardware A printer, a CD-ROM drive, a soundcard, speakers and a modem with an Internet account.

Reconciling

How to reconcile

Reconcile Bank Statement: Joint Account   ✕

1. Enter the following from your bank statement.

Opening Balance:	1,025.23
Ending Balance:	
Currency :	$

2. Enter and categorise your interest and bank charges, if any.

Service Charge:		Date:	05/05/01
Category:	Bank Charge		
Interest Earned:		Date:	05/05/01
Category:	Interest Inc		

✓ OK   ✗ Cancel   ? Help

1 To begin the process, click Reconcile at the top of the register, which displays this window. Your opening balance is entered, as Quicken remembers it from the last time you reconciled this account (assuming that this is not the very first occasion, in which case the procedure is different).

Reconciliation tip

● **Differences** If a difference remains, even when you believe you've checked off all the transactions, then your account is not reconciled. Quicken lets you make an adjustment, with different options depending on whether the mistake is in the opening balance or comes later on.

This line separates the past from the future, and is only displayed when you've entered transactions with a future date. Here, you've anticipated your six-monthly office rent.

All your accounts are shown on these tabs. The current account is selected and to its left is your credit union account, then a savings account and so on. To work with the transaction register for any account, you just click its tab. You can rearrange the tabs by dragging them with the mouse. Tabs for investment accounts don't appear on non-investment registers like this.

Clicking an Activity Bar icon takes you immediately to that part of the program.

When you receive a statement, it's important to reconcile it promptly with the data on your computer.

If you use a home-finance package to manage your checking account, it's crucial that the program data matches the account. The screenshot below shows the register of a checking account. You received your last statement on, say, March 8 and expect the next one on May 8. The Rs in the Clr column show you have reconciled these transactions. Since then, there have been more transactions that must be reconciled when the next statement arrives. The final balance, including regular future transactions, shows the amount you currently have—$13,200.

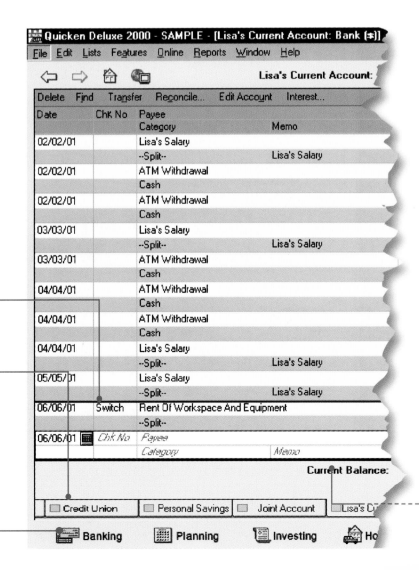

3 The window then displays all the transactions in your register that have not been reconciled. You simply click the Clr column for each such payment and deposit that appears in your statement, and a check mark appears against them.

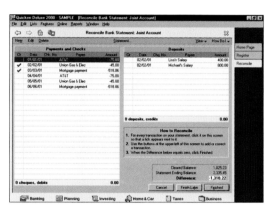

4 There may be a lot of transactions to check here, especially if your statements are not very frequent. As you check off each one, the Difference field at the bottom right gets smaller. The future transaction here is not checked off, as it's not yet on your statement. In fact, it has clearly not even been credited to your bank account yet. When the difference reaches zero, you can safely click Finished.

Reconciliation tip

● **Missing entries** You can easily add a missing transaction during reconciliation, using the New button.

Reconcile Bank Statement: Joint Account

1. Enter the following from your bank statement.

Opening Balance: 1,025.23

Ending Balance: 2335.45

Currency: $

2. Enter and categorise your interest and bank charges, if any.

Service Charge: ☐ Date: 05/05/01

Category: Bank Charge

Interest Earned: ☐ Date: 05/05/01

Category: Interest Inc

✓ OK   ✗ Cancel   ? Help

2 Enter the ending balance from your statement. If there are interest or bank charges shown on it then you can also enter those here. Then click OK.

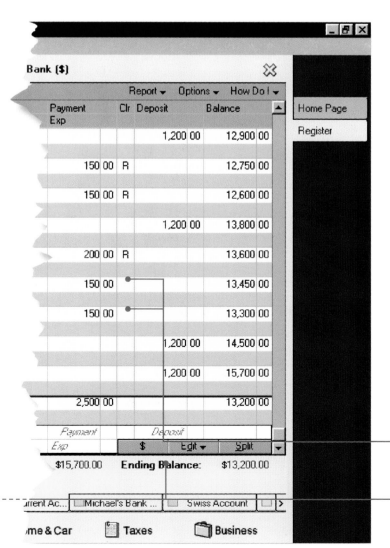

The absence of an R shows that you have not yet reconciled these two recent transactions.

Note that both your current balance and ending balance are shown. The ending balance reflects future transactions that you've entered early.

Staying ahead

How to manage transactions

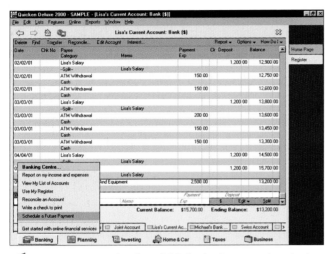

1 You can access the Financial Calendar from anywhere in the program, either by selecting Features on the top menu, and then Reminders, Financial Calendar, or by clicking the Banking icon in the Activity Bar and choosing Schedule a Future Payment.

2 The Financial Calendar appears, with the current month and some of the previous and following months visible. Here previously recorded transactions and scheduled transactions are shown.

Jargon buster

Postdated transaction One with a future date. You would use postdating to record a payment that you know you'll have to make and want to anticipate; or you could use postdating for money which you expect to receive.

Finance programs have powerful facilities for scheduling and managing future transactions.

Most people have regular expenses and deposits. You probably receive a salary every month, pay a rent or mortgage sum and so on. With a home-finance program, instead of entering a transaction on the day it occurs, you can schedule it. On the day the transaction is due, the program reminds you or automatically enters it in your register. In Quicken, there are several ways to organize regular transactions. One is to use the Financial Calendar.

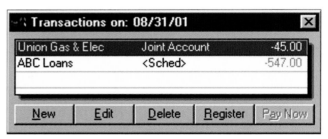

3 Right-click on any date and choose Transactions. For example, for August 31 you've already entered the payment to Union Gas & Electric. But there's also your monthly telephone bill scheduled on that date. Click Pay Now if you want to record this in the register too.

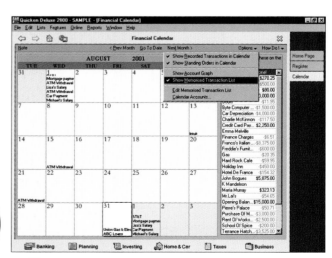

4 The Financial Calendar layout can be altered using the Options list. You can show all memorized transactions on the right. This makes several facilities possible, such as updating the calendar by using the mouse to drag and drop entries.

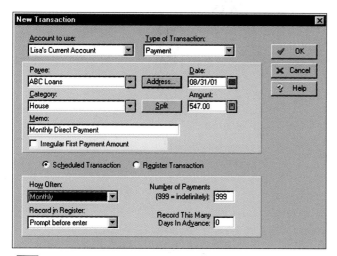

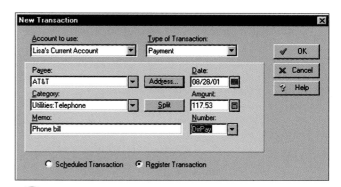

5 Suppose you've been paying your mortgage by check but now want to switch to direct payment, starting on August 31. From the transaction list, drag the mortgage entry on to the August 31 cell in Financial Calendar and release the mouse button. Choose the option to make this a scheduled rather than a one-off register transaction. This displays further options: frequency of payment, how far in advance to enter it, and whether to record it automatically in the register or prompt you first.

8 This window then appears and you use the Mark button to assign each required transaction to the group, assuming that all have first been recorded in the Memorized Transaction list. Then click Done.

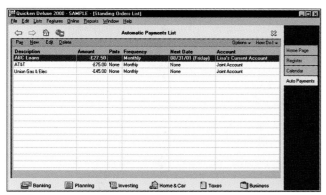

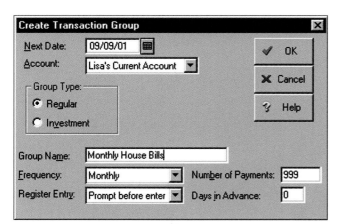

6 To check, display the latest Automatic Payments List using the top icon bar or the List menu, where the new entry can be seen.

9 Apart from scheduled transactions, many users prefer to use the Financial Calendar as their primary method for entering transactions in the account, rather than working in the register. You just drag the memorized transaction onto the required day of the calendar. Providing the date is not in the future, this dialogue box appears. You enter new transactions, with no memorized entry, by using the top line (shown in blue with the words Use This For A New One, see step 4 on page 176). Changes and alterations can all be handled from the Financial Calendar.

7 Often you'll have a group of transactions that can be paid at the same time from the same account. You can handle that in Quicken using a transaction group. Open the Automatic Payments List, click New and select Group. Enter data about the group (similar to a single transaction) and click OK.

Watch out!

It's even more important than usual to take care over accuracy when you're setting up regular transactions. You could be accumulating errors well into the future if you get things wrong. Quicken helps to prevent this because when you drag from the Financial Calendar, the mouse pointer changes to a calendar symbol to show that you can drop the transaction onto a day. If you move the pointer over a date in the past, the pointer changes to a register, which indicates that the transaction will be entered directly into your register. It is essential to check the default information that appears when you drag and drop and fill in the correct amount, date, and so on. Unless you change them, Quicken uses data from the last memorized transaction.

Stay in control

How to use Reminders

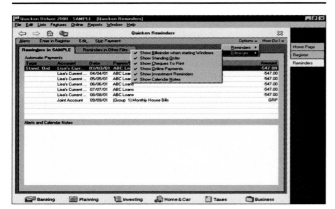

1 To get the best out of Reminders and Billminder, tailor their options. Choose Options then Reminders from the Edit menu. Alternatively, if you're viewing the main Reminders window, use its Options button. The resulting dialogue box is titled Reminders but it has a pop-up menu from which you can select either Reminders or Billminder. If you choose Billminder, you can set various options such as showing Billminder when you start Windows, plus choices of what type of information to include.

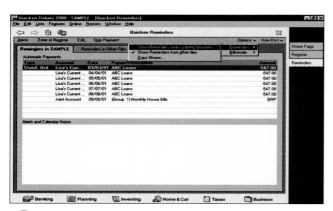

2 To view a list of forthcoming transactions regularly, click Reminders and select Show Reminders When Starting Quicken. You can also choose to see events in any other Quicken files you might have, such as separate ones for a business or partner. The number of days in advance, if any, is specified once, and applies to both Reminders and Billminder.

Scheduling tip

To disable a scheduled transaction that you'll probably use later, enter zero. Quicken won't record transactions in your register until you enter a new number, although the item remains in the Scheduled Transaction list.

Reminders can alert you to imminent transactions and exceptional account situations.

Once you've set up your calendar, your finance software can be used to help maintain control of your affairs. In Quicken, there are two features to handle this: Reminders and Billminder. There is some overlap between their functions, but the main difference is that Billminder appears every time you start Windows, while the Reminders window opens when you start Quicken if there are transactions due within the period specified. However, you can display Reminders at any time by choosing the Reminders option in the Features menu.

Scheduling tip

To schedule an indefinite number of transactions, leave the number set at its default of 999. If you know exactly how many will be made, such as 24 months against a loan, enter that specific number.

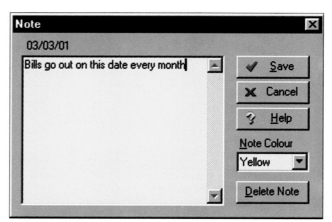

3 In addition to scheduling transactions in your Financial Calendar, you can add color-coded notes on any topic, financial or otherwise. Just right-click the date to which it refers and choose Note from the menu that appears. Choose the relevant color from the box on the right and, after you've entered your text in the blank note, save it. Quicken pastes a small colored box on the date, which you can click when you want to read or edit the note.

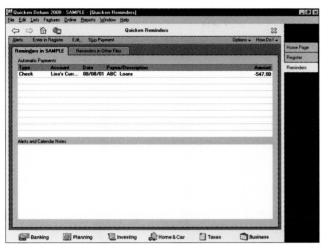

4 Here you have a reminder that a loan repayment is due.

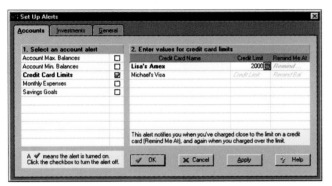

5 Reminders are accessed by clicking the Alerts... button in the Reminders window. There's considerable flexibility because for each of the areas on the left, you can enable or disable their alerts and specify details on the right. These will vary depending on the alert area. For example, in the case of credit-card limits shown here, you can specify a reminder when you've charged close to your maximum and also when you are over the limit.

6 For the Monthly Expenses alert area you've attempted to cut back on restaurant expenses, by asking for a reminder when you've spent more than $200 in any month.

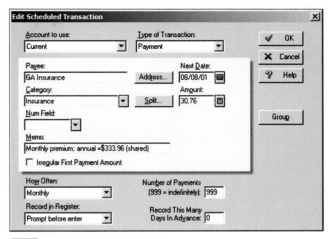

7 When a scheduled transaction such as the GA Insurance item becomes due, you select it and then decide what to do with it. You could deal with it later by just closing the Reminders window for now, or accept it by clicking Enter in Register. To ignore it this time but resume your normal schedule next time, you'd choose Skip. If you want to change something before entering it, you click Edit. This brings up the Edit Scheduled Transaction box, shown above, which allows you to change any of the details, such as the amount. However, if you want to change all future occurrences, you have to do so from the Scheduled Transactions List.

8 Remember, you can choose whether to have the program automatically enter the scheduled transaction or prompt you first, giving you a chance to change some of its information. This is an option found within the Edit Scheduled Transaction window, not in Reminder Options. Another option in the same dialogue box is Record This Many Days in Advance. You might use this to remind you a bill is due and give you time to post a check, such as before a credit-card account settlement date.

Icon bar tip

As well as the main menu and Activity Bar, you can use the top Icon bar to navigate Quicken. It's accessed from the menu displayed when you right-click a blank area. You can have the Activity and Icon bar displayed together.

Budgeting

Before tackling your budget you need to check that you have the categories you need and that they're appropriately named and logically organized.

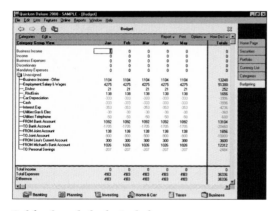

Quicken's main budget window.

Using budgeting tools you can focus on expenses that need cutting back and compare future scenarios.

One clear motive for setting up budgets is finding yourself short of money. This could be due to falling income but more often the underlying cause is that one or more expenses are greater than anticipated. If the relevant categories are not obvious, you can use your home-finance program to prepare reports and graphs to help with detailed analysis of your past expenditure.

Stick to your budget

Budgets are based on the structure and definitions of the categories and sub-categories you've set up. Before you begin setting up budgets, it's a good idea to ensure that your categories are suitably named and organized. Use the Lists menu and choose Category then Transfer. Delete any categories you don't use and add new ones to fit your income and expense patterns. Then you can create your first budget.

    Access Quicken's main budget window either using the Activity Bar's Planning icon and selecting Budget My Spending, or clicking Features then Planning on the main menu, and then selecting Budgets. Its format is a spreadsheet, with

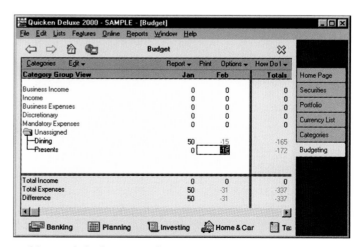

In this sample budget you're focusing on just two expense items, Dining and Presents. You can type in budget amounts for these, replacing the zeros. These appear in red and their row and column totals are calculated automatically.

inflow and outflow categories as the rows and each budgeting period as the columns. Initially it will be full of zeros and set to a monthly period.

There are several ways you can proceed. Creating a realistic budget usually takes more than one attempt, but you'll be able to alter budget values at any time. Change the format to suit your needs. For example, the View menu lets you remove the clutter of zeros. Then click Close and save the budget.

Automatic budgets

There's a facility in Quicken to calculate your budget automatically. It's accessed by clicking Autocreate from the Edit menu. You can choose the historical period on which this will be based, as well as alternative calculation methods. The monthly detail method is suitable for seasonal or trending categories, while the average approach would show an identical figure for every column, based on the historical period's average rate.

Apart from displaying and printing reports and graphs, you can also use Quicken's Progress Bar to track how well or otherwise you're doing on a daily basis against key budget categories. You access it from the Features menu by choosing Planning and Progress Bars. Then you click its Cust button on the right to select the categories and other options, such as keeping it visible at all times.

The **Quicken Home Page** gives you an at-a-glance breakdown of your finances, together with a chart showing how you're spending your money.

Budget tips

● It's easy to work with your budget in a normal spreadsheet as well as in Quicken if you wish. From the main Budget window's menu, use the Edit/Copy All command to place your budget on the clipboard. Then open your spreadsheet program and paste it in.

● Quicken indicates expenses in red with a minus sign. When you enter a new expense amount, don't enter the minus sign in front of the number. The program displays the minus sign when your cursor leaves the cell and automatically adjusts the Totals amount.

	A	B	C	D	E	F
1	Category Name	Jan	Feb	Mar	Apr	May	Ju
2							
3	INFLOWS	0	0	0	0	0	
4	OUTFLOWS						
5	Dining	-50	-50	-50	-50	-50	
6	Presents	-150	-150	-150	-150	-150	
7							
8	Total Inflows	0	0	0	0	0	
9	Total Outflows	-200	-200	-200	-200	-200	
10	Difference	-200	-200	-200	-200	-200	
11							
12							

A full budget would initially look like this. You can use the various tools under the **Edit** and **Lists** buttons to make whatever changes you need, such as eliminating rows or changing amounts.

What you're worth

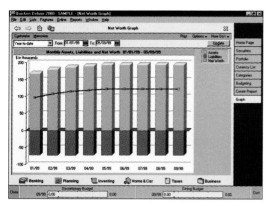

You can see your net worth as a graph. Here's a
user with modest assets and a liability apparently
stuck at around $80,000.

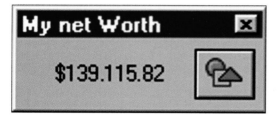

You can show the bottom line in a floating window.

It's easy to keep track of your financial net worth, either in detail or just as a single total.

Home-finance programs can integrate various
sections of your data and help you control your
affairs. In Money Financial Suite and Quicken
Deluxe there are many such planning features,
some of them advanced. One of the simplest, yet
most effective, is working out your net worth.

Your worth

Before your program can calculate net worth, you
need to set up an account for every asset and
liability that you have and ensure they all contain
accurate, up-to-date information. Apart from your
checking account, you should set up accounts for
things like interest-paying savings, stockbroker cash
accounts and credit union savings accounts. Asset
accounts can also be created for estimates for your
car and house, with a new entry made when there's
a significant change. Then set up liability accounts
for things such as your mortgage and private loans.

In Quicken, you can view net worth via the
Reports menu. For an overall perspective, you'll
want to see just the current totals. But if you want
to see how the figures have been reached, change
the Interval under the Display tab of the Customize
dialogue box to an appropriate setting.
Alternatively, you can show net worth as a graph.
For a simpler representation, Quicken allows you to
pop up a floating window showing just the bottom
line total. It will reappear each time you run
Quicken. Clicking the icon on the right lets you
customize it.

Jargon buster

Net worth The value of your assets minus liabilities.

Assets Things you own, such as your car, property and other
valuables. When a home-finance package calculates your net worth,
it treats your checking, interest-paying savings, credit union savings,
asset and shares investment accounts as assets.

Liability account The opposite of an asset account because it
reduces your wealth. Examples are mortgages and other loans.

Glossary
A Jargon-Buster's Guide

Active desktop
This brings the Web to your PC. When Active Desktop is enabled, you can take content from the Web—such as share prices, news pages and images—and use them on your desktop. To update the information you need to go online.

ActiveX
Technology developed by Microsoft to share information between applications. ActiveX controls can be embedded in Web pages for animation and other interactive effects.

Active window
The part of the screen that is "in focus"—that is, being used currently. When active, the title bar (the top strip of the window) will be a different color from that of the inactive windows.

Adapter card
Printed circuit board that plugs into a PC, enabling it to liaise with other hardware. A display adapter, for example, enables the PC to display text and images on the screen.

ADSL
Stands for Asymmetric Digital Subscriber Line. This provides a fast, always-on connection to the Internet over existing phone lines. It can share the same line as the telephone because the digital data is sent at a different frequency from the voice traffic.

AGP
Stands for Accelerated Graphics Port—an interface designed for super-fast 3D graphics cards.

Analogue
A signal that varies continuously rather than being composed of discrete steps. Sound waves and clocks with hands are analogue. Clocks with LED displays are digital. A PC performs digitally, so it uses digital-to-analogue conversion (DAC) to produce sounds, display graphics and communicate along phone lines. Analogue-to-digital (ADC) converts analogue signals, such as recorded sound, into digits by "sampling" the waveform thousands of times a second and storing snapshots of the amplitudes as numbers.

Anti-aliasing
A technique used to reduce the jagged appearance of images on screen, which is particularly noticeable when low-resolution pictures are magnified. In anti-aliasing, pixels around the edge of the image or text are given a shade of the relevant color to give a smoother look.

Anti-virus software
Software that scans for and removes viruses on your PC. You can set it to monitor for virus activity while the PC is on, or just to scan when you wish. Most anti-virus software checks e-mail and downloaded programs for viruses.

Applet
Small programs, such as the Windows Calculator. Applet is sometimes used to denote programs that can be run from within other programs only, and also refers to programs embedded in a Web page.

Application
A program that produces something, such as a word processor, spreadsheet or drawing program, rather than a utility program the main function of which is to keep the PC running smoothly.

Associate
If a file type—determined by the three letters after the dot—is associated with an application, opening the file by double-clicking on it will launch the application and load the file. Opening a .TXT file, for example, will launch Notepad. Opening an unassociated file will produce a dialogue box asking which application you want to use to open the file.

Asterisk
In a search box you can use * as a wild card to represent one or more letters. For example, typing C*.txt into the Find File box will find every TXT file starting with the letter C.

AVI
Stands for Audio Video Interleaved. A standard file format for mixed digital video and audio files.

Background
1) The area of the screen, on which letters and graphics appear. Users can change the color, shading, or pattern of the background.
2) Special tasks carried out while you are doing something else. For example, with background printing, a document can be sent to the printer while you carry on working on another document.

Backslash (\)
A symbol used to separate files and folders from the folders or drives that they are stored in. For example, C:\Windows\ Help\Calc.hlp denotes the help file for the calculator (calc) which is inside the Help folder, which is itself in the Windows folder on the C: drive. The main folder (here C:) is also called the root directory and the folders it contains are called subdirectories.

Backup (.BAK)
To make a duplicate copy of programs, disks or information. Some programs automatically make a backup of recent versions of the file and call it by the same name with the extension .bak.

Bad sector
A physical fault on the surface of a floppy or hard disk. Software such as Windows ScanDisk can find bad sectors and mark them off-limits, so that the operating system won't try to write to, or read from, them.

Baud rate
The speed at which a modem transmits data. The baud rate is the number of changes that occurs in an electrical signal every second. This isn't the same as the number of bits per second transmitted (a more accurate measurement of modem speed). Modems can compress data so there are several bits transmitted in every baud.

Bay
The space inside a PC's case where you fit a CD-ROM, floppy, tape backup, or hard disk drive. Blanking plates are used to cover spare bays.

BBS
Stands for Bulletin Board System. An electronic messaging and file download system available free or by subscription. Online services that also offer Internet access are taking over, but there are still many BBSs, including those maintained by hardware and software companies for downloading drivers and upgrades.

Bidirectional
Something that operates two ways. A bidirectional printer prints from left to right across the page and then back from right to left. This speeds up printing time. A bidirectional parallel port allows two-way communication between the PC and some hardware devices, such as a printer or scanner.

BIOS
Stands for Basic Input/Output System. This is a set of essential instructions that manage the basic functions in your PC. The BIOS is stored in read-only memory (ROM) so that it starts when the computer turns on. It tests the hardware at startup, launches the operating system and controls the screen, keyboard and disk drives.

Bit/byte
A bit is the smallest unit of information handled by a computer. Short for BInary digiT, a bit can have one of just two values: 0 or 1. The value of a bit represents a simple choice, such as on or off, true or false. By itself a bit means little, but a group of eight bits makes up a byte—which can represent one letter, digit or other character.

Bits per second (bps)
A common way of describing the speed of a link between two PCs or a PC and a printer. It measures how many bits of data can be sent every second. If you check the specification of a modem, make sure it describes bits per second, not baud rate.

Bitmap/.bmp
Images are made up of tiny dots (pixels). If you zoom in close to a bitmap image, you'll see the dots grow. Compare this with a vector image, where shapes are calculated mathematically, so they appear sharp however much you zoom in. .bmp is the filename extension given to files that store bitmap image data.

Blind carbon copy
Marked as bcc on the e-mail header. Put a friend's address in this field and a copy of the e-mail will be sent to them without the other people receiving the message knowing.

Boot
To start up your computer. When your PC boots up it carries out a sequence of instructions stored on the BIOS and loads the main operating system. A cold boot is starting up the computer from scratch by turning on the power switch. A warm boot is when you restart the computer (without having first turned it off by using the power switch).

Boot disk
A boot disk is a floppy disk with the main system files on it. It can be used to start (boot) the computer if there's a problem with the hard drive.

Browser
A program used for viewing Web pages—both on the Internet and on your PC. It can also display images, play sounds and video clips, and run

animations or small programs. In addition, most browsers let you send and receive e-mail and link up with newsgroups.

Buffer

A holding area in memory used for temporary storage of information. For instance, a print buffer can store data waiting to be printed so that you can carry on working on something else.

Bus

Sets of cables that connect parts of a PC—such as the processor and memory—and allow them to transfer information. There are three main buses: the data bus carries data around the PC, the address bus carries the memory location for the data, and the control bus carries a set of control and time signals to make sure all the components are working together.

Bus speed

The speed at which a processor communicates with other devices in a computer. Most PCs use a 100MHz or 133MHz bus, but faster ones are in development.

Cache

Pronounced "cash," this is a storage area where frequently used data is kept. The information can be accessed quicker from the cache than from other storage areas, such as the hard drive or memory. Web pages can also be cached so that when you want to look at them again they can be loaded from the computer instead of having to download again from the Internet.

Capture

In Windows, you can save the current screen as an image (capture it) by pressing the Print Screen key. The image can then be pasted into a document or paint program. To capture just the active window and not the whole desktop, press Alt and Print Screen.

Case-sensitive

Software that can detect the difference between lowercase (small) and uppercase (capital) letters. You'll find this in the Find and Replace function in some word processors. Searching for "School" won't find "school." Most passwords are also case-sensitive so be aware that typing in "John" will not be the same as "john."

CD (CD-ROM)

Stands for Compact Disc-Read Only Memory. This usually refers to a music disc that can be played on your stereo or in your PC's CD player. In the PC world, the same type of plastic

disc is used to store up to 650MB of data. CD-ROMs cannot be altered.

CD-R drive

This is used to make copies of existing CD-ROMs or to create new CDs. CD-R drives can be used for playback (reading) as well as for recording, but in general they tend to operate more slowly than conventional CD-ROM drives.

CD-RW

CD-RW (CD ReWritable) discs and drives follow on from CD-R. The main difference is that CD-RW discs can be re-recorded. CD-RW drives can read conventional CD-ROMs and CD-R discs, but they write to the new discs more slowly. Because they can re-record over the same discs, CD-RW drives are good for making backups.

Chat/chat room

Using the computer to have a written conversation in real time. When you chat with someone, you write what you want to say and then press the Enter key. Your words appear on the screens of the other people in the conversation. They can then reply to you. Most chats are done via the Internet. A chat room is a program that allows several people to chat at the same time.

Child

A small window displayed inside a main window, often used to display options. For example, if you want to change a font, the options are all displayed in a child window.

Clock speed

This is the internal speed at which a processor runs. This is almost always faster than the bus speed, sometimes by a factor of six or seven.

CMOS

Stands for Complementary Metal-Oxide Semiconductor. This is battery-powered memory used to store the vital information needed to boot your computer, such as the type of disks and the amount of memory, as well as the clock/calendar.

CMYK

This stands for cyan, magenta, yellow and key (black), the four colors used in an inkjet printer to make up any other color.

Color depth

The number of colors that each screen pixel can display at any given resolution, usually measured in binary bits; 8-bit color depth allows 256 color variants, 16-bit allows 65,536 and 24-bit allows 16.7 million.

COM port

Communication port on the back of your PC for connecting to serial devices such as the mouse and modem. You can have up to four COM ports.

Compression

A method of reducing the size of a file by squashing the data it contains. Compression programs employ a number of clever tricks to do this and the results can be impressive, with some files being squeezed to less than a tenth of their original size. To use the files or programs, they usually have to be decompressed first.

Configure

To adjust software or hardware to suit your needs. For example, you can configure Windows so that it displays a different color background or uses a larger font that's easier to read.

Control key (Ctrl)

This is a key on the keyboard (in the bottom right and left corners of the main character pad) that is used for special functions. The keys and their functions all depend on the way the software was written. In many Windows-based applications, there is a set of standard control key functions. Ctrl+S will usually save the current document, Ctrl+N will create a new document, and Ctrl+P will print the document.

Control panel

This is a collection of controls that allows you to configure the basic functions of Windows and your computer. Among them are controls to define the fonts that are installed, the display settings and the type of printer that's installed.

Cookie

A small text file sent by the server to your machine when you go to some Web sites. It can store log-on information so you don't have to re-enter passwords each time you visit the site. It also allows the server to customize the information to your interests and to keep track of the pages you visit.

Corrupt

When data is accidentally changed or destroyed, the file or document is termed corrupt. It can be caused by a software problem or by a sudden power surge damaging the hard drive. Some utilities programs (such as Norton's Utilities) try to recover the data from a corrupted file.

CPU

This stands for Central Processing Unit, the brains of your PC. It is an electronic device—an integrated circuit

board or chip—that contains millions of tiny electronic components needed to carry out basic arithmetic and control functions. The speed of the processor is measured in Megahertz (MHz) and generally the bigger the number the faster the PC.

Crash

This is what happens when your PC goes wrong and freezes up. A crash can be caused by all sorts of problems with the software, but it usually happens because the PC has terminal problems or the software you are using has bugs in it.

Ctrl-Alt-Del

Also known as the three-finger salute. Pressing these three keys together helps you get out of a crash. Press them once and a close box appears, showing the programs are running. You can then try closing the program that may have frozen the computer. Pressing Ctrl-Alt-Del twice will restart the computer.

Data/data transfer rate

Data is a general term for anything the computer processes—it could be numbers, words or images. The data transfer rate is the speed at which data can be read from the hard disk and transferred to the processor.

Dedicated

A PC, printer, program, or even phone line that is used for one particular job only. If you have a network, you might find that you do a lot of printing or that you need to store a large number of files. In this case, it would make sense to set aside one PC for printing or storage. It would not be used for anything else.

Default

The choices automatically made by a program if you do not specify an alternative. For example, if you run a word processor and start typing a letter, it will use the default typeface (e.g. Arial) and the default paper size and margins. You can change these settings.

Defragmentation

When a file is saved to disk, your PC does not always save it in a single area. If the disk is full, it might have to split the file and save it in sections in different places. This makes it slower to retrieve the file. Defragmentation utilities reorganize your hard disk so that all the parts of a file are stored next to each other.

Desktop

Desktop is the term that defines what you see on your screen when Windows first starts up.

The icons, status bar, Start button and the Recycle Bin are all located on the Desktop. Think of an office—you have folders on your desk, some open (the icons and windows), a waste bin, and a small filing cabinet which is the My Computer icon. The Desktop also has a background pattern and any windows or applications that might be open.

Device/device driver
Device is a general term for the parts that make up a computer system—such as a printer, serial, disk drive and modem. The software that controls each of these different parts is called a device driver, or just driver.

Dialogue box
A message window that asks you to do something in reply (such as press a button). It is called a dialogue box because it's the closest there is to a conversation between the computer and the user. It's usually used for choosing options, such as creating a name for saving files.

Dial-up connection
This term covers the whole process of connecting to another computer over a telephone line—such as your Internet service provider. To do this you need a modem and the dial-up software that's supplied with Windows.

Digital/digitize
Digital refers to the system whereby numbers are used to represent information, rather than a continuously changing signal. Compare this with analogue, which refers to a signal that varies continuously over time rather than taking a fixed value. PCs work with numbers only so they cannot directly deal with analogue signals. To digitize something is to convert an analogue signal—such as speech or sound—into a numeric form that can be processed by the computer. For example, a soundcard contains an analogue-to-digital converter to convert the sound signal from a microphone into numbers representing the volume and tone.

DIP switch
Sliding switch that can be moved to one of two positions—open or closed—to set options on a circuit board.

Direct cable connection
A utility or small program supplied free with Windows that allows you to link two computers together using a cable plugged into the serial (or parallel) port on each PC. The two computers can exchange files or share printers.

DirectX
Software needed to play some games. It gives applications direct access to the computer's sound and graphics hardware in order to improve performance.

Disk compression
A way of squeezing more data on to a hard disk. Unlike file compression, which is used to reduce the size of individual files, disk compression works in the background, compressing and expanding files on a disk without the user having to do anything.

DLL
This stands for dynamic-link library. A DLL is a program file that's stored on disk and loaded as and when an application needs it. That means it doesn't use up any memory until it is needed. Large applications, such as a complex word processor, might use several DLLs: one to carry out the spell check; one to manage printing a letter; and a third for formatting the text. DLL files have the extension .dll. The same DLL may be used by several programs so be careful if deleting any.

DMA
Stands for Direct Memory Access. This is a fast method of accessing the contents of memory chips. If a video card wants to read data from the main memory, it has to go via the central processor, which accesses the memory location and passes the data back to the video card. With DMA, the video card retrieves the data directly from the memory.

Document/.doc
A document is any piece of work created by a program, that has been saved to disk and given a name. Although documents are usually thought of as something written—such as reports or letters—on a computer a document can also be a spreadsheet or a graphic file. The file extension that shows files have been formatted for a word processor is .doc (it is also the default file extension for Microsoft Word files).

Domain/domain name
(1) In Windows, a network can have groups of users. These groups are called domains, which is a convenient way of referring to a set of people or resources on the network.
(2) Sections of the Internet are identified by domain names. The domain name is part of the site name (or URL) and ends with the TLD (top-level domain) category. One you'll encounter frequently is .com (commercial).

Dongle
(1) A physical device—such as a key—which has to be attached to the computer for a particular software program to run on that machine.
(2) A lock to keep a computer secure, such as a lock on the front of a cabinet which has the PC inside it.

Dots per inch (dpi)
The number of dots that a printer can print on an inch of paper; or, on a screen, the number of dots displayed per inch. The greater the number of dots, the smaller each must be and the finer the resolution. Most laser printers print at 600 dpi but the better ones can have a resolution of 1200 dpi.

Download
When you download a file from the Web you are transferring a copy of a file from a computer on the Internet (the remote computer) to your computer (the local one). This can be done either using a modem or a network. When you send files from your computer to one on the Internet it is called uploading.

Drag and drop
A feature of Windows which means you can move a file, image or piece of text from one place on screen to another by picking it up with the cursor, dragging it to where you want it and dropping it into place.

Drive
A mechanical unit that reads from and writes to disks. The drive has a motor that spins the disk and an access head that can be positioned over the disk. The access head can, in the case of a floppy or hard disk, write or read data from the surface of the disk. In the case of a CD-ROM, the access head uses a tiny laser to read the holes etched in the surface of the disc.

Drive letter
Letters are used to identify different drives on your system. For example, A and B are usually floppy disks, C is the hard drive and D is the CD-ROM drive. With the large storage space available on disk drives, your drive might have been partitioned, that is split into manageable sections. For example, if you have an 8GB hard disk drive, you might find it more useful to split it up into two 4GB partitions. The drive letters are then automatically changed to C and D, with the CD-ROM drive as E.

Driver
A special piece of software that sits between Windows and a particular device, such as a

printer or disk drive. It translates the instructions from Windows into a form that the device can understand. Some drivers come with Windows but most new devices come with drivers supplied by the manufacturer. They need to be loaded before the device will work properly. Drivers are regularly updated as bugs appear or new functions become possible.

DVD
Stands for Digital Video Disk (or Digital Versatile Disk). This is a CD format that even in its basic form can be used to store as much data as seven ordinary CD-ROMs (4.7GB). Double-sided DVDs can store 17MB. The main attraction of DVD is to distribute feature films and sophisticated interactive multimedia titles. Films are encoded for each country to prevent piracy. To view them you need an appropriate MPEG 2 decoder. DVD drives can be used to read CD-ROMs.

Dynamic
Something that changes immediately it is needed is termed dynamic, such as a Web page where the information is updated in real time.

Emoticons
These are emotional icons, better known as smileys. Made by pressing keyboard keys, they look like faces displaying some particular emotion. So J is I'm smiling while L is I'm sad.

Encryption/decryption
Encryption is the conversion of data into a secret code. Files are encrypted using a password and must be unscrambled (decoded) using the same password (also known as a key). Decryption is taking a message or file that has been coded (encrypted) and changing it back into its original form.

Ethernet
A type of network connection that allows fast data transfer.

.exe
The filename extension—short for executable - that indicates that a file is a program and can be run, usually just by double-clicking on it.

Expansion card
A circuit board that can be plugged in to expand the functionality of your PC. For example, if you want to connect your PC to a network, you will need a network card that controls the way signals are sent over the network cable. You can fit several expansion cards to a PC by plugging them into empty expansion slots.

Explorer

A program supplied with Windows that lets you manage all the files stored on a disk. With Explorer (officially called Windows Explorer) you can copy files, move files from one folder to another, create new folders, and rename or delete files and folders.

Export

To move information from one program to another. Generally, this will involve converting a file from one format to another format so that it can be read by a different program. For example, if you have written a letter in Microsoft Word and want to give it to a friend who uses Word Perfect for Windows, you need to export the Word document to a Word Perfect format file using the File/Save As option in Word.

Extension

The three-letter code at the end of a filename that generally indicates the type or format of the file. A filename might be Partyinvite with the extension .doc—the extension shows the file is a document. Similarly, .bmp means a bitmap file, and so on.

Ezine

Short for Electronic magazine, it is a magazine or newsletter that's available via the Web or e-mail, usually for free.

FAQ

Stands for Frequently Asked Questions. A FAQ (pronounced fak) is a document that answers questions on specific topics. FAQs are posted on the Internet to save technical support staff having to deal with the same questions repeatedly.

FAT

When you open a file, the operating system looks through the file allocation table (FAT) to find out where the file is stored. The FAT is hidden, so you cannot see it, but without it you cannot retrieve any of the information on your disk. Sometimes the FAT gets corrupted. To remedy this problem, run ScanDisk or another disk recovery program.

Fatal error

Often shown by the blue screen of death, a fatal error causes the system or program to crash with no hope of recovery.

Favorites/favorites folder

Favorites are a collection of shortcuts—or links—to Web sites that you want to save and go back to later. In Internet Explorer all these links are kept together in the Favorites Folder. In other browsers these collections of shortcuts have different names, such as hotlists or bookmarks.

Field

In a database, a field is an individual section that can hold a particular type of information. For example, if you have a contacts list of your friends, each entry is called a record and the various parts of each record are called fields. There would be a separate field for the name, address, phone number and so on.

File format

The way data is stored in a file. For example, every document created in Word for Windows is stored as a Word file with special codes to tell Word how the margins are set up, the fonts that are used, and whether images are included.

Firewall

A firewall is a security device to protect networks (and now individual PCs) from outside threats such as hackers. Instead of each computer linking directly to the Internet, they have to go through a separate server (proxy server) which decides which messages or files it is safe to let through.

Flag

A flag is a marker or signal that something's important or needs some follow-up action. For example, in Outlook Express you can flag a message that comes in to show it needs an urgent reply.

Flame

Red-hot passions can be aroused by messages in e-mail forums or other online chats. To flame is to send rude or insulting e-mails to someone whose opinion you don't agree with. Those who do so are called flamers.

Flicker

Images on screen flicker (appear to move) when the picture is not being refreshed often enough or quickly enough. Most screen displays need to be refreshed at 50–60 times per second in order to appear flicker-free.

Font

A set of characters all of the same style (such as italic), weight (such as bold), and typeface (design). For example, labels in Windows are normally displayed in a font called Helvetica or one called Arial. Fonts are used by computers for their screen displays and by printers for producing printed pages. Windows has TrueType fonts that can be printed and displayed in almost any size, and printer fonts that can be printed in predefined sizes only.

Footprint

The area covered by a piece of equipment, such as a PC or printer. As notebooks need to be small and light enough to carry around, they will have a smaller footprint (that is, take up less space) than desktop PCs.

Frame

(1) A moveable, resizable box that holds text or an image. (2) The parts of the Window—such as the minimize and maximize controls, scroll bar and title bar—that are controlled by Windows and not by the application running inside it. (3) Some Web pages include frames. Each frame on the page links to its own separate HTML document.

Freeware

Computer software that is given away free of charge and often made available on the Web or through newsgroups.

FTP

This stands for File Transfer Protocol and is the way of moving files backwards and forwards across the Web. Using an FTP program—such as Terrapin or CuteFTP—you can take the files, pictures, and text for your Web pages and "upload" them, via an FTP server, to your Web space.

Function key—F keys

PCs have at least 12 function keys at the top of the keyboard. These are keys that are linked to specific tasks—such as refreshing the screen. However, the keys may have different uses according to different applications, although most use the F1 key to display help information.

Gantt chart

This is found in project management software, and shows the progress of a project by listing tasks and giving a graphical representation of them as horizontal bars.

GIF file

Stands for Graphics Interface Format. This is a commonly used format for storing images and bitmapped color graphics, shown by the file extension .gif. Originally developed for CompuServe, it is now one of the most popular formats for images stored on the Internet.

Giga/gigabyte (GB)

The prefix giga means one billion (which, US style, is 1,000 million, not a million million as it is in the UK). So the latest PCs with a processor speed of 1 Gigahertz (1GHz) go through 1,000 million cycles a second. A gigabyte (1GB) is 1,000 megabytes. The storage capacity of most hard drives today is measured in gigabytes.

Graphics card

A graphics card produces the picture you see on your screen. It is also known as a graphics adapter, graphics accelerator, video adapter or display adapter. Most cards have special processors to boost performance and have their own memory in which to cache (store) the display.

Some graphics cards are best suited to 2D work (standard applications) while others have been specially designed for 3D effects in games and multimedia titles. Although combined 2D/3D accelerated graphics cards appear to offer the best of both worlds, they may not be quite as fast as cards dedicated to either 2D or 3D.

GUI

Stands for Graphical User Interface. This is a way of representing files, functions and folders with icons. With a GUI such as Windows you can point and click on an icon using the mouse rather than typing in the filename, so making it easier to use a PC.

Handshaking

A series of signals that are sent between two communication devices—such as two modems linked by telephone—to establish the way in which they should send and receive data.

Helper applications

These are programs, such as sound or movie players, which are launched by the browser to play multimedia content downloaded from the Web. They are different from plug-ins as they are not part of the browser and can be run as stand-alone programs (e.g. RealPlayer).

Heuristic

Programs that learn from what's happened in the past. For example, heuristic scanning (also known as rule-based scanning) used in some anti-virus programs, is where the scanning program compares files or programs with the virus files it knows, and decides the probability of them being infected.

Hierarchical file system

A way of storing and organising files on a disk so that each file or folder is within other folders on a disk. The main directory (folder) for the disk is called the root. The route to get from there to a particular file or folder is called the path.

Hit

Originally, this was the way traffic to a Web site was measured. The number of hits was an indication of how popular a site was. Downloading a file from a Web page is a hit, but as each page can contain lots of files (such as picture files) it can take quite a few hits to download a full page. Now the number of visits (that is individual users) to a Web site is used as a better measure of how busy a site is.

Hotspot
An area of an image that reacts if you move the mouse pointer on to it and click. You can tell when there is a hotspot in an image because the mouse pointer changes shape from an arrow to a hand. For example, if a multimedia title displays a picture of a guitar, there could be a hotspot over each string, which would enable the user to play the sound of the strings being plucked.

Hot swapping
This means you can connect peripherals such as modems or CD-ROM drives to the computer and work with them immediately, without having to switch off the PC or restart.

HTML
Stands for HyperText Markup Language. This is the markup code used for creating Web pages and saying how they should look. It's also used for creating hypertext links (see hyperlinks). A Web page has .html as the file extension. Some software programs, such as FrontPage, are HTML editors, which will help you set up and change Web pages.

Hyperlinks
Click on these to move to different parts of the page or to other Web pages. They are also known as hypertext links or hotlinks. The link is usually underlined or in a different color to make it stand out from the text around it. Pictures can also be links. When the cursor passes over a link it changes from an arrow to a pointing hand.

HTTP
This is the method, or protocol, by which Web pages are moved around the Internet. In the address bar of your browser, http is usually seen as the first part of any Web address, e.g. http://www.msn.com.

Illegal operation
This is when a program does something that the computer thinks it shouldn't. Examples of illegal operations include protection faults when a program tries to use a protected block of memory used by another program or Windows itself. Exceptions are error conditions trapped by software.

Stack faults occur when a program fills up the amount of space reserved for temporary data storage.

Infrared port
A port that uses an infrared light beam to connect to other computers with a similar port to transfer files and documents. Although there's no need for the computers to be physically connected, the ports have to be in a line with each other and less than a few feet apart for the transfer to work. Some printers also have infrared ports so you can print your documents without having to connect through a cable.

Initialize
To set up a disk or tape ready for use. This may include testing the surface of the storage medium for faults, writing a startup file and setting up an index for file information.

Inoculation
Used by anti-virus programs to check for suspicious changes in files. Programs are inoculated—that is protected against virus infection—by recording characteristic information about them. This information can then be compared each time the program is run. If there are any significant changes, the file may be corrupt or infected.

Input/Output—I/O
As it suggests, this is information that comes in and goes out of your computer. I/O cards control the data flow to and from devices such as your hard drive and mouse.

IRQ conflict
This arizes when two peripheral devices use the same IRQ (Interrupt Request) number. The interrupt is a request for attention from the central processor. If two devices—say the mouse and the modem—share the same interrupt, the processor may react to the wrong device and the system won't work properly.

ISDN
Stands for Integrated Services Digital Network. This is the standard way of transmitting digital data over a telephone network at high speed—much faster than normal modems.

ISP
Stands for Internet Service Provider, a company that offers users a connection to the Internet. The Internet Service Provider has high-speed links to the Internet and a server that stores and delivers e-mail messages to its customers.

JPEG
A standard file format you may come across if you use graphic images. JPEG is a complex way of storing images in a compressed format so they take up much less disk space than they would normally. The file extension is .jpg.

Keyword
The word that is most relevant or important. Often used for searches where any document found must have the keywords in it. In advanced searches, you can specify keywords that must be in and keywords that should be excluded (e.g. green and vegetable, but not broccoli).

KB/Kilobyte
A measure of the capacity of a storage device or size of a file. Usually written as KB, a kilobyte is equal to 1,024 bytes (210 in binary notation).

KHz
A measure of the frequency of a sound. One KHz (or kilohertz) is equal to 1,000 cycles per second. The higher the number, the higher pitched the sound. You will also see KHz mentioned in the specification of a soundcard. This can define two separate functions. The first is the range of frequencies the soundcard can output. The second is the frequency at which the soundcard takes samples of a sound when recording it on to your disk. A soundcard looks at the level of a sound thousands of times each second and so builds up a picture of it. The more times it takes a sample, the more accurate the recording.

LAN
Stands for Local Area Network. This is where several computers all within a short distance of each other, such as in a building, are linked together by cables. If your PC is on the network you can exchange files or messages with other users connected to the LAN. A wide area network (WAN) is similar to a LAN, but links computers that are miles apart—even in different countries.

Lost cluster
A lost cluster is when Windows thinks that a part of the hard drive or disk is being used by a file, but the data in it isn't linked to any particular file. It usually happens after a program has crashed suddenly.

Macro
A series of commands or operations that enables you to automate common tasks in various programs, such as Word or Excel.

Media player
A utility program supplied free with Windows that allows you to run multimedia files including sound or video files.

Megabyte (MB or Mbyte)
A measure of the data capacity of storage devices, including hard drives, that is equal to 1,048,576 bytes (220 in binary notation). Megabytes are also used as the measure of the storage capacity of main memory (RAM).

Memory
Generally, this means any device that can store information, but it's usually used to refer to the RAM (Random Access Memory) chips. These store data that can be accessed quickly as they are directly linked to your PC's processor. Electronic memory chips, like these, can remember data only while the PC's switched on. By contrast, information stored on a disk, such as the hard drive, remains even when the power is off, as it is stored magnetically.

Memory expansion
This means adding more RAM (electronic memory chips) to your computer. Your PC needs memory to run software programs and Windows needs as much memory as possible. The more RAM you have, the more programs that can run together and the faster they will work. New PCs come with up to 256MB of RAM.

MHz
Stands for megahertz. A measure of the frequency of a timing signal that's equal to one million cycles per second. The higher the MHz number, the faster the clock that's generating the signal. This normally refers to the main clock that sets the timing signal for the processor chip in your PC. The faster the timing signal, the faster the processor will run.

Modem
The name comes from MOdulator/DEModulator. A modem is a device that converts electronic signals from your PC into sound signals that can be transmitted over a phone line. To receive information the modem works in reverse and converts the sound signals back into digital electronic signals. Modems are used to connect to the Internet. Some modems are internal and fitted inside the PC, while an external modem can plug into your serial or USB port. A modem's speed is measured in bits per second (bps) and the top models currently transfer data at

56Kbps (56,000 bits per second), which is roughly equivalent to three pages of A4 text a second.

MPEG
Stands for Moving Pictures Expert Group. A set of standards for compressing audio and video files.

Multi-tasking
The ability of Windows to run several programs at once. You could be typing a letter in a word processor, while sending an e-mail. In fact, the processor handles each program one at a time but does so quickly enough to make it appear they are running concurrently.

Newsgroup
One of the features of the Internet. Newsgroups are free-for-all discussion forums. When an article is posted, all the replies to it that carry the same subject line make up a thread.

OCR
Stands for Optical Character Recognition. This is software that takes a scanned text image and converts it into ordinary text. This can then be loaded into a word processing program—such as Word—for editing.

OEM
Stands for Original Equipment Manufacturer. A company that produces equipment, such as a computer, using basic parts made by other companies. Only the biggest computer companies make everything themselves.

Outline
A software program that helps you organize lists of things to do, ideas or projects (such as Microsoft Project). Each heading can have many sub-sections beneath it, which in turn can have sub-sections or bullet points. You can view all the sections or just the headwords.

Pages per minute (ppm)
The number of standard A4 text pages a printer can print out each minute. With color printers there are usually two speeds, one for color printing and one for black and white.

Parallel port
A socket at the back of the PC that lets you connect it to a printer. A parallel port sends data to the printer over eight parallel wires. Some other devices, such as ZIP drives, can be connected this way.

Partition
A way of dividing a hard disk into sections. Each partition is treated by the operating system as though it is a separate drive.

If you buy a 20GB hard disk, you may find it convenient to split it into four 5GB partitions called C:, D:, E:, and F:.

Patch
For programs that are causing persistent problems or have security issues, manufacturers will issue a patch. This is a piece of code, often downloaded from the Web, that will correct a bug in the program.

PDA
Stands for Personal Digital Assistant. This is a general term for any small, electronic personal organizer. These may also be known as palmtops.

PDF
Stands for Portable Document Format. Many instruction books and other documents you can download from the Web may be saved in this format (they have the extension .pdf). To open and print them you need the Acrobat reader program which can be downloaded for free from the Adobe Web site.

Peer-to-peer network
A simple network in which no single computer is in control; each acts as a server to the others in the network and shares their resources.

Peripheral
Any add-on item that connects to your computer, such as a printer or Zip drive.

PIM
Stands for Personal Information Manager. It includes integrated address book, phonebook, diary and e-mail manager.

Pixel
The smallest single unit on a display, or on a printer, the color or brightness of which can be controlled. A monitor usually has a resolution of 72 pixels per inch, whereas a laser printer has a resolution of 300 to 600 pixels per inch. Pixels are also called dots.

Plug-in
A small software program that works within another one for a special purpose—for example, your browser may need a particular plug-in to play animation, video, or sound files from a Web page.

Plug and play
With most modern PCs you can plug in your new peripheral, such as a printer or modem, and when you reboot, Windows will automatically configure it to work with your system.

POP3
Stands for Post Office Protocol. This is used to get e-mail from

the mail server at your ISP. When first setting up your e-mail client to download messages from your ISP, you will need the name of their POP3 server.

Pop-up window
A window that can be displayed on the screen at any time on top of anything that is already there. They are most often used to display warning messages or to confirm a choice.

Port
A physical connector for linking input and output devices to the computer.

Protocol
A set of codes and signals that determine how two different PCs communicate with each other. For example, one simple protocol ensures that data is correctly transferred from a PC to a printer along a printer cable. Other protocols set out how PCs talk to each other via the Internet or over a network. A protocol is like a spoken language. If you cannot get two PCs to exchange information it's likely that they are using different protocols.

QuickTime
A video system originally used on Apple computers but also available for PCs. It is commonly used by interactive multimedia software such as encyclopaedias. The player for QuickTime is free and is usually bundled along with programs that require it.

RAM
Stands for Random Access Memory—a type of computer memory that can be written to, or read from, in any order. The main memory chips in your PC are RAM. RAM is short-term memory. While the PC is switched on it can store part of the operating system, and run applications and other work, but all the contents will be lost when the PC is switched off. The more RAM a PC has, the faster it will be.

Refresh rate
Measures how many times a second the picture on a monitor is updated in order to maintain a constant flicker-free image. The image on the screen is visible because tiny dots of phosphor shine. The glow from the phosphor lasts a few tenths of a second, so the dots have to be hit by an electron picture beam to get them to glow again. This process is repeated 60 to 70 times per second.

Registry
A database at the heart of Windows that contains information about every

program stored on the disk and the users, networks and preferences. You'll never see the registry, but it's worth knowing it's there in case you see an error message such as Object Not Found in Registry. This means that a program has not been correctly installed.

Remote access
A link that allows you to access another computer from a distance (it may be in a different room, building or country) by using a modem.

Resolution
Measure of the number of pixels that are displayed on your screen. The more pixels per given area, the sharper the image and the higher the resolution.

Rich text format (RTF)
A way of storing a document that includes all the commands that describe the page, type, font and formatting. The RTF format allows formatted pages to be exchanged between different word processors.

ROM
Stands for Read Only Memory. This is a type of memory device that has had data written on to it at the time of manufacture. You cannot store your own information in ROM. Its contents can only be read, for example a CD-ROM.

Safe mode
A special operating mode that is selected if Windows detects a problem when starting. Safe mode does not load many of the drivers for the peripherals, such as the printer, so these will not work. But it does allow you to start Windows in order to identify and fix any problems with the system.

SCSI
Stands for Small Computer System Interface (pronounced scuzzy). This is a high-speed parallel interface standard originally used with Apple Macintosh computers. Now it is used in some PCs.

Serial port
A port to which you can connect serial devices such as a mouse or modem. Through it, data is sent and received one bit at a time, over a single wire. Usually, data in a PC is transferred around the computer in parallel form that is 8 or 16 bits wide. However, if you want to use a modem, you need to send it the data so that it can be converted into sound signals that can be sent one at a time over a telephone line.

Server
A dedicated computer that

provides a function to a network, such as controlling who has access, storing files or printing data. On the Internet, it is a computer or program that responds to commands from a client PC. For example, a file server with an archive of shareware programs will transfer a copy of one of them to a client PC when it receives a request from the client.

Shareware
Software which is available free for you to sample. If you keep it you are expected to pay a fee to the writer. It is often confused with public-domain software which is completely free.

Shockwave
A programming language designed to bring animation to Web pages. To view its effects you need a plug-in, otherwise some Web pages you visit won't display properly.

Shortcut
An icon, usually placed on the Desktop in Windows, that links to a file, folder or program stored elsewhere on the disk. The shortcut has the same icon as the original file except for a tiny arrow in the bottom left-hand corner. The shortcut is not a copy of the original, it is just a pointer to it. So, if you delete a shortcut you haven't got rid of the file or program it was linked to.

SMTP
Stands for Simple Mail Transfer Protocol. This is used for sending messages from one computer to another on a network. As with the POP3 server used to receive e-mail, you will need to enter the name of your ISP's SMTP server when first setting up your e-mail client.

Soundcard
An add-on device that plugs into an expansion slot inside your PC and generates analogue sound signals. Soundcards are used to play back music and sound effects, such as from a wav or midi file, or CD-ROM. A wavetable card has the most realistic sound; it has samples of real instruments used to create music, rather than a synthesizer.

Spam
Junk e-mail sent to many addresses at one time or posted in several newsgroups. It is possible to set up rules in your e-mail client, such as Outlook, to filter junk mail into a special folder automatically. Check it really is spam before deleting it.

Status bar
A line at the top or bottom of a screen which gives information

about the task that is currently being worked on, such as the position of the cursor, the number of lines, filename, time, and so on.

Swap file
A hidden file stored on the hard disk, used to hold parts of programs and data files that don't fit in memory. Windows moves data between the swap file and memory as needed. The swap file is a form of virtual memory.

TCP/IP
Stands for Transmission Control Protocol/Internet Protocol. This is the network protocol used to send information over the Internet. It describes how information must be packaged and addressed so that it reaches the right destination and the computer can understand it.

Temp file
This is a file created in memory or on disk that is used just for that session and can then be deleted. For instance, when a new application is installed, it will usually set up a temporary file that will be deleted when your computer restarts. It is a sensible idea to run Disk Cleanup regularly (accessed from System Tools on the Accessories menu) to remove any temporary files that you don't want.

Template
A template is a file containing some standard features, such as text or a logo. It can be laid out in the style of a memo, invoice or other document. Once you enter specific details, such as an address, date and prices, in the relevant section, you can save it as a new document.

TSR
Stands for Terminate and Stay Resident. TSR programs load into memory and stay there even when they are not running, so they can be re-activated quickly. Because they are in memory, they can interfere with other programs that are running, or new programs being installed. To close them down, press Ctrl+Alt+Delete to bring up the Close Program box.

Toolbar
A toolbar has a row of buttons or icons that can be pressed to carry out certain features of a program, such as pressing the printer symbol in Word to print out a page. The buttons on the toolbar can usually be customized by the user. Floating toolbars can be moved around the screen and placed where you want.

TWAIN
Stands for Technology Without An Interesting Name. It is the standard way for scanners to communicate with a PC. All scanners come with a TWAIN driver, which makes them compatible with any TWAIN-supporting software.

URL
Stands for Uniform Resource Locator. A URL is the technical name for an Internet address. For example, the URL of the Microsoft home page is http://www.microsoft.com.

USB
Stands for Universal Serial Bus. This is a recent standard for connecting peripherals, such as scanners, printers, cameras, and mice. You can add up to 127 devices through a single port. USB also supports hot swapping, that is devices can be connected, or disconnected, without switching off the PC.

Utility program
Utility programs, or utilities, help you get more out of your PC. They provide file management capabilities, such as sorting, copying, comparing, listing and searching, as well as diagnostic and measurement routines that check the health and performance of the system.

Virtual memory
This is a neat trick to give your PC more memory than it physically has. Free space on your hard drive is used as a temporary storage area and information is swapped in and out of memory as needed.

WAP
Stands for Wireless Application Protocol. WAP-enabled mobile phones can view simple Web pages to look at e-mail, check share prices, or get the latest news.

WAVE or WAV file
The standard file format that Windows uses for storing most sound files. They can be recognized by the .wav extension.

Windows
Windows is an operating system designed by Microsoft to make it easier for you to control your PC. Windows uses icons to represent files and devices such as printers, and can be controlled using a mouse. Previous operating systems were MS-DOS-based and required commands to be typed in. There are different versions of Windows. The latest, pitched specifically for the home user, is Windows ME. Previously there was Windows 98 Second Edition, Windows 98, Windows 95 and Windows 3.1. For

business users there is Windows 2000, which has taken over from Windows NT, and Windows for Workgroups. The two strands will come together with the introduction of Windows XP.

Windows CE
Stands for Windows Compact Edition, a version of Windows designed for palmtop computers. The Windows CE interface is a stripped-down version of the full Windows operating system, but with some extra features for handheld PCs.

WYSIWYG
Stands for What You See Is What You Get. The user sees a document exactly as it will appear in the final version. Examples are a word processing or DTP program, where the display on screen is the same as the image or text that will be printed, including graphics and special fonts.

Zip file
A file format used to save disk space. A single Zip file is used as a container for one or more compressed files. These must be expanded to their original size before they can be used. The format was originally devised for use by utilities called PKZip and PKUnzip, but is now so common that virtually all compression and decompression programs can handle the format. Compressed files are shown by the file extension .zip.

Zip drive
A high-capacity disk drive from Iomega which can store from 100MB to 250MB of data on sturdy, pocket-sized removable disks. Because of their capacity they are useful for backing up day-to-day data.

Index